Making Figures

Making Figures

Reimagining Body, Sound, and Image in a World That Is Not for Us

Bruce Bromley

DALKEY ARCHIVE PRESS
CHAMPAIGN / LONDON / DUBLIN

First edition, 2014

Library of Congress Cataloging-in-Publication Data

Bromley, Bruce.
Reimagining Body, Sound, and Image in a World That Is Not for Us / Bruce Bromley.
-- First edition.
pages cm
Includes bibliographical references.
ISBN 978-1-62897-056-2 (acid-free paper)
1. Woolf, Virginia, 1882-1941--Criticism and interpretation. I. Title.
PR6045.O72Z5638 2014
823'.912--dc23
2013041809

Partially funded by a grant from the Illinois Arts Council, a state agency, and
New York University's College of Arts and Science

www.dalkeyarchive.com

Printed on permanent/durable acid-free paper

Table of Contents

To
Michael Harris Bromley
1958–2010

Introduction
Keeping Watch

Keep here your watch, and never part.
—Nahum Tate: *Dido and Aeneas* (1684–1689), 4.

Life is not susceptible perhaps to the
treatment we give it when we try to tell it.
—Virginia Woolf: *The Waves* (1931), 267.

[D]ead ideas . . . are inconsistent and unmeaning in their new environment and necessarily come in conflict with the new ideas which new circumstances have brought to life. But the old is nearly always stronger than the new, and the dead than the living. Thus you have the tyranny of the dead mind.
—Leonard Woolf: *After the Deluge, Vol. I* (1931), 34.

La méfiance à l'égard du vécu, elle est philosophique—
on postule que la conscience nous trompe sur nous et sur
le langage et on a raison: seule façon de les *voir*.
[Mistrust with regard to lived experience is philosophical—one
postulates that consciousness deceives us about ourselves and
about language and one is right: this is the only way to *see* them.]
—Maurice Merleau-Ponty:
Le visible et l'invisible (1959), 235.

What has neither wit nor wisdom and is indifferent to itself solicits no respect. Awe before nature's mystery gives way to the disenchanted knowingness which grows with the success of the analysis of all things into their primitive conditions and factors. The powers that produce those things are powerless to impart

a sanction to them: thus their knowledge imparts no regard for them. On the contrary, it removes whatever protection they may have enjoyed in a prescientific view. The implication this has for man's commerce with the equalized manifold is obvious. If nature sanctions nothing, it permits everything.
—Hans Jonas: "Seventeenth Century and After: The Meaning of The Scientific and Technological Revolution" (1974), 70.

I could compare my music to white light which contains all colours. Only a prism can divide the colours and make them them appear; this prism could be the spirit of the listener.
—Arvo Pärt: *Alina* (1999)

The artist is the canary in the coal mine.
—Joni Mitchell: *Woman of Heart and Mind* (2003).

We are all players, and we are all being played.
—Keith Jarrett: *Radiance* (2005).

Imagine, with me, that we are at Glyndebourne in 1996, watching act 2, scene 4 of Handel's oratorio *Theodora* (1749), which Peter Sellars stages as a near-opera, updating fourth-century, Roman-occupied Antioch to the America of our present time. Just before the scene begins, we have learned that the president, by obliging all citizens to burn incense at the altars of the gods in order to honor a recent military success, conflates the state and religious observance, without reference to denominational complexity. We have learned, too, that Theodora and the members of her pious community have been jailed due to their non-compliance with a presidential dictum that disregards devotion to a God unrecognized by the state; that, as she was born into a prominent family, Theodora will be forced to submit to the following admonitory punishment: in the morning, she will be raped, in public, by those who guard her. Finally, we understand, according to the ways in which Sellars has staged the music, that Irene, the head of Theodora's devotional sect, has been murdered in her cell for failing to pay what obeisance required of her.

But now, while the scene opens, our gaze falls on Theodora, imprisoned in the middle hours of the night before an admonishment she will not outlast, lying, fetus-like, in a cone of light, her face oriented towards us, eyes closed. She does not see Irene, upraised, lingering in the shadows far behind her, does not watch Irene seeming to float in the direction of that radiance of which Theodora herself is unaware, while she sleeps. Yet we do; and, watching the figures irradiated at center stage, we listen to Lorraine Hunt Lieberson sing Irene's aria as if its first notes were always there, though we had not noticed them, hear the melodic line rise to Theodora's defense, imploring that "angels spread / their viewless tents around her bed" so as to "keep her from vile assaults secure." We observe how image and sound appear to angle towards what cannot quite be seen or spoken with sufficient adequacy, how both utilize vocabularies centered on the visible, on the sayable, as a means of adumbrating their apparent opposites. Looking at Irene's hair, falling over the body of Theodora, at Irene's arms forming two curves that surround this body, still asleep, we find ourselves hypnotized by what they effect: a sleeping arm rises into the light and stays there; Theodora's guard, into whose ears Irene vocalizes her plea, turns, unseeing, his eyes moistened, lit, even in the darkness. Throughout, Handel, his librettist, Thomas Morell, Sellars, and his players prohibit our forgetting the palpability of the dead, of the living, the two intermixed beyond the logic of explanation, an intermixture that, were all involved to acquiesce in it, might reorder the morning that is almost here.

I begin with a sonic picture of our need to acknowledge what we may resist considering because much of the work which follows my introduction concerns interminglings, intervolvings by which our world would only be enriched, if we could consent to admitting them. Admittance results from a kind of seeing; what we see, we can act on; and, given that we live in the midst of a climate change produced largely by our own behaviors, "to refuse to act," as Elizabeth Kolbert warns in *Field Notes from a Catastrophe* (2006), is not to free ourselves of "consequences, but to rush toward them" (187). Yet, since behaviors issue from desires, yielded to or checked, since desires play on persons, to reconceive the performer is to allow for the possibility that his performances may submit to transformation. Once we combine that potential transformation with the notion of interrelationship, with the concept that the human cannot be an "itself," isolated from the outside of which it must be a part, from an interdependency with entities animate and inanimate, we arrive at the near comprehension that we may be other than we know, that our actuated desires fail the world into which we insert them when we operate under an impoverished vision of what relation means, one grounded in simple equivalence or opposition. Thus, the effort to shift our sense of the relational can guide us to shifting the personhoods by which we thought we were defined, to modifying the ways in which we bear on the many things among which we live. As a work of art manifests an approach to the envisaging act, represents that act, we ought to be capable of transferring the closeness of our attention to it, regardless of its difficulties, because of those difficulties, to the world, which, on the edges of any text, merits all the attending we permit ourselves to imagine offering it. And this admixture of attentiveness and imagination leads me to my primary subject—Virginia Woolf.

I organize my investigation of Woolf's thinking around *The Waves* because the latter arises from the imperative of interrelatedness, the challenges of interrelatedness we stand so in need of, whether or not we recognize them. I also believe that

Woolf's questioning the singularity of selfhood answers for her lifelong interest in generic fluidities, in how one art form touches on another, that touching, with respect to her readers, reshaping the reading mind that commits itself to contemplating liquidity and its troublesomeness. It is not obvious how we can distinguish one thing from another under the press of that onrush, how we can discern things as separate from one another when they appear to merge. Yet merger need not be identical with erasure, just as the thing that touches us, by doing so, cannot be our equivalent.

Indeed, Woolf embodies this emphasis on the toil of discernment amid the interrelated, very powerfully, in the manner by which she represents her narrator's interventions in the narrated. Though I respect much Woolfian scholarship, awareness of a mobile, narrating presence, with regard to *The Waves*, has often been strangely eliminated from discussion: *Virginia Woolf and the Visible World* (2001) shows Emily Dalgarno consistently citing, for instance on page 22, the language of Woolf's characters as though the words were not reported by the implicit intermediary whom the text takes care to register; Ann Banfield, in *The Phantom Table* (2000), declares that the novel's "structure" alternates "unoccupied perspectives . . . with occupied ones" (309), even as such "perspectives," with their proliferating figuration, presume a seer; for the whole of *Cézanne and Formalism in Bloomsbury* (1987), Beverly H. Twitchell refrains from connecting Cézanne's portraits of objects seen by an advancing eye with Woolf's transiting narrator; J. Hillis Miller, in *Modernism Reconsidered* (1983), finds all Woolfian narrators "a fictional replacement of God" (180), an assertion that such presences could only deny, in view of how they intervene between character and reader, never demonstrating complete access to what they describe or that nothing persists outside their activities. No: Woolf's mediating narrator can be none of these.

The elimination from view I am articulating supports the requirement that we should look again, read again, ascertain the ways in which we intervene in things, how they intervene in what we call ourselves, how the two fields must be interdependent so that both endure. Woolf's narrators, in the fiction and the nonfiction, may figure a means of meditating on such endurance, but its noting is not merely delivered to us, not rendered transparent for us; we must labor for it, accept that, like the world in which it occurs, envisioning is never finished. Incompleteness can only be its wonder and our problem, so long as we mistake the world for what we demand of it and ourselves for being always on the verge of a completion which is yet another sort of stopping. In my ensuing materials, I explore how we might look at bodies, at things, at what we do to them, at how we might listen to and image them in new ways, all in the light of Woolf's exemplary struggles to re-envision what seems so simply to be the case. Yet, since to reimagine the relational is to thwart the linearity implied by mere equivalence and antithesis, since that thwarting points to an understanding of relation in multiplex terms, indirect because not self-evident, the reader will find that the indirection of my approach to what Woolf asks of us is consonant with an indirectness suggesting that our valued concepts need to be investigated once more, challenged once more. A signal gift of indirection lies in the inferences it exacts from us: what we see inferentially can neither be already given nor predetermined, so that the inductive process fundamental to drawing closer necessitates our comprehending how we order, how we experience, proximity. Thus, when the reader marks that my Woolfian explorations are surrounded with, interrupted by, deliberations over the work of Oscar Wilde, Plato, Isadora Duncan, William Butler Yeats, Sophocles, Iris Murdoch, Simone Weil, and that of many others, I hope she will concede that what appears to be an interruption, an intrusion, honors the difficulties of Woolf's re-evaluative thinking by exhibiting that such thinking has a long history, however indirect, one worth our watching over it. And I maintain that to "keep watch" enjoins our recognition of the reciprocity without end through which the world that is not ours for the having may survive, for keeping "watch" must be reciprocal—or become a nothing whose making will be ours.

1.
The Figure: Between the Mover and the Moved

> On ne se fait pas un bonnet de coton d'une métonymie; on ne chausse pas une comparaison en guise de pantoufle; on ne se peut servir d'une antithèse pour parapluie; malheureusement, on ne saurait se plaquer sur le ventre quelques rimes bariolées, en manière de gilet. [We cannot make a cotton cap out of a metonymy; we cannot put on a comparison like a slipper; we cannot use an antithesis as an umbrella; unfortunately, we cannot lay a few gaily colored rhymes on our body by way of a waistcoat.]
> —Gautier: Préface, *Mademoiselle de Maupin* (1834), 191.

It should not be difficult to imagine him, imprisoned, bound, just as the suggested title of what later becomes *De Profundis* (1905) verbally pictures for us, its Latin (*In Carcere et Vinculis*) lucidly situating Oscar Wilde in a place from which he may not move. There, without evident succession or extension—for time moves so "slowly" that it may not be said to proceed at all, and the lineaments of the world are constrained by the architecture of his cell—he begins "the day by going down" on his "knees and washing the floor" of his cell (921). Indeed, one thing becomes a metonym for another: the day, its "very minutest detail like its brother," endlessly repeatable, duplicated by its twin and thus vulnerable to the substitution of twinship, resembles the "one long moment" of time, physicalized in "an unchangeable pattern" so that time, space, and the man bound by them persist without differentiation (904). And yet the day—*a* day, *some* day—begins, and he falls to his knees in order to wash the stone floor of his cell. Behind him, the "small iron-barred window" yields little light, rendering the space beyond and bound by the window homologous (904). Later, sitting beneath the window, he will begin to write, only to turn what he produces "over each night to the warden"; this work, as Richard Ellmann informs us in the biography (1988), will not be "returned to" him the "next day"(510). Originating in a place where "motion is no more" (*DP* 904), how can the word review the immobility of its conditions? How can the writer's "heart" resist the "stone" all around him (921)? What would such resistance sound like?

To explore these questions, it is important to begin with a discussion of the culture out of which *De Profundis* emanates, the culture whose judgment Wilde strives to order. This is a culture, H. Montgomery Hyde reports, which, with the advent of the second trial, charges Wilde with committing "indecent acts" (153), a culture whose judicial representative—Sir John Bridge—rejects Wilde's application for bail with the declaration that "there is no worse crime" than that with which Wilde has been "charged" (157). How is the legal prosecution of "the gravest of all offences," whose perpetrators "suffer from a species of insanity," logically constructed (99, 197)? To grapple with this question is to contextualize Wilde's recasting of the terms on which his culture's jurisprudence is founded. For such jurisprudence, such knowledge of law, purports to be organized by logic—by the *techne*, the art, of reason. And yet it is precisely the art of reasoning, the means by which we construe the phenomena of our world, which Wilde adverts to when he asserts that "the fatal errors of life are not due to man's being unreasonable," but "to man's being logical" (*DP* 894). This logic, this "common sense" (Hyde 115), this mode of subsuming the particular under the weight of the general, is grounded in a causality arising from a series of equivalences: heterosexuality = normality; normality = virility; virility = the breed of "common sense" which understands these equations to be self-evident, and under the operations of which the regularized world *continues*. What follows from this is the need to categorize human behaviors which will not fit the equivalences ordained for them, so that homosexuality = abnormality, abnormality = effeminacy, and effeminacy = aestheticism, the latter becoming a kind of *de facto* figuration of same-sex relations. Such figuration claims that same-sex relations are dangerous, that what ensues from them is a cessation of community, a disintegration of community, propagated by those who will not consent to fit the correspondences by which humankind values and recognizes itself.

Moreover, the work of art and its maker, under the auspices of this logic, subsist in a synonymy from which there is no removal because the interstitial, the intervening space between one thing and another, has been deemed unworthy of being made room for. Thus, the "corrupt" (Hyde 114) book is a surrogate for its author, whose "sodomitical habits" themselves, Hyde tells us (349), were historically inaugurated on Anglo-Saxon soil by the "Normans" (349): hence, sodomy becomes a signifier of incursion, the product of a virally configured invasion whose peril is that the virus is *contagious*. The aforesaid pathological model and the ostensible 1:1 ratio between art-object and artist are identically constructed, so that to proclaim the veracity of either model is to affirm that there is nothing beyond, nothing outside the operations of, this logic, "fatal" because it denies relationship by withdrawing its constituents from the world of differences in which our species may be said to live. Indeed, in this system of equivalences, the human subject is effectively erased, obliterated by its alleged representations; therefore, nothing may be predicated of it. And it is much of the work of *De Profundis* to declare the merits of the particular human subject whose predications are broader, more compassionate, than the "fatal logic" by which that subject has been judged. By means of the word, then, Wilde pronounces the potential for the subject—whose frailties, knowingly or unknowingly, are answered by our own—to exist at all.

But the potential for the subject to exist, to speak of the toil of its existence, is, like all human potentialities, a problem; for, "if life be, as it surely is, a problem" to Wilde, he is "no less a problem to Life" (*DP* 917). And this is precisely the point, that the human subject and "Life" are engaged in a dynamic, reciprocal relation whose problematical nature does not require a solution but a way of honoring, by the angle of vision embedded in the use of the word, the imperative that the subject should "feel itself alive" (899). The dynamism of the problem is written into the "great things of life," which are "what they seem to be, and for that reason . . . are often difficult to interpret" (901). Given that we are "entirely free, and at the same time entirely dominated by law," it is "the eternal paradox of human life that we realise at every moment" (891), and *how* we "interpret" that "paradox" "reveals" us (901). The entirety of our freedom is enfolded into the "law" under whose domination we move because the "law" has not been produced by spontaneous generation, but originates in us: it codifies the moves that we can imagine ourselves making. Therefore, the "law" could be imagined differently in such a way that it fosters our "own development" (916). "To forget" how we participate in the structures that we make, in "the good as well as . . . the evil" that we do (916), is to remove ourselves from our capacity for "imagination" (887), from our responsibilities to ourselves, to one another, and to the energy field of the "Life" all around us. Indeed, without the tensions of the "problem" in which each of us is implicated, nothing could be said to happen: there would be no impetus for transformation, no "means for development" (921). "To forget," here, is to embark on the "Eternal Negation," to attempt to tame the "problem" that will not be tamed (897).

Ellmann states that "the most important thing about *De Profundis* is that it is a love letter," one whose "climax . . . describes

Christ without recognizing his divinity" (515, 514). Wilde's work has often been abused by being forcibly tethered to models which diminish its scope: Ellmann assimilates Wilde's letter to amorous discourse as though such assimilation made sense of the "problem" of the text, just as Smith and Helfand, the editors of *Oscar Wilde's Oxford Notebooks* (1989), assimilate the latter to the Hegelian method, which presumably attests to Wilde's intellectual merits. To envelop the Wildean text in mere generic concerns, or in extra-theoretical discourses, is to erase what the text *does*. I am arguing here that what *De Profundis* does, for its author, for its addressee, for its community of readers, is to show the costs of our removal from participating in our own "development" in order to "realise both" the costs themselves and how our separation from the relational—the world of selves in which we live—may be reconfigured (916). In the *Oxford Notebooks*, Wilde quotes the *Hecuba* of Euripides: "Stand off and view my sorrow as a painter might" (137); in reference to *De Profundis*, to share in this painterly vision is to "view" how that "sorrow" has been made, and to comprehend its structure implies the ability to conceive that this "sorrow" may be made *differently*. Wilde's prose affirms the "motion" of the word, the word that testifies to "all things" being "of equal value and of equal size," at once capable of differentiation and connection (904, 879). Sorrow signifies the revelation of relationship: if "there is nothing that stirs in the whole world of thought or motion to which sorrow does not vibrate in terrible if exquisite pulsation," sorrow—vibrating, pulsing, resonating—announces the relationship of which it is compounded (905–906). To vibrate and to pulsate are responsive acts, and these acts speak of the world of other people, of mutual responsibilities, in which we move.

Wilde must "write" Douglas's "life to" him as a means of picturing how that life may be transformed (896); the picture of the life and the work of sorrow enunciate the language of suffering, out of which rises the narrative of Christ, who is a type, an embodiment of "imaginative sympathy" through which we can enact the claim that "soul and body are one and indivisible" (923, 919). If Christ "took the entire world of the inarticulate, the voiceless world of pain, as his kingdom, and made of himself its eternal mouthpiece," one of the functions of this is to model for us how "sorrow and suffering" are "modes through which" we may "realise" the "conception of the beautiful" (927).

And this leads us to what the "symbol" (922), to what the "Form reveals" (919): an "idea" has no value until it "becomes incarnate" because, by virtue of its incarnation, the "idea" can be read, sensed, learned from, and—by extension—enacted in the world (927). Ellmann's reading of *De Profundis* thus diminishes the breadth of the text, for as Wilde envisions the voicing of the "voiceless," the articulation of the "inarticulate," he braids together the aesthetic and the divine, and attests to—under the aegis of the speaking "image" (927)—the "dynamic forces" in which each of us participates (934). Indeed, to "remember that imagination is the quality that enables one to see things and people in their real as in their ideal relations" simultaneously renders us adequate to the "burdens" of our "problem" and reconfigures their very nature (953, 955). This is what the word, fueled by "imaginative sympathy," can do. As a way of grounding the pedagogy of Wilde's oratory here—for to guide our vision is nothing if not a pedagogical project—I situate the rhetorical procedures of *De Profundis* among the work of Plato, Aristotle, and Cicero. Each author argues that "the end of life must be realised through the means" (Wilde, *Notebooks* 142), and Wilde—a Classics scholar, after all—endeavors to affect the "soul," the "body" of his audience. I do this not to quiet the text, but to indicate that its valued "imaginative sympathy" has a history.

In the history of rhetoric, under what auspices can the body be said to function? The individual orator, like the body politic of which he is a part, becomes a reservoir for the interconnectedness of the heavenly, earthly, and corporeal realms. The fact that, according to Marjorie Hope Nicolson in *The Breaking of the Circle* (1960), "each of the three worlds" has "its individuality, yet each" is "involved with the others," describes the simultaneously singular and combinative stamp of these relational domains, intricately ordered by the medical model—the trope for classical oratory—which makes of the human body a community of relations (125). The humoral body is vital to a discussion of the orator as physician, because that body—governed by blood, choler, phlegm, melancholy, in proportions relative to the system in question—is founded on, rendered *recognizable* by, the balance of opposites so significant to the rhetorical project. Proportioned by fluids that persist in a species of dialectic, of conversation, figuring "in little all the sphere," the body, together with the relationships by which it is constituted, forges the social structures of a community (125). It also, by virtue of its beneficial use in the world, permits those structures to continue. The orator-physician ministers to the body politic by means of the *techne* of his rhetoric in order to craft a conversation among citizens, each of whom is individual and involved with his neighbors. Here, to value the external object—the community at large, the compounded corpus of sky, earth, and body—is to signify that internal and external territories are relationally bound together, so that it is the work of the therapeutic, rhetorical act to voice the breadth of the relationships through which the community construes its world. Through the process inherent in the medical model, the orator-physician at once solidifies, enunciates, and extends the relationships of which his culture is made. To balance opposites is to claim that evidently oppositional elements are relatable; implicit in the medical model is the contention that physicality and speech, orator and body politic, entail each other. Indeed, they are unthinkable without reference to each other and to the community engendered by them.

In the *Phaedrus*, Plato presents the interlocking of oratory and community in an organic fashion. Here, the medical model that certifies such an interlocking is figured even further as a journey, a way; medical and expeditionary models are homologous because both are procedural. Through the process of narration—via narrative, the therapeutic act becomes communicable to an audience of present and future "patients," and it is the nature of a journey to be told—these models are capable of instructing and benefiting the body of the orator's audience. The instructional note is important because in this text Plato renders the procedures of oratory analogous to medicine, journeying, and pedagogy, making the orator embody the triad of physician, traveller, and mentor. This figuration consequently characterizes the audience as patient, fellow voyager, and student, citizens embarked on a dialogue through which any community may be said to develop.

But Socrates and Phaedrus, orator and auditor, significantly begin in the same place. Sharing situational "turf" fosters dialogue: meeting him in the street in Athens, Socrates asks Phaedrus "where have you come from . . . and where are you going?" throwing Phaedrus—and, by extension, the reader—into the narrative act and all that may be expected of it (227). We are about to hear Phaedrus read a speech by Lysias, a "clever" production originating in the "best writer living" (227–228). By virtue of wandering from the seat of *negotium* to that of *otium*, Socrates and Phaedrus describe what is particular to each location: the city, replete with the business of daily life, offers the gift of sudden encounters, while the country affords the peace required for expectant contemplation. The balance necessary between these two poles is itself a species of dialogue, and delineates the specific conventions with which city and country are associated, conventions which speak to the community that propounds them. These conventions, their attendant expectations—and the community that is their origin—make it possible for Socrates to formulate his restorative, pedagogical irony. Without common ground, of place, of discourse, the revisions and reversals of Socratic irony would not be possible: irony rests on shared context. The *stasis*, the beginning-point of common ground, enables Socrates to travel—through the *ductus*, the way of the text—towards the *skopos*, the target of reconfiguring the work of oratory.

Because rhetoric and its oratorical expression are shown to us as already being in a state of decline, Socrates is able to effect the multiple labors of his ironic project. For Lysias's speech, "clever," founded on the *telos* that "an admirer who is not in love is to be preferred to one who is," communicates merely its own self-referentiality, where the guile of the performance is valued above all else (227). Its status as an object, as a written *thing*, eradicates its ability to accommodate its audience: simply inhabiting the page, Lysias's speech is without the power to speak and be spoken to, to live as a voice among other voices. It cannot, therefore, ameliorate the humanity of its audience; its singleness reveals its debasement. But the merit of this debasement resides in its offering Socrates the opportunity to vocalize its opposite. Socrates, "still in ignorance about" his "own nature," positions himself in the place of "ignorance," a region, a route to knowledge: to identify "ignorance" of the self is an epistemological act, as the act of naming requires a kind of knowledge (230). The proclamation of "ignorance" here is a marker for irony—it is, after all, the great pedagogue who speaks through the labor of Plato's hands—and this irony is work, a proceeding, full of the suffering and restlessness attendant on identifying the beginning-place of unknowing. If Socrates makes himself the "object" of his "investigations," he does so as a gesture towards the process of gaining knowledge through dialogue with others who are involved in an analogous "ignorance," questioning the self and what that self owes to its kind (230). Irony, "ignorance"—and the rhetoric that grants them life—are necessarily ameliorative, medicinal, setting the speakers of the dialogue on a course in the direction of knowledge communally worked for, argued over, moved towards.

When Socrates produces his initial oratorical answer to Lysias, its properties are the direct "opposites of all the bad qualities . . . attributed to the first" (241), exemplifying that Socrates has manufactured an inversion of Lysias's "clever" display without submitting that display to an altogether radical reconfiguration. At this juncture, the "power of divination" manifests itself; receiving "the supernatural sign," Socrates seems to hear "a voice declaring" that he "had committed a sin and must not go away" until that sin should undergo expiation (242). This passage is significant in manifold ways: it indicates that rhetoric operates under the injunction of "sound doctrine" (243), that the soundness of that "doctrine" speaks of "unity and plurality as they exist in the nature of things" (266), "things" that can be named, discussed, divined if inspiringly read under the aegis of "Love" (242). Love, here, is humoral; like the humors of the body, it is built on a pattern of relationship and functions as an overarching trope, tying all relations together.

Physician/patient, mentor/student, lover and loved, all typify relations crafted in order to evince the benevolence, compassion, and concern between self and other that make our world knowable as world. If "there is not nor ever shall be . . . a genuine art of speaking which is divorced from the grasp of truth" (260), that "art of speaking" is predicated on the truth-values of its effectual use: its imperative is "to influence the soul" (271). The process of influencing the soul begins in amatory "madness," with the proviso that it "comes as the gift of heaven" (244); this gift renders the orator a conduit for the efficacious workings of the divine, and entails the amplification of the rhetorical/medicinal act into a kind of purgation (243), a sowing of the orator's "seed in soil that suits it" (276), and a generation through which our "kindred come to birth, as they should, in the minds of others" (278). But the knowledge and truth so fundamental to these figures of delivery—and vital for both self and community—are themselves procedural, speculative, for through "speculation" we may arrive "at a knowledge of reason and unreason" (270). Working for, moving towards, this knowledge, the orator devises a speech with "its own organic shape, like a living being" (264), a "living being" that is a testimony to the relations from which it has arisen and which confirms that its community will continue.

For Aristotle, in *The Art of Rhetoric*, the speech itself is "comprised of three factors—the speaker, the subject and the listener—but it is the 'listener'" who is privileged by virtue of his capacity for weighing whether the orator's speech has achieved its object (1.3,135b). The audience here is of supreme importance because it is comprised of individuals who have undergone the same educational process, in which different modes of discourse and different disciplines are connected; these materials of study, through being contiguously taught, are rendered of equivalent value: the pedagogical model, then, is not hierarchical. Orator and audience stand on a common ground of socially defined, shared knowledge; the audience becomes a *creature* whose humoral balance may be reaffirmed by the orator's "detection" of the "persuasive aspects" of the "matter" (1.1,135bff.), given linguistic form through being demonstrated. But demonstration proceeds, M. F. Burnyeat tells us (1996), by "advancing considerations for the audience to think about" (93); allied to invention, inciting the cognitive work of thought, demonstration often utilizes the enthymeme, which "embodies the claim that the clash of opposing arguments in deliberative and forensic gatherings is a positive expression of human reasonableness in a world where issues are complex and deciding them is difficult" (Burnyeat 91). Standing on their common ground, orator and audience are not homogeneous: to invent, to demonstrate, to argue both sides of an issue—and, analogously, to listen in order to enact judgment—do not produce homogeneity because the heterogeneous must be made room for in a "complex" world where decisions are "difficult." Here, the imperative of room for the "difficult" accommodates the emotions which we—orator and audience—simultaneously share and which articulate the gradations of our differences.

Aristotle, on the basis of Martha Craven Nussbaum's reading of him (1996), identifies emotions as "forms of intentional awareness . . . directed at or about an object, in which the object figures as it is seen from the creature's point of view" (303). Since emotion and "object" define each other, in order to account for the experiential fact of the emotion, "one must mention the object to which it is directed," characterizing "the object as it is seen by the person experiencing the emotion, whether that view is correct or not" (Nussbaum 304). Truth, therefore—the correctness of the person's flush of feeling—is not an operative value; on the contrary, what remains of the utmost value is the struggle for the "virtue of moderation," which "requires psychological balance" (Nussbaum 305). If we must learn "to take appropriate objects," it is the orator's project to "produce these emotions in an audience," to reveal those emotions' "complex cognitive disposition" (Nussbaum 305): the audience must not only see the "object," but experientially double the person's appetitive contact with that "object." These processes are humoral on multiple levels. The lecture notes of the *Rhetoric* give us the artist, Aristotle, and the corollary of his student-apprentices who must, through the work figured in the text, absorb how "emotions can in fact be created and taken away pretty reliably by discourse and argument" (Nussbaum 306). The pairs of artist/apprentice, physician/patient, orator/audience are connected by procedures in which one thing is answered by another: to elicit feeling is to know the potential for our own created feeling to be answered, so that the elements of these pairs, by "cultivating the emotions," may "keep themselves in health and even become healthier" (Nussbaum 317) through "acknowledging their vulnerability before the circumstances of life" (Nussbaum 312). The orator evokes feeling in his audience in order for that body—"the giver of judgement"—to be brought into what Aristotle calls "a certain condition" (2.1), predicated on the belief that "life can do something to us, and that this something matters" (Nussbaum 312). From the point of view of this "certain condition," the audience is a human "we," capable of coming to appropriate, compassionate judgment, an act that substantiates that the aforementioned "something" profoundly "matters."

The palpable nostalgia with which Cicero invests *De Oratore* poignantly clarifies that "life can do something to us." For this text exemplifies that we live, as Cicero lived, in a world always in danger of moving away from us; as the text begins, rhetoric is virtually already lost, and this state of being nearly lost signifies the old world that is on the verge of vanishing. Crassus and Antonius, the representatives of the "faculty of speaking" (212), embody "the real power of eloquence" that "embraces the origin, the influence, the changes of all things in the world, all virtues, duties, and all nature, so far as it affects the manners, minds, and lives of mankind" (213). Encompassing all of nature, originary and procedural, its use affecting every component of that nature, oratory conveys—through the "faculty" of speech—the linked chain by which all the "things" of the world are connected. If oratory is a connector, fuelled by the theory of rhetoric, the orator's project is to enunciate the texture and breadth of those connections; doing so, his speech becomes a trope for the synapses of the mind whose joinings carry the thought that emerges as the communicable word. Cicero theorizes the kinship of mind and body, and—by extension—the worldly community of minds and bodies, for "all the powers of action proceed from the mind, and the countenance is the image of the mind, and the eyes are its interpreters" (258). Here action "is, as it were, the speech of the body, and ought therefore the more to accord with that of the soul" (259). Such theorizing merges medical and neurological models for the work of oratory, since action "by its own powers displays the movements of the soul" and "affects all mankind" (259): affecting "all mankind," the actions of the orator and audience are joined together in order to effect oratory's "necessary use" (244). But if the present in which *De Oratore* begins is a time where rhetoric and its *techne*, oratory, are virtually lost, the enactors, the carriers of these connections, persist in a spatial/temporal realm out of balance with the action of the "necessary" word. In an attempt to right this balance—humoral, medical, cognitively structured—Cicero portrays the health of the past as a means of potentially regaining health in the present.

What does this effort to right the balance make of the text? The text becomes an indicator of "the way" to return to health, a "finger" held "out . . . toward the spring" of the past (61). "Knowledge of all subjects that contribute to form" the "wisdom" and the "force of oratory" springs from the mouths of Crassus and Antonius, so that the text is a medium for rescuing "their fame, now upon the decline, from silence and oblivion," to "render their fame . . . imperishable" (84–85). Their "fame" must be seen to be "imperishable" because of the connectives for which Crassus and Antonius stand, "the very system of the universe and of nature to be constituted with a view to the safety and preservation of the whole," which it is the business of oratory to perpetrate via the "action" of speech (244). To "contemplate and call to mind" (6), to generate "the recollection of an old tradition," is to write nostalgically (7), and to write nostalgically is to bring the past back through the agency of the word. *De Oratore* mutually embeds historical and literary incidents, as Crassus's "plane tree . . . diffuses its spreading boughs to overshade this place" (13), so that the "Tusculan country seat" mirrors the contemplative position of Socrates and Phaedrus (12), whose dialogue is similarly situated. The memorial text performs—actively, medicinally—the meaning that it carries, and is a "repository for all things," the memory that is "the keeper of all matter and words that are the fruits of thought and invention" (10). The vessel for recovered memory, Cicero's reader is endowed with the capability of delivering—and amplifying—the value of the nearly lost.

While all these texts are memorial to varying degrees—and belong to the genre of commemoration—in *De Profundis*, Wilde memorializes the past by subjecting it to the lens of a comprehensive vision, not to recover the lostness of the past but to "look on" it with "different eyes" (957). He does this as an expression of the premise that "a thing *is* according to the mode in which one looks at it" (957), as a way of arguing that the "irrevocable" (956), the evident givenness of the past, can be remade by the work of the directed gaze. The gaze, then, is a vehicle for writing the perceiver's present—and his subsequent future—into the object of the past, so that the temporal model here refuses linearity; on the contrary, it presents itself as a kind of synaptic construction, conceptually enacting the interwoven connections it honors.

Wilde infuses this synaptic vision of time into the language of the letter's initial sentence:

> Dear Bosie, After long and fruitless waiting I have determined to write to you myself, as much for your sake as for mine, as I would not like to think that I had passed through two long years of imprisonment without ever having received a single line from you, or any news or message even, except such as gave me pain. (873)

The coiling of the tenses here, each wrapped round the other, is as multiple as the audiences Wilde addresses: Doulgas, the intended recipient of the letter, will presumably read in the present Wilde's portrait of their shared past, while future readers will gain access to the text by means of Robert Ross, who will be given instructions "to have" the letter "copied" (Ellmann 515). "At first . . . given separate sheets to write on," Wilde—at some undisclosed juncture—is permitted to compose in "a manuscript book" (Ellmann 510), so that the writing process itself is of an axial nature, the present of each separate sheet at once a continuation of prior work and an icon for starting over. The turning of Wilde's tenses, the twisting of present perfect, conditional present, past perfect, past progressive, initiates Wilde's ethos—his character and credibility—for his multiple audience. Time has become a multiply factored *thing* to twist, to turn, and his language performs this twisting-turning in such a way that language bears its own thingness. We—and this "we" is as complex as the language addressed to us—are meant, I think, to understand that Wilde, the persuader, is someone who has undergone "something" that "matters" (Nussbaum 312), that the significance of this "something" announces itself in his syntax so that syntax and semantics merge.

Wilde's rhetorical procedures in the narrative of selected scenes from his life with Douglas work in three registers: concurrently deliberative, judicial, and epideictic, their operations are exhortative, accusatory, and concerned with blame. Through a kind of narrative accretion, Wilde adjures Douglas to kill his "vanity" by picturing the ceaseless rapaciousness of that "vanity" (873), how it is founded on a paralysis of the "imagination" (876) where "nothing remains" but what has been "eaten," what has been "drunk" (877)—where "nothing remains" but the inventory of the merely *used*. He accuses Douglas of "an entire lack of imagination" (887) in which "desire without limit" originates (909), how such desire treats "everybody"—and everyone—"alike" because, without the catalyst of "imagination," desire cannot recognize the pith of its own objects (931). Douglas's illimitable hunger causes Wilde's exhaustion, and it is this for which Wilde blames him, the wearing "out" which attends the human subject whose treatment renders it an object en route to a satiation that fails to occur (878). The triad of Wilde's exhortation, accusation, and blame serves to incite in us the pathos of inhabiting, as readers, the nearly compulsive nature of these desiring narratives; it is excruciating to read them because our reading replicates the experience of being pulled into the "certain condition" (Aristotle 2.1) of an appetite which "anything will feed" (*DP* 893). Wilde's appetitive narratives perform their very import, emblematized in the emotions they elicit: they make us yearn for something outside, something beyond, for a way *through* them.

It is not my intention to assimilate Wilde's procedures to the work of oratory, but to contend that Wilde strives to persuade us, his explicit and implicit readers, of the value of the logos, the argument his letter demonstrates. The circularly desiring narratives, while building our persuader's ethos and fostering our pathos for him, with him, become a *ductus*, a way to bringing our emotions to the "profusion" of the world that is not a mere thing to be imbibed, not our equivalent, but to which we are related (876). We, like Doulgas, must "try to see" (898) that the costs of our desires, the "sufferings" they cause us, are not "without meaning" (913), and that this is the injunction in which they involve us. For things that *mean* speak of a world of relation, a world of distinctions, while meaninglessness would engender an absence of distinctions, a gluten of phenomena before which our language would be useless, given its basis in the relational. When Wilde avers that "where there is Sorrow there is holy ground" (906), he indicates that our "sufferings," if we grant them meaning—and such granting is one of the "powers of action" which "proceed from the mind" (Cicero 258)—direct us to the "Sorrow" that adumbrates the "turf" of the relational, the scene of meanings where "whatever happens to another happens to oneself" (923) because our "sufferings" link us, connect us, and the emotions they awaken. And these emotions entail our responsibility to them; they are a "revelation" (919) of the "imaginative sympathy" (923) through which we can discern what we have "never discerned before" (919). So "to forgive" and to be forgiven (912) are acts whose "necessary use" (Cicero 244) is that they honor the world of feeling, a world typified by Christ in whom "the outward is expressive of the inward" (919), and who manifests—in a mortal body—the connectivity of the divine, the aesthetic, and the ethical. To mean, then, is to try "to realise" the breadth of that connectivity (933).

As Gautier instructs us, it is not possible for the figures of our language, for metonymies, antitheses, to protect us from the thingness of the world. If, however, "the real power of eloquence" is that it "affects the manners, minds, and lives of mankind" (Cicero 213), how we deploy the instrumentality of our language can announce our capacity for seeing these "manners, minds, and lives"—in all their "irrevocable" thingness—with "different eyes" (*DP* 956–957). This, in turn, implies the potential reconfiguration of that thingness. One of the merits of *De Profundis* is Wilde's attempt to persuade us that such an act is possible.

. . .

But if there are no stories, what end
can there be, or what beginning?
—Virginia Woolf: *The Waves*, 267.

A woman in off-white muslin stands positioned at the back of the stage. It is difficult to see her, to discern with any certainty whether her apparent stillness conceals a slow, deliberate motion.

In the odd half-light, only the scooped neck of her costume gleams; this proves, however, to be a trick of the light, or a product of the woman's concentrated pose, for it is the skin bounded by her costume that appears to pulse, so that the woman's sternum, throat, and head rise out of muslin in a single plane. The Allegretto of Beethoven's Symphony no. 7 in A major begins (1812), its repeated notes in the strings emphasizing the focused intensity of the woman's figure. If she is moving, her movement occurs at a pace the eye cannot measure. Indeed, she seems to resist the means by which we identify if one thing rather than another may be said to happen; in her, motion and stillness become two simultaneous considerations, just as Beethoven's exposition of his first theme resonates with the palpitating beats of repeated pitches, so that the theme—and the woman's figure—inheres in two alternatives, which are not mutually exclusive but concurrently present.

I turn to this ekphrasis of Arnold Genthe's 1920 portrait of what Ann Daly qualifies as the "full, postural movement" of Isadora Duncan's body (1995, 153), because that body at once strives to remove itself from "the old bondage of exteriority," as Arthur Symons phrases it (1899, 9), and throws into question the discursive nature of the language by means of which we can articulate our experience of the figure poised before us. For a figure is, has been, there, one which reveals—as Edward Gordon Craig asserts in *On the Art of the Theatre* (1911)—"by means of movement the invisible things, those seen through the eye and not with the eye, by the wonderful and divine power of [m]ovement" (46). If movement is a marker of "invisible things," the seen and the unseen persist in a dynamic relation, where one realm structures—and is structured by—the other. As a maker of movement, the body, in this conceptual model, also announces the contiguity of the visible and the invisible, that announcement being effected "through" the eye, with Craig's preposition transfiguring, idealizing cognition as a process beyond the scope of individual agency. The body, the signifier of the official reality of *things*, becomes a vessel through which animation moves, enacting a "divine power" necessarily posited by the instrumentality of the dancer's quotidian body. In this case, the difficulty, the impossibility, resides in distinguishing between the mover and the moved, between motility as a suffusing energy field and the implement of Duncan's body.

The "symbolic reality" here may depend, Frank Kermode insists (1962), "always upon the body—upon the power of the body not to express emotion but to objectify a pattern of sentience" (1957 27). Nevertheless, that patterned "sentience" depends on the dancer's gift of ceding the medium of the body to the motion that actuates it, as what is required of us—the viewers of that body, the readers of Yeats's early poems—is our acknowledgement that "it is the business of art momentarily to mend" the "process of dissociation" that "mind and body, form and matter, image and discourse have undergone" (1957, 2). This momentary mending may be one of the "stories" valued by Virginia Woolf, but it has fuelled much of the significant work of Duncan, Craig, and Yeats. Beginning with Genthe's vision of a late Duncan solo, I ponder the reconfiguration of agency articulated *through* the dancing body and the utility of connecting Yeats's early, symbolist work with the mythical method so fundamental to the later poems. Indeed, to associate the given and the "divine," the seen and the unseen, is to tell a different story whose telling challenges the supremacy of discursive thinking in the very language of discursive thinking.

As symbolism emphasizes the linkages among conventionally discrete objects, it reorganizes mimesis as a portrayal of the interfusion of external and internal domains. It is the work, then, of language—and of the dancer's body—to evoke these linkages in the reader's receptive mind. For Yeats, however, this linking is fraught with valued tension: while "it is only when the intellect has wrought the whole of life to drama, to crisis, that we may live for contemplation" ("Hodos," 287), it is our readerly project to observe that this tethering together of antinomies is founded on the usefulness of the "crisis" on the page, on the stage, and *in us*. As Duncan's body, in her late solo, becomes a vehicle for moving beyond mere sensory perception, so Yeats's symbolism deploys a language usually intimate with time—in the syntactic sequence of one element followed by another, in the predication of divided subjects and objects—in order to summon a world beyond time. We, in our sequentially ordered world, with our language grounded in the distinctions between one thing and another, are asked to inhabit a "crisis" of impingement. Rather than seeing the "Yeatsian symbol" as affording a "reconciliation" of "the opposites of action and contemplation" (Kermode 1957, 43), I find that symbol—untamed, undomesticated—compounded of the impingement of its antithetical components. It is as though one were to say: without the reciprocal relation of impingement, nothing identifiable may be said to happen. The gnostic nature of this discourse, its emphasis on a muscular, difficult approach to knowledge, is as continuous as the discursive project it repudiates. The "crisis," for poet, dancer, and reader, is without end because time—under the auspices of this vision—is without the *telos* of linearity.

If myths are narratives generated for the benefit of a community—and are non-linear by virtue of their ceaseless retelling—the narrator of those myths has situated himself within the community he addresses. In his early work, Yeats gives us a community of symbols operating under the aegis of reverie; the mythical method of the later work proportions the symbol and the givenness of the world—customarily transfigured by the symbol's breadth—in such a way that the given is vivified, energized, by myth. The impingement of the symbolist program is retained, only both components (the frailty of earthly things, together with their linguistic translation, *and* their propinquity to mythological narrative) merit significant value. There is a pedagogy here: privileging the myth over its proximity to the real, if that term is equivalent to the sequentially given in time, Yeats's mythical method nevertheless yields us work which does not jettison the given as being unworthy of consideration. On the contrary, this is a pedagogy that reviews an empiricism predicated on the declaration that things—in their vulnerability to our inspection, their being present before us—are merely knowable, and hence assimilable to *the known*. Yeats, reviewing the empirical model, sees it differently, and it is in that difference that we can discover the method's pedagogical impetus.

While myth narrates a vision of the breadth of our world(s), its narration inserts itself as mediation between the life of the community and the forms of life that are possible for us to know; and knowing, here, does not cease with the object, but delivers the local object to us as an instance of perennial breadth. This interpenetration of the local and the perennial is notated in much of the vernacular nature of the later work's language and in the poet's persona, which struggles with the weight of its pedagogy. If the "terror is in recognition, the strength in the image which compels assent" (Blackmur 1952, 122), Yeats's method neither capitulates to nor erases the object. Rather, the object is reverberated, its dignity enriched by those reverberations. We are implicated in this project: as readers, we are urged to participate in the work's revision of the world of things in which we read.

It is interesting to hear Eliot subdue the freighted tensions of Joyce's mythical method—and, by implication, that of Yeats—in his 1923 review of *Ulysses*. For Eliot, this method is "simply a way of controlling, of ordering, of giving a shape and a significance to the immense panorama of futility and anarchy which is contemporary history" (Eliot, 177). But to found the value of the method on the claim that "contemporary history"—standing here for a present replete with its own lateness, its own anarchic futility in relation to an unrecoverable past—must have order conferred upon it by the "continuous parallel"-ling (177) of the contemporary and the ancient, is to retain a vision, explicit in empiricism, of the impoverishment of the object. Indeed, the object's supposed poverty is proclaimed by our need to redeem it. This paralleling avows not that these temporal modes are contiguous or even associable, but rather that it is the writer's work to make "the modern world possible for art" (178), to consign the "possible" to an order ordained by the writer, who thus becomes an "Einstein" (177), a discoverer who reconfigures our deployment of the real. Science consequently propounds a means of recovering—and, by extension, *supplanting*—the real by virtue of the splendor of its representations. This appears to me to be an empiricism which replaces the object with the use to which it can only submit.

Conversely, for Yeats—who "adumbrated" this method (Eliot, 177)—"all the ladders start / [i]n the foul rag and bone shop of the heart" ("The Circus Animals'," 39–40); we are "lost amid the labyrinth" that we have "made / [i]n art or politics" ("Nineteen Hundred," 70–71): we piece "our thoughts into philosophy / and [plan] to bring the world under a rule," we "who are but weasels fighting in a hole" (30–32). These lines clarify that Yeats, who "commonly hovered between myth and philosophy" (Blackmur, 122), generates such hovering in order to connect myth, philosophy, and the given with which they are concerned. Yeats's histrionic imagination recognizes conflict as a value, an engine for sustaining energy, and all the while the creaturely *thing* is made room for, honored even in its exposure, because its creatureliness cannot—in contrast with Eliot's paradigm—must not be, transcended.

Yeats's mythical method, then, rather than ordaining an essentially static order, originates in a "troubled mirror" ("Nineteen Hundred," 62) which is, after all, what we may be said to have. Antithetically structured, revering the toil of conflict, Yeats's procedure offers us a plenitude of temporal modes resting on a breed of association which does not impugn the merit of differences *and* similitudes; the differences themselves are given to the reader in order to spur cognitive work in a time which does not posit a resolution of the tensions between Homeric song, for example, fabricated in a kind of elongated time, and the "meaning" of "all song": "Let all things pass away" ("Vacillation," 70–71). If, for Eliot, to "parallel" the present with the mythical is to remand the present to the representation that orders it, for Yeats, the method propagates a linguistic enactment of the contradictions, the conflicts, of which time—and, by extension, space—is made. And this delineates a restatement of community: the reader, like the writer, works associatively, inhabiting the associations by means of which his world is recognizable.

In order to investigate the development of the mythical project out of the early symbolist poems, I begin with a discussion of "The Secret Rose." The speaker's summoning calls up a separate world, a domain transfigured by desire in contradistinction to will, for will is teleologically grounded—and therefore moves towards its termination—while desire fastens things to itself in a species of endless accrual. The rose, "inviolate" because of the certitude of its having-been-summoned (1), simultaneously figures propulsive desire and encloses the poem's constituents in a symbolic circuit linguistically operating under the aegis of all that its "great leaves enfold" (7). The architecture of this circuit is comprised of three sentences, all but the third burgeoning with many subordinate clauses, and two final questions. Importantly, the terminal question ratifies the enclosed nature of the poem, duplicating as it does—in its close—the poem's first line. So first and last things are made to meet by their equivalence on the level of language; the body of the poem, however, swells with syntax that graphs the relationship between subject and object.

The following excerpt exemplifies this relationship:

> And him who sold tillage, and house, and goods,
> And sought through lands and islands numberless
> years,
> Until he found, with laughter and with tears,
> A woman of so shining loveliness
> That men threshed corn at midnight by a tress,
> A little stolen tress. . . . (22–27)

The enfolding of the roses' "great leaves" is composed of a slowness that permits us to see the subject of this clause as an attenuation of the movement at work in the language. The sibilants, so prevalent throughout, stretch the sonic life of these lines, affording us the opportunity to linger in them, to inspect the way in which this stretching works in a kind of counterpoint to the heroic couplet, which is—after all—the marker of an acoustic procedure so abundant in the eighteenth-century, the century that fomented the empirical project. But subject and object, here, are not hierarchically configured: the adhering of the subject—"him" and its permutation—is deferred by means of interpolated phrases, elongating the space between subject and object in order for us to note rhythm as a suspension of movement. In that suspension, we can nevertheless observe how subject-object relations have been built; we can acknowledge that the one is not subsumed under the pull of the other, with deferral notating the dilation of desire, and interpolation encouraging us to identify a subject and object connected even in their syntactic separation.

The Cuchulain in "The Secret Rose," the Cuchulain originating in "he that's in the sun" who "begot this body / [u] pon a mortal woman" (*On Baile's Strand*, 294–295), becomes, in the late "Cuchulain Comforted," a representative of both the divine and the human. It is significant that this doubleness of origin is emphasized because it renders Cuchulain an exemplar of the simultaneity of *chronos*—the succession of one moment after another—and *kairos*, a point in time charged with the significant circumstances of an event whose capaciousness is beyond mere succession. Mythical figure and a human agent, Cuchulain illustrates that, as Wallace Stevens declares (1951), "no fact is a bare fact, no individual fact is a universe to itself" (701). Indeed, the "fact" of the divine mortal dying is given to us as a confluence of universes, formulated in a sonic structure that enacts the confluence with which it is concerned.

The following quotation shows us the pattern, the "unit of poetry" that is "*the poem*" (Davie 1955, 19):

> A man that had six mortal wounds, a man
> Violent and famous, strode among the dead;
> Eyes stared out of the branches and were gone.
> Then certain Shrouds that muttered head to head
> Came and were gone. He leant upon a tree
> As though to meditate on wounds and blood.
>
> A Shroud that seemed to have authority
> Among those bird-like things came, and let fall
> A bundle of linen. . . . (1–9)

There are profound differences and similitudes articulated here. Cuchulain, in the process of dying, strides among the dead who are busy with coming, with going, as though the one act were a translation of the other. This conceptual equivalence of the two acts is mirrored by Cuchulain's passage: meditating on the tactile specificity of "wounds and blood," he is going into a death which announces itself as a voice arising from the first-person plural, a community in which everything "must" be done "together," (17), "in common" (24). The significance of the singular and the communal is echoed by the rhyme scheme, an apparent triadic structure where common tones are retained from stanza to stanza while a new acoustic element is introduced. The "dead face which has another kind of life"—so important for Kermode's reading of Yeats—the life "of being as against becoming" (*Romantic* 91), here interweaves "being" *and* "becoming" in an assertion where the state and the process entail each other.

This mutual entailment of "being" and "becoming" returns me to Genthe's portrait of Duncan at the end of her 1920 solo. She moves towards or is situated at—the two options, process and state, are both indistinguishable and present—the front of the stage. We have heard Beethoven build a sonata form without a development section, yet the themes as they resound are developmentally varied in such a way that the movement seems to value stasis and kinesis. What is certain is that—standing before us, an audience of eyes and ears, joined—Duncan raises her arms. Or, to rephrase this discursive formulation: the mover and the moved meet. It is a movement without evident end, even as the music terminates.

And it is precisely these visions of the human body, weighted with the generation of movements which at once terminate and fail to terminate, that launch us into territory so vital to *The Waves*. We have seen the Wildean body of *De Profundis* stooping to scrub the floor of its cell, suffused with the "sorrow" which actuates that body, its representation resisting the conventional hierarchy of subject and object. We have watched Duncan raise her arms so slowly—after moving across the stage seemingly beyond the scope of mensuration—that we do not know how she has come before us. Indeed, we cannot know what she is, if defining the body requires pinning word to thing, as though the thing were spatially fixed by the single name we give it. We must revise our looking, re-see what we have seen. But how can we name, render legible, the body that is more than its own singleness?

By connecting my texts, I maintain that each begins with visions of the body, with what we can imagine the body doing and with what is done to the body. And as Woolf goes to such lengths in the fiction and the essays to rhetoricize the body, to consider how words rise from it, she urges us to rethink the evidently isolable nature of our materiality, contending that the individual and the community cannot be fruitfully separated, that to reconceive our corporeality will transform our experience of the world in which we stand. As a constellation of figures, each valuing the effort to speak in another way, Wilde, Duncan, Craig, and Woolf can be yoked together by Yeats whose belief in the "occult," Woolf affirms, entails that all his "writing depends on it," hangs on the struggle to typify how the hidden and the unconcealed, the invisible and the visible, orient each other (*Diary 4*, 256). It is true that Woolf writes only sparingly of Wilde, categorizing his work as "persuasive and lucid" ("South Wind" *Essays II*, 126), importantly adverting to Wilde's emphasis on rhetorical procedures which reorganize the distance between writer and reader. It is also the case that Woolf and Yeats knew each other, that Yeats admired Craig's set designs, which so significantly spurred Duncan to reimagine her approach to moving through theatrical space. And if "modernist performance," as evidenced by the Ballets Russes, "was rife with anomalies . . . depersonalized yet replete with emotion" (Garafola 1989, 87–88), such valuation of the anomalous can be traced to Duncan's body, traversing the breadth of a stage as though that body were simultaneously single and permeated with the force of a motion finally beyond her, larger than what it moves.

It is not for these reasons alone that I position our texts in a species of impingement, but because each enacts Woolf's assertion, in an essay on Thoreau, that "the common things are so strange," that the "usual sensations" they evoke in us are "astonishing" (*EII*, 135), and that strangeness and astonishment are valuable for us. For one of the virtues of the "common things" being "strange" is that their perceived strangeness alerts us to their complexities, urges us to consider that the local, the so evidently given thing, is intricately compounded. We can think of the body as an exemplar of the commonness of "things," and it is fitting that Woolf begins *The Waves* where we begin, in the body.

Yet as *The Waves* formulates the origin of the body, we find the body itself in multiple manifestations. Thus, each corporeal entity is attended by, doubled by, paired with, another from which it cannot finally be disjoined, so that the ground of our inception—the thingness in which we start—confutes any notion of a single point of origin. A consequence of this is that while it may be impossible here to speak of one thing without reference to another, impracticable to trace our way back to a body's inaugural moment, the world of things is compacted of the relations that render it discernible, representable. And what is describable—sonically, pictorially—can be read, permitting us to ascertain the proportions in which things persist under the work of our readerly gaze. As early as 1917, Woolf notes the "dominion which writers have over us," how "it is their actual voice that we hear in the rise and fall of the sentence; their shape and colour that we see in the page, so that even their old shoes have a way of being worn on this side rather than on that, which seems not gossip but revelation" ("Flumina Amem Silvasque" *EII*, 161). Nevertheless, this "dominion" is one in which we participate, gaining a sense of the body by means of the word. Through the act of reading, we bring our body to bear on the physicality Woolf envisions in the page, and meet that physicality with our own. To read, then, is to be included in the "revelation" of a community of the body, for we are paired with the page before us.

Even the body of the sun, with which *The Waves* begins, cannot be separated from what it affects. "Not yet risen" (7), the sun's photic work is implied by what happens to the sea, "indistinguishable" from the sky, "slightly creased" (7) from the pressure of a radiance not yet precisely visible. The novel originates in a viscosity in which one thing sticks to another, weighs on another, a viscidity comprised of bodies whose presences we can infer from the glutinous creasing of sun on sky on sea. This emphasized creasing announces the relational nature of weight, how each object leans on the world of things contiguous to it. Indeed, the procedural nature of weighing—like the italics out of which the novel arises—figures a moment italicized by its own portentousness, as Woolf's narrative urges us to consider an initiatory pressure of one body upon another. If the act of weighing involves us in determining how bodies proportion one another, and if we start with the logic of sight (with identifying the visible, the invisible), *The Waves* demands that we interrogate how we determine what we see. For we are evidently given a chronicle of the originary moment to which all ensuing phenomena can be traced, and yet we commence with the indiscernible body of the sun. So we know where we are by inferring the presence of what we cannot see; we think we identify our location by reading, by deriving, the invisible from its opposite. *The Waves* may situate itself, and us, in a vision of the three original bodies—sun, sky, sea—to whose distinguishable forces the weight of human life will be added; however, something breaches the primordial scene: we can deduce its shifting from what we read. Can we conceptualize the moment of origin in which a recording eye intervenes?

Such intervention signifies that the originary, when narrated, is necessarily subject to mediation, that the depiction of our starting place is not produced in a vacuum. The narrative, like the body, begins somewhere; a signal virtue of narration, however, is that it bears the marks of its own telling. Unlike the fleshly body, narration testifies to the method of its construction, so that to read the embodied text is to chart the means out of which the thing before us issues. The first words of *The Waves* may yield a picture of the magnetism shot through sun, sky, and sea, but something interposes itself between the picture and our gaze. Unnamed, invisible, this interposing object is nevertheless figured by, italicized by, its verbal procedures. Thus, we are given an (implied) object, an eye whose moving, deciphering glances result in a subject, speaking. As here one body is never isolated from another, so we find ourselves in proximity to a presence written into the words we read.

We can infer the narrator's presence, trace the residues of a reporting subject by means of the protasis so prevalently marked in the A sections comprising half of the two-part, repeated structure out of which *The Waves* is built. From the Greek for "before stretching the proposition," protasis names a clause expressing the condition in a conditional sentence, often marked by "as if" (OED). When we are told that the sea was "as if a cloth had wrinkles in it," that the "cloth became barred with thick strokes moving, one after another . . . pursuing each other" (7), we inhabit a page organized by the logic of the protatic, which analogizes, under the aegis of "as if"—and following the original Greek in an effort to stretch the proposition—sea and cloth. Yet the sea, the thing whose activity such language documents, metamorphoses into cloth so that the thing is enveloped in its figuration. This metamorphosis, this lengthening of the proposition that the thing can be overtaken by its linguistic representation, works in multiple ways. The envelopment of the syntactically marked "as if" in the figure it engenders instances how verbal procedures seem driven on, rushed on by all that they entail, thus rendering language the disposing-subject into which the human object has been encoiled. Encoilment obscures for us any vision of a path through which we can locate the narrator who uses, or is used by, the protatic clause, while this apparently present narrator, word-enshrouded, necessitates that we realize the richness of what is made.

We can best follow that injunction by marking what language does through the human vehicle we cannot see: "each bar" of the sea accrues to a "they" (7), fuelled by an animism that burgeons into human figures. Under the operation of the simile, the "wave" resembles "a sleeper," while after mounting protatic clauses the horizon, figured by "the arm of a woman," becomes a "she" who raises "her lamp" (7). Indeed, if simile and protasis require a human voice to announce them, even though we cannot distinguish the body behind the voice, we find ourselves in the initial section of a novel which sutures together presence and absence, the natural domain and the human lives that proceed from that domain. Yet proceeding, here, is a problem: we do not know how we have arrived, but we can articulate what may follow from our arrival. And such suturing together of problematic elements produces the body of the book we read.

Woolf, then, sets us within one pair of opposites, only to ramify the oppositions themselves so that we appear to sit in, to be delimited by, a world of refractory pairs. Confronted with the couples of origin and lateness, the present and the absent, narration and the narrator whom we cannot name, we seem to be offered—under the binary logic of the problematical—the choice of privileging one term over the other, as though the dynamism of the valued term subsumed its partner under its own magnetic pull. Some further examples of binaries at work in *The Waves* are: stability of genre/pluralized genres; consistent patterning/the pattern, broken; the single self/community of selves. The relations between these terms are problematical because the novel checks our readerly need to resolve one term in the other, thus making it impossible for us to stabilize, to simplify, how we weigh the terms themselves. If the problem is irresoluble, we cannot transcendently surpass it: Hence, how can we shape our experience of the mobile relations that structure the novel we read? But the "method of intensification" at work in *The Waves*, the "method" whose "results are the reverse of simple" ("Thoreau" *EII*, 135), resists what often succeeds the identification of a problem; the novel spurns taming: the problem will not be transcended.

The prime pair within which we find ourselves, and from which all the correlatives ensue, is that of the problem and its transcendence. Yet we inhabit a novel with resistance "in the centre" (*TW,* 153), where—as Woolf asserts in 1918 of *Hakluyt's Collection of the Early Voyages*—"different people write the book, but they have the same outlook, the same manner of speech" ("Trafficks and Discoveries" *EII,* 333), thus balking, in the novel's B sections, our compulsion to raise the separable self over the selves against which we discriminate individuality. So "imposing shape upon the tumult" of her "material," confronting the "ludicrous incapacity of words to repeat even a simple emotion exactly," Woolf's project "to abstract and exalt" the emotion arising from the problematical presses us to acknowledge our concomitant need that the problem should be transcended ("Mr Howells on Form" *EII,* 325). But "to abstract and exalt" emotion, in the perceivable pattern of ramified pairs so significant to *The Waves*, is tantamount to rendering visible the "form" of the problem "everywhere scattered about us" (*EII,* 325). We can discern the lineaments of the pairs; we can rank one component over another, evidently resolving our quandary. However, the very form of the book shirks our potential ranking. For the body of the novel—its treatment of genre, its patterning, its vision of the isolable human frame—continually presents us with a problem which will not be climbed over or surpassed, which rebuffs the transcendent by which the problematical is structured. Indeed, the two terms order each other, and to opt for one is to choose a stasis beyond the book, outside the book itself, a location we will have *made*. *The Waves* argues that we should remain in the kinesis of where we are.

Such kinesis is rendered apprehensible by means of how *The Waves* thinks about generic concerns. Woolf's negotiation of genre here is particularly verdurous, abundantly "green," given that the reader moves through a novel which performs the claim that "the germs of an equal susceptibility [to literature], to painting and to music" instruct us that the "gifts should go together; all three are perhaps needed to complete each one" ("Coleridge as Critic" *EII*, 223). Thus, the many are interfused in the "one"; the "one's" copiousness is affirmed by its reference to multiplicities. As *The Waves* enacts the interconnectedness at work in the *poesis* of literature, painting, and music, so the novel associates the species subordinate to the genus of literature itself. Such association has its analogues in antiquity, whose pedagogy hooked together the various disciplines via the ways in which each incarnated thinking, as though the overarching genus were thought, hurtled through the neural pathways of its particular but akin embodiments, a story well-told, for example, in *A Short History of Writing Instruction* (1990). If the specific manifestation of thought in *The Waves* is that of the novel, Woolf nevertheless entangles the ostensible singularity of the novel in the genres with which it is associable. So the "one" integrates the many: the novel's A sections present us with the lyric, a genre whose vocabulary rhapsodizes over the opulence of the visible, sung here by a voice which notes phenomena shifting over time. Yet the subsequent B sections spring from the reasoning of the epic—and its familial incarnation, the romance—whose *epos* describes the plenitude of a world sufficiently prolific to be susceptible to refashioning, chanted by a self discernibly there before us. But these generic integrations return us to the problematical, for the A sections' singing self is written into her song, so that we cannot stably find her, while the self who offers us the B sections' dramatic, epic voices—the latter often utilizing poetry's elevated diction and pointed syntax—is concealed in her recording work.

The Waves rebukes, then, our potential choice of resigning pluralized genres to the seeming supremacy of the novel; we are asked to consider that the many will not merely surrender to the "one," as both categories are bound in mutual relationship. The body of the book, as evidenced by its generic vision, thus materializes Woolf's conjecture—in 1919—that "if one were free and could set down what one chose, there would be no plot, little probability, and a vague general confusion in which the clear-cut features of the tragic, the comic, the passionate, and the lyrical were dissolved beyond the possibility of separate recognition" ("Modern Novels" *EIII*, 33). If the mind's *poesis* labors to "recover beauty, and impose order" upon the "raked," the "dishevelled soul," such "beauty" and "order" are as manifold as the mind that summons them (*TW*, 161). Indeed, the summoning of "order" affords "beauty" its recognizability, and it is by means of pattern that the corpus of the book evolves.

Before detailing the pattern out of which *The Waves* arises, I want to dwell on Woolf's implicit admonition that we ponder how pattern functions for us, as how we conceive of sequential patterning will proportion our experience of the design that engages us as we read. The evolution of patterning may raise the body of *The Waves* before us, but that pattern itself need not engage in the propulsion so indispensable to teleology, to the convention of design's achievement being gained through an unaltered repetition of its component parts. To comprehend a pattern awakens us to where we are within it, and such legibility demands that the pattern should be terminable: it must begin and end somewhere, however eventually resumed. So the consistency of pattern gives us the gift of a figurative home, a nearly spatialized domain marked off from all others, whose consistence renders it intelligible.

Yet constancy of pattern is nevertheless liable to violation; thus, the *telos* of any pattern, the end towards which pattern propels us, is attended by design's vulnerability to dissolution, so that teleological achievement may be adjourned. We can pronounce such adjournment a failure; in our pusillanimity before the imperative that the pattern must continue, we can elect not to consider that the pattern, broken, delivers us to a space cleared for—replete with—reflection. To do so, however, is to operate as though "centered in a self which in spite of its tremor of susceptibility never reaches out or embraces or comprehends what is outside and beyond" ("Modern Novels" *EIII*, 34). For *The Waves* prompts us to judge that the "balance between the inner and the outer is, after all, a terribly precarious business," given that "they depend upon each other with the utmost closeness," a closeness of relation which the book patterns and interrogates ("'Madeleine'" *EIII*, 109).

As we follow Woolf's construction of her twofold pattern, where A follows B, where the ekphrasis of sun rising over sea is antiphonally answered by six speaking characters striding from childhood to adulthood, we inhabit a breed of Socratic elenchus dilated over time and over distinguishable—but contiguous—domains. While elenchus comes from the Greek for "cross-examining, testing," as Richard A. Lanham instructs us in *A Handlist of Rhetorical Terms* (1991, 62), G. B. Kerferd and *The Sophistic Movement* (1981) are helpful regarding its Platonic incarnation, which the textual Socrates so ripely enacts:

> Elenchus consists typically of eliciting an answer to a question, such as what is Courage, and then securing assent to further statements which are visibly inconsistent with the answer given to the first question. On rare occasions this leads to something approaching an acceptable modification of the first answer. But far more often the Dialogue closes with the participants in a state of aporia, unable to see any way forward or any escape from the contradictory views in which they are enmeshed. (65–66)

Corresponding to the ways in which elenchus adjudicates the verity of related propositions, the rhythmic declaration of A and B sections models a cross-examination of how "the immitigable tree" (152), the thing we refute at our peril because its presence will persist beyond our refutation, and our "perspective" pertain to each other (154). Here, truth—the truth yearned for, the truth expectantly written into the very procedural nature of elenchus itself—is equivalent to "the thing that lies beneath the semblance of the thing" (163). Yet our instrument, and that of Woolf's characters, for eliciting the identification of the "'abstract,'" the "'eyeless'" (154), the "'unvisual beneath'" (156) the phenomenon of "'the thing,'" is a language invested in the mandate that the "'sequence returns; one thing leads to another—the usual order'" (155). Nevertheless, to break, to fracture that "'order'" is to grant us a view of how "'we have made a dwelling-place'" by exercising the language that frames our experience (164).

Such fracturing is another way of posing the two-part question of Woolf's "pertinacious pupil" in "The Art of Fiction" of 1927: "What is this 'Life' that keeps on cropping up so mysteriously and so complacently in books about fiction? Why is it absent in a pattern and present in a tea party?" (*The Moment,* 109). So, midway through the nearly ten announcements of its pattern, in the B section's fifth occurrence, *The Waves* truncates its six voices to three; so, soon after, this truncation is mirrored by another, as though to emblematize Woolf's pronouncement that "all that fiction asks of us is that we should break her and bully her, honour her and love her, till she yields to our bidding, for so her youth is perpetually renewed and her sovereignty assured" ("Modern Novels" *EIII*, 36). So to "break" and to "bully" couples pattern and variation in a kinship which affirms, which reflects on, the sovereign power of the "fiction" that speaks through us in the embodied stories we can imagine ourselves telling, and enlarges the perimeter of what we deem intelligible.

Yet to widen the boundaries of the decipherable, the sayable, corresponds to a revision of the body that moves within the limits of what we see. If "prose takes the mould of the body and mind entire," it is through the transactions of that "prose" that we can regard the tissue stitching together the "body" capable of moving and the "mind" that conceptualizes movement ("Reading" *EIII*, 157). Predicated on the effort to re-see, Woolf's method desires at once "to be rid of realism, to penetrate without its help into the regions beneath it," and to retain the "shapeliness of the old accepted forms" ("The Tunnel" *EIII*, 12). But "to be rid of realism," to evacuate the novel of its sycophantic aping of the "machine," whose applications conventionalize our experience of the visible (*TW*, 154), requires the very tools of "realism," for, without them, our method would be incommunicable. Thus, *The Waves* supplies us with the mimesis by which we gain knowledge of where we are—the narrative, however anomalously deployed, enacts a species of linearity—and amplifies the scope of the mimetic as a means of reviewing how we organize where we find ourselves.

And so we begin in childhood, at seven in the morning, with tissued-together senses, with senses concatenated by the bodies that experience them, each body voicing the world of sensation that verifies the sutures between self and other. Yet "'leaves'" are "'moving,'" as "'heart'" and "'legs'" move: What ensures that "'leaves'" should "'go on moving, though there is nothing to move them'" (13)? If the unseen—instanced here by wind—registers itself in the palpitations of the visible, how can such registry be imagined? We can visualize ourselves, as Louis does in the novel's initial B section, "'standing by the wall among flowers'" whose "'stalks rise from the black hollows beneath'" (11). We can say "'I hold a stalk in my hand,'" declaring further that "'I am the stalk'" whose roots burrow "'down to the depths of the world, through earth dry with brick, and damp earth, through veins of lead and silver'" (12). However our declaration strives to substantiate the discernible "'fibre'" originating in the "'depths'" we cannot see (12), we remain—our very physicality propelled by the invisible—in our struggle to conceive, to *say* the unseen. Our six characters, sitting "'together, close'" may "'melt into each other with phrases'" (16); nevertheless, the figure "'there in the centre,'" the Percival whose Arthurian name notates the work of questing (and whom, like the narrator, we never see), can only be deduced from the galvanism he effects on those around him (153). Hence, we appear to be rooted in the undecidable nature of the ways in which "'the centre'" shapes the (patterned) things that move around it. Indeed, how we weigh undecidability here will engender what we do with it.

The critical issue for us is to realize that our manner of ruminating over the evidently undecidable elements at work in our reading, the ways in which the seen and the unseen dovetail into each other, tests both our capacity for weighing what we read and our acknowledgement that such weighing shapes our experience of the thing before us. And the thing before us—the "'whole flower'" of *The Waves*—examines our ability to comprehend how the object is that "'to which every eye brings its own contribution'" (127). Thus, by arguing that the narrator is our surrogate, our double, at once mediating what we see and only by implication present in her mediation, I assert that the novel insists we recognize how we remove the mediate from our consideration, fracturing, splintering the connections between the seer and the seen. Such connections—in their very difficulty—"remind" us of the "duties and responsibilities" that are ours "in this business of writing books," just as to privilege the "division between reader and writer" impoverishes the "spirit we live by," the "life itself" that shudders through us and among the words available for our use ("Character in Fiction" *EIII*, 435–436).

To claim, then, that in *The Waves* we are faced with a looming aporia, an impassable loss regarding how we value the problematical and its hoped-for transcendence, is to generate an interpretation while behaving as though no such act had been committed. Yet, "'swept now into this large figure'" (*TW*, 103), we are offered the potential to permit all the components of the novel's pattern to resonate without resolution, without the boundedness that resolution and mere doubt only seem to yield. For "'after all, the problem remains'" (*TW*, 58), and how we tolerate that "remaining" figures our engagement with the "'problem'" itself. And so we question the relationship between the discernible and indiscernible, the bodied world around us and the forces that animate it, finding that the galvanism of the Percival we cannot see, the Percival who "'does not need us'" because "'he is never at our mercy,'" is nevertheless subject to the act of dying, which binds each of us together (*TW*, 70). So bound, we are led to the vision that one of our "duties" is to awaken ourselves to the questions that need asking, to stay in them, honoring that, together, we are within the "problem," and not finally outside it.

In an effort both to evince that Duncan's solo has a history and to represent "'some common emotion'" which ropes each of us together, even in our differences, I move to a final ekphrasis (*TW*, 126). It is 14 June 1926: Woolf and Vita Sackville-West are walking—"with the dark blue sky overhead" (Sackville-West, 151–152), the sky that emblazons "how it is not oneself but something in the universe that one's left with" (Woolf, *D3*, 113)—in order to see one of "Stravinsky's new ballets" (Lee, 495). They are about to take their seats, to find before them the Ballets Russes performing Nijinska's vision of *Les Noces*, which at once reveals "a new and cogent classicism" by referencing steps belonging to "the traditional lexicon" (Garafola, 127), and defies pointe's "conventional usage" as the dancers' toes will rhythmically thump the ground (Garafola, 128), emphasizing the downward jabbing of the foot rather than the knee's arced lift, as though plunging into the surfaced depth that supports us, that binds us to where we stand upon it. As her brother did in *Le Sacre du Printemps*—where "human sacrifice" secured the "continuity" of "primal" man and tribe (Garafola, 63)—Nijinska will give us a dance "predicated on the very absence of the individual," embodied by an "ensemble" of "human pyramids, phalanxes, mounds, and wedges" (Garafola, 126), marking how we gather ourselves into the structures we make, into the designs that speak of how we can conceive of making.

For the curtain rises, exposing a mound of female bodies encircled with the braid of the bride-to-be, who is merely one of a company of women, and whose "tresses" will be combed out, pulled, plaited again, signifying—as A. H. Fox Strangways will later argue in *The Observer*—that this is an "epic" in which "things happen once, and once only, and they can't be undone; the family counts, after all" (Macdonald, 329). But the family's "counting" is a product of how we imagine familial procedures, and soon—when the music begins—Stravinsky will enfurl us in a "family" of sounds whose initial octaves will ring in bars, the beats of which shift from three, to four, to seven, a sonic world where the soloists do not sit in individual roles, but slide from one role to another within the order that contains them. Even so, that order's conclusion will not simply repeat its beginning: into the bell-like resonance of four pianolas, harmonium, and percussion, something will be added. Within, around the octaves' reverberation, we will hear the donging chime of a major second—coupled with its permutation, the major ninth—as though sonically decreeing our addition to what we see, attesting to our place in the choral dance in which we will have taken part by means of our senses. If "glasses we wear, though we cannot see them" ("Not One of Us" *EIV*, 466), Woolf and Sackville-West nevertheless gaze at Nijinska's women whose pyramidal form illustrates that to configure the problem we are in pictures how we inhabit it, that to regard a moving picture may waken our responsibilities to what we see. But now—slowly—the figures seem to open their mouths and surrender, as will the characters of *The Waves*, to an amalgam of speech and song.

2.
Sounding Figures

It is inevitable, as well as desirable,
that we should bear each other's burdens.
—E. M. Forster: "The Eternal Moment," 294. (1928)

The actors in *Antigone* open their mouths. The sounds that pass between their lips, combined with the resolute immobility of their bodies, with the way in which each declaration answers another and reflects the very thinking it amends, as though syntax, syllabled out, were capable of attaining a physicality equal to that of the body—all this assumes the fact of our presence, given that the argument before us appears to exact a judgment of each individual's strategy for participating in the whole of which he is a part. But what do we owe to the whole whose expanse our eyes cannot measure? How can we "bear each other's burdens" if we fail to recognize their urgency?

The sentry has escorted a young woman to the palace, stiffly grasping her arm, though the woman has not balked the judicial imperative of being guided. Indeed, she submits to the weight of the sentry's grip as if submission logically followed from everything that preceded it. When her cry, out in the noonday heat, covered over the "great empty air" (462), when she "poured a triple stream / of funeral offerings" and "crowned the corpse" of her brother with all that had been refused it (474–475), she saw the consequences of her choice: the charge of an arresting arm; the cast of Creon's body, buttressed by the law for whose rectitude he stands. She saw, too, the inevitability of the scene arising from her efforts to honor the ligaments connecting the living and the dead, how the public world extends beyond what we see, proportioned by the "Justice" which "lives with those below" (495). She saw that to separate the public "proclamation" (494) from the "Justice" which ordains it renders that "proclamation" a nullity, a heap of words thrown in air as though nothing stretched beneath it. But now the chorus—in which each distinguishable voice is enfolded in a speaking whole—asserts that Antigone "does not know / how to yield to trouble" (516–517); while, in the sunlight, her body draped but for the shaft of her neck, her face surmounted with a mask, we see Antigone briefly close her eyes. We can imagine all her dead ranged behind her, the father guilty of parricide and incest, the brothers equally embraced by the "god of death" (570). So that when she opens her eyes, announcing that it is her "nature to join in love, not hate" (576), Antigone proclaims the struggle "to join" what must be joined equivalent to a yielding that cannot be repudiated, a yielding acknowledging the very "trouble" of its cost.

But what species of joining "love" is this, so freighted with the "trouble" of apparent disconnection? And what vision of community does such "love" enact? For Antigone, the present becomes an apostrophe to the past, a kind of mobile locution directed at the ways in which the ancestral and immediate pasts must remain undivided, as both inundate the fact of the present moment, making of time a vessel which cups together the familial and the singular self in a breed of mutual flood. Thus, the identifiable, particular self cannot be seen without reference to the selves who are her origin. To attempt to sever the living woman from the dead who endlessly modify her would be tantamount to positioning her in an incoherent category whose terms she could only choose not to recognize. Moreover, to admit those terms—their import, their utility—would necessitate that she should be separated out from the corporate body which orders her, would entail her expulsion from a temporal plenitude in which each choice embodies our commonality with the dead.

So removed, expelled, Antigone would find herself in a domain where everything is always the present, impoverished, diminished by its lack of common ground with all that antedates it. Such impoverishment would, in turn, vitiate the work of "piety" (574): we perform our "reverence" for the dead (1001)—dutifully, taking the "trouble" to give what must be given, to honor the bridge between the outside through which we move and the "below" where our dead await us—or we are nothing.

Hence, asserting that "there is nothing worse / than disobedience to authority" (726–727), Creon renders himself the physicalized criterion by which all phenomena are organized, without context, the past effaced by the minatory "discipline" to which we can only pay obeisance (730), and the future a tautology for the present, without end. Before the illimitable extension of such a present, Antigone commits herself to the "love" that claims to rupture the relation between the laws "of God" (978) and worldly "authority" requires that we should give "precedence" to our duty to the lost (970), a duty less adventitious than mere "authority" by fiat. Indeed, to obey the quotidian decree without consideration of divine law is to proceed as though we were not bound to share the burdens of our dead, as though all we had left was an "outside," unshadowed by something that exceeded it. But giving "precedence" occasions its trail of losses: an Antigone "unbedded, without bridal" (974); the suicides of Haemon, of Eurydice—all ensue from dicta in collision. Nevertheless, joining those "below," Antigone embraces the community—the interlinking of past, present, and future—in which we start.

Yet how does *Antigone*, as a model of the philosophical system on which classical drama rests, exhort us to imagine the relation between first and last things? Are the two territories—one the scene of our arrival, the other that of our recovery of everything we have lost—conceived so that they amount to a single dominion whose seamlessness contains all things, without differentiation? Rather than conceiving a junctureless structure, depicting the provinces of the living and the dead locked in mere metonymical correspondence, *Antigone* argues that the two precincts are bound in a proportionate relation: the individual's actions above the ground are weighted with, contiguous to, his mnemonic debt to recall those "below." And this presents us with a double burden whose capaciousness we must be stalwart enough to carry—we must shape our actions with regard for our obligations to those adjacent to us, while choosing not to forget that we do not act alone, in a kind of quarantined isolation, but find ourselves fastened to the bulk of those who have preceded us. Even so, the conceptual system here models room for difference and for solidarity, as we are free to abjure the encumbrance of realizing that the self is not a world segregated from all other phenomena, however costly such abjuration may be for us. We are free to imagine ourselves detachable from our dead, and to proceed as though disentanglement were equivalent to defining the scope of what it means to be an individual. But no matter how we adjudge the relations between self and other, others remain around us, as the dead persist below us; hence, to posit the self in sequestration affirms that we move always alone, that the terrain of the dead is a pleonasm for that of the living, duplicating the self's cloistral environs. Yet, at the conclusion of *Antigone*, when Creon avows that he does "not know where to turn" his "eyes / to look to, for support" (1416–1417), the play gives us a new form of proclamation: the king who stepped through the world as though the operations of selfhood were identical with equity, with right adjudication, awakens to the fact of his bereavement. Bereft of community, of son, of wife, he cries out at being sealed in the detachment on which his self-conceptualization was predicated. And his cry sounds the need for our "support," given that the chorus around him stands for us, for the solidarity between self and other, for the common ground whose amplitude embraces the generality of the living and the lost.

Crafting the relationship between the particular and the general directs us to Woolf who, in "On Not Knowing Greek" (*The Common Reader*, 1925) and *Three Guineas* (1938), puzzles out the virtues of being "for ever drawn back to Greek," to the "impersonal literature" of classical drama ("On Not Knowing," 24). Puzzling out the nature of an "impersonal literature" necessarily entails a consideration of what we mean by the primary terms of "personal" and "impersonal," and summons their corollaries in a kind of convocation. For, as we define the characters of the personal and the impersonal, we place those characters under the auspices of the particular and the general, conferring spatial breadth on the purviews in which these associated terms operate. Hence, the particular, as manifesting the personal, can be assimilated to the local "life indoors," the "inside," which seemingly affords us the option of secluding our selfhood from the community that formally regulates it ("On Not Knowing," 33). The life "transacted out of doors," under the aegis of the generalized "community," logically follows from this, detectable in the "common stock" from which, grooved "for centuries," customs "have arisen," tethered to "hilltops and solitary trees," to the "outside" permeated with the accumulated drama of our shared experience (25–26). But such accumulation postulates that we infuse, inscribe the turf outside us with what we say of it, and that what we permit ourselves to say of it *matters*.

The act of saying, then, the energy that propels the act of saying, redistributes the relations between our primary terms and the associative net arising from them. For if "legends have" customarily "attached themselves to hilltops," to "solitary trees" (25), the single voice that raises itself in speech at once stitches together, by a type of reverberatory knitting, the personal and the impersonal, the inside from which the voice ascends and the outside it addresses, the particular, vocalizing self and the general nature of the ritualized word. It is critical here that we note Woolf's syntax: to contend that "legends have attached themselves" to the territorial markers of "hilltops" and "trees" argues that "legends" precede the speakers found for them, that the "legends" themselves spur the generation of human speech into which they are enfolded, and by which the verbal and the physical are looped together. Thus, Woolf's contention rearranges the conventional order by means of which speech is said to function, and simultaneously reviews the ways in which the personal and the impersonal are habitually aligned. "Legends" become the principal agents, the subjects that inaugurate the sonic arc of the voices shot through with them, while the scenes of their narration are permeated with all that we consent to tell of them. The propulsive force at work in the act of saying consequently renders human voices the instruments of the "legends" whose scope includes *and* surpasses the speakers who can countenance yielding to the gift of orchestrated sound. Indeed, our work is to accede to uttering the "legends" that move through us, which narrate how the general breaches the particular, and which sound out the "great fund of emotion" from which we may profitably draw (27).

But to draw from that "fund" is not without its risks. While the things of the earth resound—lingeringly, memorially—with the "legends" that human voices have sung of them, it is nevertheless the project of "each new poet" to weigh, to stress the commemorative reservoir of "emotion" in "a new place" (27). Taking Sophocles as an exemplar of the "new poet," Woolf exhibits the imperative that Sophocles, under the impetus of "those legends . . . known to every one in outline" (26), should "at once impose his stamp" upon them (27). To "impose" our "stamp" on the communal store of "legends" fostering our capacity for song shows us how Woolf elaborates her vision of the kinship between the impersonal and the personal: generalized, legendary stock may initiate song, but the singer must fashion what he sings so that—marked with him, interleaved with him—it testifies to the way in which he serves the narrative heave of his material. The general and the particular reveal their interdependent affiliation as the "new poet" shapes the swell of the tale which simultaneously predates him, transfuses him, only to be re-forged in the work which will signify how he leaned, how he stood on the ground which once widened beneath him. Reflecting on the instance of Sophocles and his *Electra*, Woolf visualizes the "design" which affords the poet his opportunity for interlarding himself with the venerable curve of the tale he treats (27), and it is here that we confront potential failure. For the mythical Electra, like Antigone, is antecedent to all her figurations.

Indeed, Electra's tale—so prevailing, so globally allied to the house of Atreus—serves as a kind of preface to the play to be made of it. We know her story in such a way that our knowledge adumbrates a breed of foreknowledge, which generalizes the foundations of our familial drama and particularizes its narrative incarnation, without the testimony of a single verbal source as Electra, herself, appears precedent to the stories told of her. And yet we see her, the daughter of Clytemnestra, the sister of Iphigenia, who must have been schooled by the vision of Iphigenia's sacrifice not to mistake parental caprice for an injunction forbidding individual action. So we see her transporting Orestes to safety, only to find brother and sister avenging Agamemnon's death by killing Clytemnestra and her lover, as though vengeance rounded off the involutions of one narrative without inciting those of another, however finally resolved by the rescinding of the ancestral curse. The elements of Electra's chronicle, in their very priority to Sophocles's treatment of them, seem to typify the task at hand: How do we bend ourselves to what is always before us while honoring the integrity of our act?

Woolf pronounces that the "genius" of Sophocles belongs to the "extreme kind" in that it marks the prominence of "design," of fabricating a concentrated whole whose failure would be disclosed in "gashes and ruin, not in the blurring of some insignificant detail," and whose success "would cut each stroke to the bone, would stamp each finger-print in marble" (27). Importantly, Woolf's metaphor renders corporeal the "legendary" Electra who materializes as both "bone" and "marble," susceptible to and inspiriting the shaping work of Sophocles's hands. By implication, Woolf asks that we register how each modeling sweep, each sculptured twist of his material shows us the particularity of Sophocles positioned within the generality of the "great fund" from which Electra emerges. "Each movement must tell to the utmost" because each has the "whole weight" of condensed design—of "legends" both figuring the personal and overtaking the merely personal, together with the language by which we know them—"behind it" (27). The peril here, the hazard that identifies this as "the dangerous art where one slip means death" (27), lies in the poet's obligation always to remember the impersonal "stuff" which his making negotiates, so that the personal and the impersonal are conjoined in mutual predication, mutual anchorage: we radiate from the impersonal, which nevertheless requires us to speak of it.

It is as if Woolf teased out the ramifications of her father's assertion, in *Hours in a Library* (1904), that "if I take my village for the world, I cannot distinguish the particular from the general" (Stephen "Charlotte Bronte" vol. 3, 281), extending Stephen's claim to demand that the "particular" and the general" should constitute a concordance which it is the toil of "art" to embody. Woolf turns, in "On Not Knowing Greek," to classical drama since it describes its makers and its audience as a people "living in the open," "out-of doors," struck by the "carriage of the body and the proportion of its parts," capable of looking "directly and largely rather than minutely and aslant," adroit at stepping into the "thick of emotions which blind and bewilder an age like our own" (35). So the ministry of the new poet, for Woolf and her readers, resides in his gift for envisioning a whole of "emotions" in which we can participate and whose scope maintains that the self is not a synonym for isolation. Arguing that "in the vast catastrophe of the European war our emotions had to be broken up for us and put at an angle from us, before we could allow ourselves to feel them in poetry or fiction" (35), Woolf articulates a prime felicity of classical drama: the "impersonal literature" models how "poetry or fiction" can picture a whole consisting in the "proportion of its parts," reminding us that "proportion" continues to be possible, that the general and the particular are as extensive—and extensively related—as we can sanction ourselves to feel them.

Yet how can we acquiesce in feeling, in the imagination at work in feeling, when the general and the particular—the public and the private—are at such odds that the one appears to swallow, to obliterate the other, so that the world seems to be one thing and one thing only? At the heart of *Three Guineas* (1938), Woolf lodges the figure of Antigone, the woman whose speaking frame pledges that the public and the private mutually potentiate, precipitate each other, and whose bodily sufferings assure us that when one term usurps the legitimacy of another, our peril is in misjudging usurpation as being identical with the world as such. Licensing the engulfment of one word in the enclosure of another repeals both the coordinate nature of words themselves and their coordinating labors: without its complement, the magisterial word telescopes our vocabulary and the aptitude it affords us of conjuring a world as expansive as ourselves. Woolf installs, in the center of her argument, "Antigone's five words" (82)—"My nature is to join in love, not hate." "Worth all the sermons of all the archbishops" (82), at once diminutive and comprehensive by virtue of the compass they betoken, Antigone's words signal the reach in striving to "join in love" without negating love's correlative, without lopping off the companion-term by which each is comprehensible. And unlike hate, love founds itself on the affirmation that self and other are coextensive; the other remains ineffaceable because he is so eminently *there*. Hate, however, or the act etched in the word, blurs the fact of the other, consigns the latter to seeming indistinguishable from the sentiment that rubs him out, as though he could be obliterated by a word.

And such potential swallowing is where *Three Guineas* begins, as Woolf offers us a "collection" of images sent by the "Spanish government" at the advent of the Civil War, photographs detailing "what might be a man's body, or a woman's," so "mutilated" that it might be neither; yet those figures "certainly are dead children, and that undoubtedly is the section of a house" (10–11). So we dismember one another and the houses that cohere us, that demarcate the space we have staked out as our own in a world of other houses; so we tender one body as the analogue of another, disseminating "abomination" and "barbarity" due to our failure of imagination before the limpidity of others who are not ourselves (11). But "the eye is connected with the brain," and the "brain with the nervous system," which "sends its messages in a flash through every past memory and present feeling" (11). These concatenations, Woolf implies, concurring with Leslie Stephen's meditation on the merits "in seeing facts through the medium of the imagination" ("Charles Kingsley" *Hours in a Library* Vol. 3, 323), can educate us in reorienting the way in which we see and how we speak of seeing. For if "every past memory and present feeling" is charged with connectivity, the way in which we brook such saturation is capable of transfiguring how we sit in the world around us.

As in "On Not Knowing Greek," when she correlates the Platonic project of *The Symposium* with that of Sophoclean drama, asserting that Plato "had the dramatic genius" (34) because his text animates the contention that "truth is various," that "it is not with the intellect alone that we perceive it" (33–34), so Woolf grounds *Three Guineas* in the drama, in the "ancestral memory" of Antigone's cluster of little words, uttered by a woman who tutors us that "without private there can be no public freedom" (120). What follows from this—as we look again at the mauled human figure in one of the aforementioned photographs—is that "we cannot dissociate ourselves from that figure," that "we are not passive spectators doomed to unresisting obedience but by our thoughts and actions can ourselves change that figure" (142). To behave differently will be to ruin "both houses," the "public and the private, the material and the spiritual, for they are inseparably connected" (143). And so Woolf's performance, coupling epistolary and dramatic structures, becomes—in Proustian terms—an "incitation," an incitement to the riveting together of thinking, feeling, and action (Preface, *Sésame et les Lys CSB*, 176). When Proust declares that "la lecture est au seuil de la vie spirituelle; elle peut nous y introduire: elle ne la constitue pas" (178), he presages the engagement which Woolf requests of us when she mobilizes classical drama as her template. The readerly act may summon us to the threshold of contemplative action, but we must embark on the task of awakening to the "figures" that we could be, should we risk purling together the state of predication with all that can be made of it. Such is the urgency of bearing our own and others' burdens.

I want to linger here on the ways in which Woolf's consideration of Greek literature resonates with Forster's dictum, as well as with Proust's insistence on the vitalizing force that potentially attends the act of reading. The inevitability and desirability that we "should bear each other's burdens" can be stamped on the "design" of the work itself, engraved by the manner in which the text meditates on its very frame. And such double intensification—the intensity of conceiving the book as a shape and of fashioning the disposition of that shape—charges the term which Proust so clearly celebrates. For the maker of the book, moved, exhorted by the stimulus of "incitation" to foment the book's schema, finds herself stirred by the incentive (echoing the Latinate substratum of the word) to "set the tune" she rouses into form. If "incitation" and "incentive" resound with each other by virtue of their being verbal kin, the combined actions of rousing and singing that produce the book may, for us, bear the potency of re-disposing the song we sing of the world we know. Thus, by extension, reading may stimulate our ability to "change"—to amplify, to re-set—the "figure" of the world we experience.

I dwell on the potential for transmutation fundamental to the making and the reading of the book as, in "On Not Knowing Greek," in *Three Guineas*, Woolf's recourse to classical drama imbues her diversification of the essay with elements of the poetic, the dramatic, and the imagination enacted in them, so that the essay can be seen to bear the "burden" of other generic forms. Indeed, when she muses—in "On Not Knowing Greek"—on the "undifferentiated voices" of the Greek chorus (30), Woolf foretokens the value of knotting together classical and musical models as the scaffolding for *The Waves*. Enjoining us to ruminate over how the merging, inseparable voices of the chorus are equal to a "means" by which the "general and poetic" can be "freed without interrupting the movement of the whole" (30), Woolf prepares the ground for the chorus in *The Waves* whose vocal instruments "sing" in the "pauses of the wind" (30), in the variation of the tonal and typographical contrasts at play in the novel's A sections. I maintain that the service—for Woolf, for us—of integrating models drawn from the domains of music and classical drama rests in how such integration magnifies the "burdens" that the novel and its discursive procedures can be said to bear. And what does generic coalescence make of the book itself? *The Waves* becomes an avatar of the "new poet's" possible fruit—to reapportion the relations between the personal and the impersonal, to augment the boundaries of the sayable and all that we may ponder *doing* with the sayable.

It is appropriate at this moment that we should listen to Leslie Stephen caution us, in 1876, concerning the fructuous nature of the "new poet's" program:

> You seek for absolute truth? Then you must admit that the world which we perceive, is an illusion—a mere screen of transitory appearances which hides the permanent realities behind; and you must retire to the world of transcendental reality, where, indeed, it is possible to obtain absolute truth, but truths which cannot by any ingenuity be brought into contact with the facts of perception, or made to influence our conduct. (*History*, 70)

Stephen furnishes us with the spectacle of a seeker aspiring to realize a "truth" whose absoluteness would be verified by its disinterment from the flux of sensory phenomena. Such a "truth"—so disinterred, so loosened from and elevated above the camouflage of shifting "appearances" at which we gaze, hypnotized by the act of looking—would explain "appearances" as impedimenta to be cast off, sloughed off, negligible through having been permanently parsed away. But what would explication mean in this case? Would it involve the seeker in being invaded by a kind of afflatus whose breath confers a comprehension beyond the linguistic operations that materialize explication? For Stephen shows us a "transcendental reality" ulterior to the ken of language and to the region of things which language substantiates by describing; thus, transcendence becomes a literal Utopia, a no-place, a non-word to be divined in unthinking silence. If Stephen's seeker returned to the world of flux, he would soundlessly open his mouth since nothing but air could be pushed out of it, as the transcendent opposes how language steeps itself in the fugitive, the variable, in the once-having-been. And, isolated in his own muteness, the seeker could only fail to "influence our conduct," to guide us in re-proportioning what we seem to know and what we can imagine of the knowable.

I underscore Stephen's distinction between the transcendently real and the "world which we perceive" in order to claim that the distinction itself and the very caution it appears to offer us comprise much of what *The Waves* confutes. Woolf devises a novel whose verbal deployment springs from the alliance between the classical chorus—the human "many" who speak as one of the "transitory appearances" in which each of us is immersed—and a "design" that musically bestows its constituent materials. If music remains uninhibited by reference to things as such, unlike linguistic discourse, Woolf forces us to interrogate whether *The Waves* intends that we should hold up the musical as an icon of the transcendent, as a terminus to which we must aspire. But to argue for this intention would be to discount the union from which the novel we are reading rises, to disassemble the affinity between the quotidian through which the chorus moves and the music that orchestrates movement. By performing such affinity, Woolf's novel instructs us to examine how the "transitory" and the transcendent can penetrate each other—reverberating the relation between the "new poet" and the "legends" that are his and more than his—so that the supra-linguistic can resound in what we do with the common word. And resounding, here, implies that the two evidently discrepant zones are capable of sharing each other's burdens.

Woolf posits—in 1909—that music compounds the dominions of the transcendent and the "transitory" by the palpitations of the phrase:

> The more beautiful a phrase of music is the richer its burden of suggestion, and if we understand the form

> but slightly, we are little restrained in our interpretation. We are led on to connect the beautiful sound with some experience of our own, or to make it symbolize some conception of a general nature. Perhaps music owes its astonishing power over us to this lack of definite articulation; its statements have the majesty of a generalization, and yet contain our private emotions. Something of the same effect is given by Shakespeare, when he makes an old nurse the type of all the old nurses in the world, while she keeps her identity as a particular old woman. ("Impressions at Bayreuth" *EI*, 291–292)

The "beautiful" character of the phrase becomes a double vessel, carrying its ripeness for formal augmentation and suggesting, as it spirals through the air, the presence of the listening mind in which it will be borne through the world. If music "submits the claim of content to that of form" (Donoghue *Walter Pater*, 128), the auditory architecture of form at once attests to how the composing voice dispenses its energy in a sonic shape and predicates the fact of our tactility, we who will be the inheritors of that shape. The way we inherit the contours of what we hear may be dictated by our education in musical structure, but the latter's notation assumes the possibility of performance and its reception by the thinking ear. However "little restrained in our interpretation" by our failure to "understand" the integral function of the phrase, we nevertheless find ourselves anchored in the method by which the phrase circulates through the aggregate which modulates and contains it. So the circulation of the phrase is steered by the orbit of the whole; so our particularities—as listeners, as receptors for sound—are invited into the audible figure that houses us. And here Woolf begins her compounding of the transcendent and the "transitory": as the "beautiful phrase" thwarts the "what-ness" of meaning—for we can expatiate on its advancement while its signification will elude us—the phrase appears to typify the breadth of the musical enterprise itself, where the part transmits its commitment to the whole and mutates into a "generalization" ample enough to embrace our "private emotions," we who are delimited by our evanescence.

However we shake our syntax at its phrasal behaviors, music adverts to the transcendent because it repels our imperative that it should *mean*, if meaning subordinates the bulk of the thing at which we point to our system for denominating it. For Woolf, the primacy of music is its "power" to embody the flux of phenomena while evading the circumscription of "definite articulation" by which we—in the very grammar at our disposal—restrict ourselves, reckoned by the "content" of the language that conciliates our yearning for perspicuous self-definition. Yet, Woolf intimates, as we attend to the swoop of a musical phrase, our particular brevity adjoins the sonic comprehensiveness we cannot confine within the limits of a word.

What would it mean to disburden the word of its capacity for limitation? Such disburdening would be founded on the assumption that the language we speak simultaneously represents and mediates our experience, so that the way in which we transact the repertory of linguistic conventions accessible to us permits us to figure our experience, even as those conventions constrain what we may say of it. And if my language functions as an assembly of verbal customs, such customs affect how I can deliver myself to the experience I am permitted to call mine. But who is this "I" that speaks? To disburden the word of its ability to curb both our deliverance to experience and how we compose such deliverance would necessitate a revision of the "I" who conceives of speaking. I argue that *The Waves* demonstrates how Woolf reviews the tradition of individuality—the tradition averring that I am distinguishable from you, that my distinction is in being apart from you, and that my apartness defines me—

by means of presenting the "I" as a community of voices whose phrasal constructions foreground connection over division. Thus, Woolf's investigation of classical drama nourishes her depiction of the individual as a collocation of voices, a "type"—like the Shakespearean "old nurse"—of the vocalizing act itself. If the "I" becomes a chorus, it follows that its pronouncements will abstain from honoring the conventions of language which render possible the preeminence of the "I" as a subject always sundered from its objects; moreover, by such abstention, Woolf displays the tenability of utilizing the instrument of sound in another way. While the Greek chorus assists her in expounding the self and its utterances, Woolf requires a method for setting those utterances in motion, a means of affording the choral-word a formalized duration. And this is precisely how music serves her. For Woolf's vision of the morphology of musical structure, how the phrase spins out over the expanse of an aural shape, produces the "design" with which she will "stamp" the application of her speakers' words. Indeed, Woolf's drawing out of a musical form reinforces the purport of her characters' verbal delivery, for music sustains a congregation of voices. Though Wagner's *Lohengrin* launches "Impressions at Bayreuth," Woolf proliferates, from 1913 onwards, anti-Wagnerian material in the *Letters*. I therefore propose the work of another composer as a model for Woolf's conceptualizing the fecundity of sonic organization. That composer is Beethoven.

We know that over five days in April, 1921, Woolf attends Beethoven Festival Week at the Aeolian Hall, during which all sixteen string quartets are played in chronological order; that she "knows the tunes" (*Diary 2*, 114); that she impresses upon us, in *The Voyage Out* (1915), the mind of Rachel Vinrace entering into "communion" with the "spirit" of Beethoven as it fathoms the intricacy of connection between the two movements of the final piano sonata, op. 111 (29). We know, too, that in December, 1930, while listening to "a Beethoven quartet"—and at work on

The Waves—Woolf begins to imagine merging all her characters' "interjected passages into Bernard's final speech," so that Bernard will "absorb all those scenes," all the chanting voices and personalities soon to be sunk in his ruminative declarations, ordaining Bernard the pitch whose vibrations will incorporate the intonations of the friends nominally separable from him (*D3*, 339). This "speech" may show that, unlike "the waves" themselves, "effort, effort, dominates" (339); it also reveals Bernard as the "absorber" who distends the patterned system that supports him.

Yet, thinking that we are "mosaics," not "immaculate, monolithic, consistent wholes" (*D2*, 314), Woolf rears a novelistic form whose elasticity flexes rhythmic repetition and—in the case of Bernard's concluding "speech"—sectional tumidity, allowing "design" to replicate the composite of human character. And we know that for Woolf music develops the ability "to stimulate and suggest" (*D2*, 320), to exhibit a "sensibility" " become externalized" (*D2*, 193), as though the capacity to feel, formally delivered, could "exist independently" of its agent, rendering the agency "externalized" by form a type of pluralized dominion whose tensility included both maker and listener (*D2*, 221). When we hear Beethoven affirm that "good singing" is his "guide" (1810, 25), that he "must accustom" himself "to think out at once the whole, as soon as it shows itself, with all the voices," in his "head" (28), we can sense the value of being conducted by the articulations of the voice, the value of a "whole" buttressed by voices, that he and Woolf share. I offer the third movement, the canzona of the Fifteenth Quartet, op. 132, in A Minor (1825), as Woolf's exemplar of the "mosaics" that sound can join together, because it shapes a "whole" out of evident inconsistency and steers us to comprehend that a "whole" can stand, even while it seems to come apart.

Though the canzona emanates from the solo voice, from the first violin's major sixth—echoed in graduated entrances by the quartet's remaining constituents—the inaugural A section appears to sound out a totality whose comprehensiveness renders it at once a proclamation and a summation. It is as though each bar provided us with the following report: this is, this was, and will be. Two affiliated methods of organization permit us to experience the initial thirty-one bars as both a crying-out and a summing-up. Rejecting the key signatures customary to Beethoven's time, the music is ordained by the F Lydian mode (whose subdominant becomes a tritone, rather than a perfect fourth) and by polyphonic procedures that sling its pitches into motion. The modal ordination of what we hear spurs us to remember that the church modes—and their ancient Greek incarnations—originated in the resonant declaration of a vocal line, while polyphony subdues a plurality of voices so that each part traces the contours of a privileged melodic turn and legislates that every voice will sound together. Thus, we are given a statement, a melody that proclaims its ability to knot all contiguous voices together, repeatedly summarized by the corpus through which it moves. But if we listen to that corpus, to that body of sound, we may waken to the variousness at work in all we hear.

Listening again, looking again at the score that pictures sonic events, we find a tension between the deployment of the vocal line and the seeming homophony issuing from the coincident ringing of the quartet's voices. If we choose merely to attend to melodic behaviors, isolating each vocalization as it travels along the horizontal axis, we see that the voices engage in a species of primordial canonic imitation, given that the imitation itself declines to enact the strictures propounded by definitively contrapuntal writing. Each voice, in relation to its acoustic "neighbor," draws a kind of aural shadow whose outline generalizes the characteristics of the first violin's inceptive utterance. We can trace back the emphasized looseness, the fluid variability of such imitative motion, to the modal system that orders the deportment of the voice: signified here by the Lydian scale, the modal world proposes a voice at once chanting and improvising on the pitch-components of its melody. Hence, the quartet, as it quadruply magnifies the fact of the horizontal axis, presents us with a melodic structure amplified by its almost-improvisatory treatment. But the subject itself, the tune that submits to modification, appears to describe a stillness, a constricted sense of movement. After its leap of a major sixth, of a perfect fourth, the line sung by the first violin circumambulates around the tonic, around the F that signals the acoustic home from which its attendant voices—and we who hark to them—need not move. This hovering around the site of rest occurs five times, each occurrence lasting for nearly seven bars, so that the initiatory A section and its phrasal negotiations value the uneven, the evidently off-balance. And yet the notion of imbalance is shaded over by what the quartet's vertical axis so plentifully gives us—a range of pitches striking together as chordal incidents. We can opt to foreground apparent homophonic motion, however delimited, and to immerse the horizontality of vocal lines in the successive chords such lines occasion. While the music may appear to ask this of us—this forgetting of one element in the hoisting up of another—such a listening would diminish its very object.

As Theodor W. Adorno insists (1969, 1993), Beethoven may reduce musical work to "elementary forms" so that the work "no longer manifests itself as material at all," but reduction serves to articulate a "positive negation: discard, that you may acquire" (*Beethoven*, 39). I would qualify Adorno's insistence by adding that the challenge for us, the canzona's listeners, remains that we must not "discard," must not submerge the vividness of melodic variation in the homophony that simultaneous voices appear to engender. To do so would be to remit ourselves to an only seeming acquisition at the expense of the text outside us. It would also fail to prepare us for the appearance of the B section whose startling nature has nevertheless been implied by what we have heard—if, indeed, we have attended with care to all that the music demands of us.

I pause at this point, at the work's tacit superscription that we confer upon it the vigilance of our regard, in order to interpose a term I borrow from Iris Murdoch. Through a series of essays in *Existentialists and Mystics* (1997), Murdoch examines the beneficence invoked by the act of "attention," a word she adopts from the writings of Simone Weil ("The Idea of Perfection," 327). To cede our "attention" to an object—if the latter names a thing existent in the world outside us—expresses "the idea of a just and loving gaze directed upon an individual reality," with such ceding understood as the "characteristic and proper mark of the active moral agent" (327). For if "I can only choose within the world I can *see*," the "struggle and the progress" inherent in looking at, in listening to, in assenting to the fact of the sensible thing "implies that clear vision is a result of moral imagination and moral effort" (329). "Attention" thus enjoins on us the "infinite difficulty" of "apprehending a magnetic but inexhaustible reality" (333); indeed, we may qualify apprehension as ethically-based since it requires us to realize that the thing in the world fails to mime us, to replicate us, so that its distinguishing feature remains its separateness from us, which in turn becomes a kind of saving distinction. I say "saving" because the thing that resists us forces us to work at looking, at listening, at what we owe to its inexhaustibility. When Murdoch maintains that the artist creates a "quasi-sensuous thing" ("The Sublime and the Good," 219)—whether the "vibration" of voices patterned by *The Waves*, or a "sound" ordered by Beethoven's composing mind ("On 'God' and 'Good,' 353)—she identifies "aesthetic situations" not as "analogies of morals" but as "cases of morals" ("The Idea," 332), given that "the consumer of art" embarks on a "task" similar to that of "its producer: to be disciplined enough to see as much reality in the work as the artist has succeeded in putting into it"

("On 'God,' 352). Hence, making and attending to the art object afford an "adequate entry" into "the good life," if "good" equals the "checking of selfishness in the interest of seeing the real" ("On 'God,' 352). "Pre-eminently outside us," resistant "to our consciousness"—and therefore analogous to the particularity of a creature to whom we give the gift of our regard—the art object pictures what our "consciousness cannot take over, swallow up, deny or make unreal" ("The Sovereignty of Good Over Other Concepts," 373).

Murdoch considers, in "The Sublime and the Good," the relations between the beautiful and the sublime as given to us by Kant in the *Critique of Aesthetic Judgement.* Associating the beautiful (pattern untainted by historical or human particularity) and the sublime (elements of nature eliciting our sense of the "otherness" of what we see) as tied together in the art object, she declares that the latter connects the beautiful, the sublime, and the good since the object fosters our potential for freely choosing to regard the "itselfness" of the work of art (219). Though Murdoch criticizes Woolf, as an avatar of "Bloomsbury," for absenting the good from her vision of the art object, I propose that, for Woolf, the transformative character of the object may significantly alter how its reader/listener/viewer grasps the world we share (332). And this alteration demonstrates the ethical hope so central to Woolf's project.

Moreover, if "quality of consciousness matters," the thing that "alters" our mode of looking in the "direction of unselfishness" and occasions our "unselfing" can rightly be "connected with virtue" ("The Sovereignty," 369). One of the virtues of vigilant "attention" is that its object does not transcend us, does not inhabit a domain to which we have no access: the thing may persist outside us, but it is not by definition beyond the toil of our attending to it. Thus, claiming Beethoven's late music shows us "transcendence" as the "full working-out" of its "origin," of everything its constituent "stuff" implies, Adorno renders the work something that can only cease to serve us (113). Shunted away from us due to its transcendent status, the art object disallows the assumption that our "attention" will be proportional to the music. On the contrary: by suggesting that the advent of the canzona's B section compels us to look for signs of how it has been made, I submit that the movement testifies both to the "inexhaustible" nature of the "real" and to our need to tend to the implacable thing before us.

As we enter the B section's dominion, we will find ourselves in foreign territory if we forget our passage there. Though we have moved from a modal pitch world to the more acoustically recognizable D Ionian scale—and from 4/4 to 3/8 time—our motion has been prepared for us by the first violin's inauguratory leap and by the A section's instancing its 31 bars as a disequilibrium we start from. Thus, if we can remember that the shift from F Lydian to D Ionian describes the interval of a major sixth, that the A section presents us with imbalance as a kind of ground, we can apprehend the source materials through which the B section may be charted. Our apprehension necessarily implies that apparent imbalance, of phrase and section length, can intimate the potential to think of a state-of-balance in another way. Such thinking, however, presses us to ask: What are the elements poised here? For the theme announcing the B section's initiation hinges on the (dominant) A that previously constituted the mediant within the precincts of F Lydian, so that the significance of the note common to both tonal systems, Beethoven drives us to consider, can be modulated if the nomenclature which organizes it alters. In consequence, nomenclature becomes a way of seeing whose modification revises the function of the "thing"—the repeatedly sounded A—whose identity we imagined had been fixed for us.

Indeed, we are in a realm of things, as D Ionian can be understood to mark the sonic conventions of the early nineteenth-century, together with that period's advancement of the empirical ethos in which objects are always exposed to our probing, to our investigation, to our use of them. The very theme, in the broad scope of its pitch-contents, in its residing so confidently in the first violin's upper register, exhorts us to identify it as a subject; nevertheless, these behaviors comprise a sonorous mask—the thing we hear consists in the object of scale-material punctuated by underlying accompaniment figures. And as the B section's rhythmic structures originate in a diminution of those so prevalent in the preceding section—for eighth, sixteenth, and thirty-second notes attest to the diminishing of the A section's quarter-note base—the music requires that we think back to our prior position in order to comprehend the league between A and B sections. Such looking back acts as a method for moving forward, for realizing that these two locations—however disparate on the surface—condition each other. But, to identify the nature of the balance in play here, we must reflect on subjects, objects, and the mind that calibrates their relationship.

If we recall the canzona's beginning, we see that the thematic subject seems strung through each of the quartet's voices, ostensibly heralding that our attention focuses on the supremacy of a subject, multiply reinforced. Listening further, however, we perceive that each part manipulates, maneuvers, varies the rudiments of the theme's acoustic shape, treating that shape as though it were an engine for conversion—for diversifying the material that appeared so invulnerably singular due to the Lydian preeminence of its subjecthood. But what we have categorized as a motif, capable, in its primacy, of decreeing that each part should capitulate to the ringing out of its aural contour, now appears an entity ripe for treatment, for the usage to which any quarry must submit. Hence, the canzona tenders us a subject that subsequently transmogrifies into an object. Yet which of these entities, subject or object, remains predominant? And what force incites such metamorphosis?

Before examining the latter questions, we need to note that here Beethoven's music assembles an argument concerning the affinity between subjects and objects, a rapport whose difficulty calls for our deliberation, given that the perceptible thing—in this case a melodic construction—is both one and manifold. The music's arguing over the character of materiality permits us, I think, to understand the theme and its behaviors as typifying our own predicament, for we, too, are speaking things. So that when we arrive at the B section, when we confront the division between the first violin's subject and its colleagues' accompanying gestures, only to fathom the theme itself as the trilling of a D major scale, as an implement for figural invention, we return to our original dilemma: the subject is simultaneously an object; our quest to identify the crux of our attention endures. Such endurance testifies to the abiding problem of how we nominate the many things on which our concentration pivots, and confirms the integrity at work in what we hear. While Adorno claims that the "fragmentariness" in the "last quartets" is "achieved by the abrupt, unmediated juxtaposing of bare axiomatic motifs and polyphonic complexes" (152), I suggest that perceived abruptness follows from a dismissal of the argument at hand regarding what it means to be a subject, an object, and how we might heed their affiliation. Moreover, Beethoven's labors perform the import of Murdoch's vision, in *Metaphysics as a Guide to Morals* (1992), that "the object" at once "requires and guarantees the subject" (148), a guarantee signifying that both are bound in a mutual pledge whose fulfillment denies the fragmentary character of their relation, as well as their mere isolation. The canzona will declare to us, if we stay in the arduousness of its declaration, that subject and object may be envisioned as commensurate, mutually proportionate, reciprocally dependent, and that their dependence demands the galvanism of our attention since how we conceive their reciprocity will affect the world we see and move in. But, intra and extra-textual, arising like its listeners from the province outside the score, a tertiary element hovers among the notes: a residuum of Beethoven's contouring mind, which points to what it makes, to the utility of a concordance (however peremptory its perceivers' burdens) communicable by the act of composing sound.

Yet how might consonance be said to serve us? To posit a concord, a conjunction, admits that we face organisms other than ourselves, and that the sphere in which we live extends us the opportunity to recognize how we subsist among distinguishable things. If the world is "inexhaustible," it follows that the elements of which that world is composed may be deemed equally illimitable—in their import, in their capacity for being known, in the potential for experiential contact they offer us. Such concord also acknowledges what Brian Stock, in *Listening for the Text* (1996), appoints the "problem area *between* subject and object, with conscious thinking as the mediator" (89), given that mind and world "jointly make up the mind and the world," and that the world is *there* (105). Hence, the "conscious thinking" by which we envisage the intervening space between subject and object characterizes our facility for wakening to how we comport ourselves, signifying that our comportment influences the life of the differentiable things we inch towards as we move through the "area" where we may enact the "problem" of choosing to pound out, through a sort of mental erasure, the interstice between one thing and another.

One of the merits of the fellowship with which Beethoven presents us lies in its provoking our consistent effort to experience the possible liaison of subject, object, and the mind that designs the manner of their association. And, while we struggle with the fraternity reverberating throughout the canzona, we may come to understand that Beethoven spurns the customary antipathy of its component parts. As Stock advises us, "social reality"—the reality of things and human behaviors—describes a "compromise between an objectivity that cannot be known *in toto* and a subjectivity that cannot be wholly reflected upon while it is being experienced" (87). Yet Beethoven's music in this case performs the interdependence of "quasi-sensuous" materials whose score affords us a duration on which we can expend our vigilance. We can reflect on the way in which the themes repeal the prescription that a thing should *mean* in one way and one way only, for as each subject appears, it is varied by the arbiter of its variation; we can discern the evidence of this thinking-arbiter in the composite quality of the whole he conveys to us, how his design coordinates ABA structure (conventionally allied to the lyricism of a subject rising up in song) with theme and variation form, where the motif's receptiveness to transformation witnesses its fertility. On thematic and structural levels, we can see how subjects and their formal distension annul unitary meaning—that for a thing to *mean*, its music must signify in multiplex ways. We can take note of Beethoven's aligning discontinuous temporalities due to his rendering adjacent the antiquity of the modal world and the present of a D major scale referencing the classicism by which nineteenth-century sonic vocabularies were codified. Such alignment becomes a testimony to how one thing orients another, to how things—musical themes as well as the minds that treat and perceive them—verge on entities transcendently other than themselves, if transcendence names an otherness resistant to definitive summation. All this can our watchful attention yield to us—if, notwithstanding its transitory duration, we elect to look, to listen.

I wish to transfer the freight of attending to Beethoven's canzona to an investigation of Woolf's linguistic deployment in *The Waves*, to a probing of its import and of what that import presupposes. My reading of Beethoven assumes that the work of our imagination under the auspices of art may be seen to adumbrate our manner of generating worldly action, that the process by which we fabricate figures prepares us—and what Murdoch calls our "consciousness"—for the inclination to act. My reading further assumes that the discursive procedures which embody our making-imagination speak to the world beyond them, outside them, the world they cannot exhaustively represent but to which their gestures may conduct us, so that the worlds within and without the work persist in a contiguity whose serviceableness for listeners, viewers, readers, resides in its reminding us that we do not abandon the world while we attend to the art object, but vouch for the latitude of our participation in it. Thus, my assumptions reach beyond the fact of their evidential springboards. This deictic quality of the imaginative product, how it points both to itself and to what outdistances it, returns us to a view of the relationship between the transcendental and the quotidian, the transitory stuff among which we move. Though the work by definition can only fail to offer us access to the transcendent, it can nevertheless give us figural manifestations of its magnitude. If transcendence refers to that which surpasses us, to a conclusive otherness somehow beyond the edge of linguistic limits, our negotiation of aural, verbal, and pictorial languages may still demonstrate a pushing up to the edge of the expressible in remembrance of the fact that there are two sides to any limit.

Beethoven indicates such a pushing with his use of modal practices, which advert to a musical history precedent to him, to an orality in which the voice swelled with song and honored a plenitude it could call to but which it could not contain within its melodic frontiers. Yet the canzona's conjoining the systems of F Lydian and D Ionian connects the orality and literacy from which each respectively proceeds, prefiguring Stock's claim that "there was no orality without an implied textuality," no "literacy without the primal force of the spoken word" (4). And, as though Woolf's listening to Beethoven edging up to the verge of the ineffable functioned as her generative model for reimagining how language demarcates its own boundary together with the unreachable on the other side of it, *The Waves* reorganizes how we can permit ourselves to see the relationship between our recourse to words and all that recourse may conjure, between our impermanent selfhood and the permanence of an otherness at which we may—with difficulty—aim.

Woolf aims at correspondence on macro and microscopic levels, correlating the former unit with the locale of the transcendent and the latter with that of our daily straining through time, which, multiplied, becomes a life. The problem, the snarl we must brave facing here, is one of terminology. To define the transcendental and the fleeting by reference to "locales" treats both as though they were equivalent to distinguishable districts, to insulated vicinities, their placements spatially anchored by how our terms point to them. This effort on the part of language and its users to impute a referential tactility, a fixity of position, to discriminative objects may involve us in the belief that our terminologies stabilize the things they designate. As words transmit the thinking illuminated by their use, assigning word to percept I appoint the latter a thing, a discoverable particular. What we need, and what Woolf's congruity between permanence and impermanence instructs us to posit, is a vocabulary of forces indicated by Murdoch's valued "magnetism" and "inexhaustibility." If we are "mosaics," composites, we stand in proximity to that which at once structures our visibility and transcends the phenomena it shapes. But we and our available diction truck with things, so it often follows that our mode of naming the energies, the forces that order the disposition of our component parts—and whose yoking together allows us to be discerned—renders its referent a mere entity, bridled by the act of calling. Nevertheless, turning first to the macro-formal level, we can identify how Woolf exhibits the way in which the zones of the permanent and the impermanent may be intermingled, with regard to representation, by virtue of the potency of their invocation.

By its very form, by the rhythm punctuating the sequential nature of its constructive parts, *The Waves* mobilizes a vision of how the object at which we gaze may seize us. For if the object "requires and guarantees the subject," in its corporeality, its ripeness for perception, for being wandered-over by our eyes, the object answers for the possible achievement of our congress with it and can secure us against the loss implicit in the belief that the subject remains defined by its exile from proximity to others. Indeed, the novel requires that we think of things under the concept of propinquity: we may hypothesize segregating one wave from another, but it is through their corporate, serial character that waves are knowable and on which we train our attention when we summon the forces at play in them with a word. *The Waves* extends this by bringing the thought to bear on the human subject—we may detach the individual from his group in an effort to palpate the phenomenon he embodies, yet the illusion of detachment here consists in the implication that we can reasonably divide the knower from the known.

In order to annul such division, the novel agglutinates one thing with another, in the title by which it is invoked, in its portrait of humankind, in the sequence of A and B under whose locomotion its form develops. While we may segregate each A and B segment due to the tenet that segregation would fortify the driving thrust of our regard, Woolf presents admixture—of segments, persons, and domains—as a value. Echoing the kind of procedural "glue" by which Beethoven's canzona manifests a seeping of one section's rhythm and register characteristics into that of another, *The Waves* tests the stamina of our gaze by admixing A and B, the transcendence and flux of their respective domains, the dynamisms permeating them, together with the discourse-systems with which each may be associated, as though the power of one element could only surge in exercising its ability to figure the power of another. While exploring these concerns, we need to observe how they picture the relationship between the seer and the seen, the maker and the made, committed to a mutual seizing, which suggests that agglutination arises from a way of looking at the usefulness of connecting the putatively segregable. Our observation, however, evokes the following question: What causes such adhesion?

I will postpone replying to the latter question in favor of moving from effect to cause, for inverse motion stresses the musicality that superintends the novel's language employment. We need here to remember the exemplary function of Beethoven's canzona, how it exhibits the sinews by which music demonstrates the endeavor to *mean* at all. A single tone cannot attain to meaning; solitude expunges its capacity for resonating together with other tones. So music schools us that meaning cannot be given, but only made. Indeed, out of the relations between one tone and another, the ringing character of the whole underpins our comprehension. Such accreting of signifying elements becomes an analogue of the way in which *The Waves* administers the confluence of its A and B sections. The former visualize the discharge of energies fired through sky, sun, and sea, emblematizing the "given" quality of the scene that precedes and outlasts us. The authority of A lies in a continuance we cannot check, absolute in the sense that the forces powering the triadic bodies do not *stop*. But the typography that represents this ceaseless intensity alludes to the stopping inherent in the fact of literacy: italicized, the words arise from what Marshall McLuhan, in *The Gutenberg Galaxy* (1962), specifies as an "explicitness," a successive unfolding which "means the spelling out of one thing at a time, one sense at a time, one mental or physical operation at a time" (18). Before us, materially there, Woolf's italics—even in their succession—permit our focus to pause over the cargo of the emphasized word. Thus, modifying the canzona's work, the novel immediately foists upon us an amalgamation over which we must deliberate.

To appraise the labors of amalgamation, I juxtapose McLuhan's "explicitness" with two claims from Walter J. Ong's *Orality and Literacy* (1982): "there is no way to stop sound and have sound"; "sound cannot be sounding without the use of power" (32). If we cannot "have," cannot probe, cannot scrutinize sound without reference to its auditory flux, our junction with the sonic rests in its continuous propulsion through air. Yet the "power" whose "use" fuels our experience of the aural field remains divisible from its utterance, for the latter functions as the effect of a diffusive cause towards which our language may pilot us, but which will not be subordinated to our trawl-net of names for it, among which we will find "power." Hence, there is always a brimming-over, a residuum untrammeled by the nominal act that cannot be menaced away as it exceeds our very ordinance. Nevertheless, I nominate what Ong terms the "sound world" as the sphere of the novel's A sections because it guides us in the direction of a vibratory power which will not be held, to a recoil from custody which we can analogize with the problem of the visual (32). Are sky, sun, and sea identical with the forces they harness? This question, whether or not the discernible object is equivalent to the stimulus that energizes it, leads us to the process of amalgamation: while the A material expounds notions of indissoluble forces, it must somehow represent them, and literate procedures—with their tacitly fixed point of view, their ability to occasion rereading—afford us a sense of what we cannot hold, of what balks at the prospect of a final capture. Thus, Woolf's A sections convene the seemingly disparate as a means of shaping half of a two-part, consonant form whose musicality disposes distinguishable elements in apposition, only to advance the vigor of their aggregation.

Yet, after drawing us to the "sound world," after angling our eyes on its incarnated, typographical assemblage, the focus of *The Waves* appears to vary. Since its B sections supply us with the procession of six human lives, when we turn from A to B we may feel obliged to swerve from one nub of concentration to another, as though our movement lacked the ballast of modulation. But a shift in focus need not foster a revolution of the gaze, for—if we listen—we hear chorusing voices, individuated to the extent that each is concatenated with a proper name, whose diction and syntax nevertheless redouble our sense of their acoustic consanguinity and prompt our impression that these voices sustain a saturation originating in a cause which will always outstrip its effects. Over the course of the novel, our transit from A to B tempers the "sound world's" visualized pulse with the throb of its resonant transcription, alerting us to acknowledge the pulsatory force which at once produces differentiable phenomena and connects them. But it fails to follow from this that a shaping dynamism can be equated with its visual and sonic manifestations; in its evident lurch from one concentrated field to another, *The Waves* prevails upon us to linger in the task of apprehending association and of remembering that linkage is not a synonym for identity.

Attending to the B sections and their voices, we find evidence of the toil inherent in detecting the associative without subsuming the latter's components under the category of equivalence—it is so easy to elide the distinguishable points of view at work among each character's words that the language may seem to require this of us. To surrender to such elision, however, would be to vacate the novel of the ways in which its method supports its signifying power, to smudge out the rhythm of what we read. Rather, we must see the B material as a permutation of the A sections' locus, given that in both the phenomenal emerges from the vibrant. We must see the human permeated with a discursive energy that surpasses it, absorb how this preponderating vibration resounds with Woolf's insistence that the "new poet" should deliver himself in supplication to the "legends" whose "great fund of emotion" his song will punctuate in a "new place," if he petitions the "common stock" to direct the circuit of his sound. To innovate, then, is to consort with the cadence of the "common," just as to permute—for Beethoven, for Woolf—presumes a springing up from a groundwork of repetition.

My reiterated "must" proposes how the novel executes the imperative that rhythm begins with fraternity: moving from A to B, from B to A, we correlate sectional emphases and durations, confederate the "sound world" and the literate maneuvers that embody it, a confederacy our reading repeats and from which variants may potentially evolve. Hence, to repeat—to bound into rhythm—in *The Waves* is to enunciate a set of familial relations, to utter the interdependence of the supersensible and the incarnate, the general and the particular, the "common" and the individual, together with their attendant confraternities. And confraternity necessitates that we distinguish it from mere dualism. If dualistic terms denote two principles, two magnitudes incommensurable because they lack a common measure, each remains independent of the other, padlocked by the opposition we conceptually tauten between them. Yet the novel, as though augmenting the purport of Beethoven's canzona, butts against the stasis inherent in the oppositional, given that A and B, in concert with the magnitudes they image, participate in each other by virtue of how the one bestows on the other a foundational ground. This accentuation of the coordinate character of grounding—for to point to the ground implies the kin which magnify it—carries us back to a sense of the way in which rhythm vaults from a "bank" of silence, of how repetition (by extension) renders the rhythmic identifiable. Recapitulating A and B, *The Waves* heralds the relational sphere from which variations emerge; so that, within the expanse of its almost ten-fold pattern, the novel diversifies dyad into triad, duo into trio, AB into ABA and BAB, a diversification permitted by the continuity immanent in repetition and which our reading equips us to envisage as a cognate of the repeatable. And we can monitor such stress on the cognatic by following how the figurative diction of one section drenches that of another.

I suggest, as a case of this, the sound of waves keeling over on sand. The second A segment gives us the way in which "the concussion of the waves breaking fell with muffled thuds, like logs falling, on the shore" (29). Here, we gather how the sonic soaks, transfuses, the visual, a soaking the subsequent B material enlarges when, through the vehicle of Louis's voice, "concussion'" becomes the "'sullen thud of the waves'" (58). But the process of transfusion does not stop: metaphorical federation transfigures the "'sullen'" sound into "'the chained beast'" which "'stamps on the beach'"; indeed, transfiguration is founded on the continuous, the repeatable, on the thing so plenteously there that we may see it again, for the "'beast'"—once imaged—"'stamps and stamps,'" without curtailment (58). Some pages on, we see this saturating of the acoustic and the visible, the perceiver and the perceived, the word and the verbal coalition netted to it, in Rhoda's fathoming of the "'present moment'" as "'part of the emerging monster to whom we are attached,'" time (like waves) securing the sequential even while its energies overflow their apprehensible effects (65). And the "'emerging monster,'" by the time we reach the fifth A section, sounds—while one wave falls after another, while the "'present moment'" descends into the heft of the past, while one word always supplements another— "like the thud of a great beast stamping" (150). Yet to affix "great" to "beast," to collate how one figure unendingly begets another, demands a collator, just as language, together with the "legends" suffusing it, requires a human agent. The issue of agency causes me to reformulate my question: who, or what, produces such linguistic collation?

Such a question supposes that discourses require practitioners, that discourses themselves precede their users, and that both shoulder the bulk of practice over time. *The Waves* may fail to award a name to the assembler of its materials, but we can spot her evidentiary train. We can site her, however partially, in the A sections' predominate figuration, since the verbal figure exacts its generator, even if the latter appears to dissipate in the generation she offers us. We can position her as the transcriber of the choric voices in which the novel's B sections consist—though, like Percival, hers is a voice we cannot hear without impediment; and, again like Percival, she remains a body we never directly see. Yet we can dwell on what she effects: how, throughout the A sections' cumulative palpitations, the "sound world" pulsates, its representation ordered by the ascendancy and dispersal of a single day; how six voices resonate, from childhood to middle age, through the B sections' progress. Our dwelling must nevertheless attest to the transverse motion intrinsic to such double ordainment. For—in terms of discourse—orality governs the "sound world's" moment-to-moment sequential character, while literacy supplies us with the text we read, so that the A constituents' literate negotiations particularize the general effusion of energies which erupt into sensible phenomena. Indeed, within each A element, we can instance the tension consequent on the crossing of two discursive systems, as the language seems to advance omnisciently in the third person, but all its figuration executes a free indirect discourse that resounds, through the entirety of the A material, like a second voice. With regard to the novel's B components, their literate, textual fact generalizes the particularity of the utterances reported to us: the species of orality here may originate in transcription, yet each voice accords with another in diction, syntax, and in the rhythm they precipitate. The narrator persists, throughout, in being only typographically signified by the quotation marks from which we can derive that she was there.

Thus, we encounter a whole built of the crisscross of discursive organizations, of the chiasmus at work when synchrony and diachrony intersect, when the sequence of the day meets the transcriptional cavalcade of six lives through time. But what is the "I" at the heart of these transverse gestures? Bernard, in the novel's third B section, may help us when he contends that "'I am not one and simple, but complex and many'" (76). The chiastic form of his declaration shows us an "I" enveloped in the inestimable persons who congregate under the shadow of the pronominal sign. It follows that—if "I" am intricate, ceaselessly extensive—in application and utility, mind, body, and the objects they hold fast to may be similarly manifold. Keeping to the ground of such logic, we discern that the narrator who disposes A and B in crisscrossed accordance may claim a diversity equal to that avowed by Bernard. But this discernment leads us to reflect on what lies behind our narrator whose coordinative presence we can merely infer.

Behind *The Waves* and its narrator lies their dispenser, the woman who, Forster declares in "Virginia Woolf" (1941), "had, very profoundly, the conviction that mind is in action against matter, and is winning new footholds in the void" (253). To assure us that "mind" and "matter" are encaged in an adversarial relation endorses the autonomy of both: thus, each enacting its own law within the self-enclosure of its name, each defined by deficit, "mind" can only be without "matter," "matter" without "mind," the two subsisting in a "void" irremediably dilated between them and characterized by the antagonism of Forster's preposition. In order to dispute Forster's assurance, I contrast it with remarks Woolf addresses to Vita Sackville-West during the inception of *The Waves*. In early 1929, when Woolf discloses her belief that "it is one brain, after all, literature," that "it wants change and relief," she suggests an image of word-abounding "mind" in which a writer partakes by virtue of her verbal productions (*Letters 4*, 4).

Yet here "matter" springs from human congress with a "mind" whose bounty of variegated forms the writer shares in, draws from, given the exemplar of her work. We can trace the tenor of Woolf's vocabulary to Platonic thinking—to the instance of the *Republic*, which, like the *Symposium* contemplated in "On Not Knowing Greek," originates in Plato's middle period and argues for "the whole partnership of body and soul" (462c). Such somatic and psychic "partnership," in the partnered world in which we find ourselves, contravenes the torsion of Forster's "against" as it ventures to summarize Woolf's outlook on the possible conclave of "matter" and "mind." Moreover, in the voice of Socrates, Plato pictures another "partnership" when he insists that the materiality around us and what we make of it must be judged by, seen in the light of, the formations of "an ideal pattern": "turning our eyes" to those formations, "the nearer we approximate to them, the more nearly" we may be said to "share in their lot" (472c-d). Hence, the case of a writer's book fails to reproduce the single "brain" of "literature" even while the work rebounds it. To shift the metaphor into acoustic terms: reverberating a preliminary intonation, the book exemplifies it.

I emphasize the imperative of this introductory intonation because it presides over Woolf's understanding of how rhythm encircles "mind" and "matter." In spring 1926, "crammed with ideas" and "visions," Woolf "can't dislodge them" for "lack of the right rhythm" (*Letters 3*, 247). Going "far deeper than words," rhythm rises sequentially: a "sight, an emotion, creates this wave in the mind" long "before it makes words to fit it"; yet "in writing" we have to "recapture" the "wave," only to "set" it "working," so that while "it breaks and tumbles in the mind," the "wave" may adjoin "words" to its sonic swell (247). If we juxtapose this passage with Forster's declaration, we see how the rhythmic "wave" begins with the "matter" of a "sight" outside us, with the "matter" of something in the world that jolts our "emotion." Indeed, within and without—psyche, soma, world—embark on an inflection, a conjugation whose character will not be distilled by the "against" Forster marshals between theoretically irreconcilable fields, even as alleged Woolfian "conviction" decrees their antipathy. For rhythm, breaking its "wave in the mind," echoes that mind's contact with a locomotive stir beyond it, with the "outside" where rhythm starts but in which the writer finds her "share" when she recasts, reforms, the falling "wave" in the auditory shape of words. Such reforming can only countermand the notion of a combat terminating once "mind" should annex "matter" to itself, repulse the notion of a "mind" interned in the struggle to think away all that it is not.

But, rather than describing loss, Woolf extends to us images of gain. Picturing what rhythm does, she constellates "mind,""matter," and the sensate thinking that re-voices the experience of their alliance by means of words. And what participates in alignment commits itself to an apportioning, to a sharing, of burdens. In this way, the Platonism of literature's "one brain" becomes an ideal to which generic manifestations approximate; nevertheless, our various literary forms must sustain the responsibility of demonstrating, however imperfectly, the magnification of the "one." Yet, Woolf implies, we fail to own genres themselves as well as the language that engineers them: Both belong to the "brain" thinking its way through them. So that brought to, "set" in, the condition of language, the "many" embowered in Bernard's "I" are in communication with a "oneness" to which the rhythm of their words is incompletely, approximately, fitted.

This incomplete fitting educes how the "outside," signified by the ideality of "one brain," cannot be recapitulated by its representations: it will always overstep them. Overstepping thus confirms an act of salvage, for if the "one" will not be encapsulated—in scope, in magnitude—by its particular embodiments, the very concepts of within and without, of "mind," "matter," and the "brain" that soaks through what we say of them are saved from the wreck of obliteration. After all, to save our concepts entails the potential saving of the actualities for which concepts stand, the rescue from elimination of the "outside" with which we are teamed whenever we raise our eyes. Notably, Woolf chooses not to treat rhythm as a mere equation: epitomizing its behaviors, its effects, she does not pinion rhythm to the identity-making work of "is." And, in *The Waves*, preferring not to restrict the identity of her narrator, Woolf safeguards her from limitation, figuring only how she intervenes in the domains of A and B, how she modifies and is modified by the words through which we intuit her.

My use of the feminine, however, is speculative; unnamed, unsexed, Woolf's narrator becomes our proxy, so that the very industry of her interventions counsels us to recall the pairings of in and out, the book before us and a "brain" vast enough for the seeming contradiction of plurality. The extra-textual nature of *The Waves*, how its narrator—like her readers—is both within and without the book, returns me to the Murdoch of *Metaphysics as a Guide to Morals*. The "limited surround" of "art" may provide us with the "consolation" of feeling punctuated by form; yet "human fates" will always "exceed art," just as, according to Woolf's argument, the individual case of "literature" will be exceeded by the "brain" superordinate to it (94–95). Hence, the book, any book, possesses "an open texture," a "porous or cracked quality": "the object is as it were full of holes through which it communicates with life, and life flows in and out of it" (96). The virtue of porosity lies in its redeeming the fact of the book and the world, the fact of "mind," "matter," and the "outside" ambit that encompasses them. Reclaiming each, porosity reminds us that we need them all.

Let us listen now to a passage from the sixth A section, which performs the applications of the porous:

> The topmost leaves of the tree were crisped in the sun. They rustled stiffly in the random breeze. The birds sat still save that they flicked their heads sharply from side to side. Now they paused in their song as if glutted with sound, as if the fullness of midday had gorged them. The dragon-fly poised motionless over a reed then shot its blue stitch further through the air. The far hum in the distance seemed made of the broken tremor of fine wings dancing up and down on the horizon. The river water held the reeds now fixed as if glass had hardened round them; and then the glass wavered and the reeds swept low. Pondering, sunken headed the cattle stood in the fields and cumbrously moved one foot and then another. In the bucket near the house the tap stopped dripping, as if the bucket were full, and then the tap dripped one, two, three separate drops in succession. (165)

Piloted longitudinally, our regard moves from "the tree" to "the bucket," with the latitude of the "horizon" interposed between the two, so that we see in both height and depth. But something appears to happen to our mode of seeing as we proceed from the first sentence to the last. Taken separately, each sentence describes the myopia of viewing things from a frontal vantage point in which objects loom, nearly abutting the eye; taken together, the sentential whole engenders an admixture, a coalescence of altitude and volume. We discover the combining of the closely and the volumetrically seen, for example, when "the distance" fuses with the "fine wings" of the "dragon-fly" that dances "on the horizon" whose remoteness does not hinder detailed vision. And, in its verbs, the passage exhibits a familial integration: "crisped," "rustled," "flicked"; "poised," "held," "fixed," "hardened"; "pondering," "stood," and "stopped" present us with three verbal sets joined by the "paused," qualifying "birds" so stuffed with sound that they perch—silent—on branches of "the tree." Thus, by means of a traceable lineage, the nouns married to these verb-sets—"tree," "birds," "dragon-fly," "river," "cattle," and "bucket"—are intermixed, their merger resulting in the efflux of three "drops" whose descent renders "the bucket" an agent of association. We detect this underlining of the associative as sentences one through seven display coordinate constructions of subject followed by verb phrase; while eight and nine, after introductory material, repeat the clausal structure of subjects and the verbs strung to them. Only when we near the vicinity of water and its attendant vessels of riverbank and "bucket" are we given the parataxis announced by "and then," as though consecutive "drops" and the totality of water were our end, imaged by the additive work of "and," by the consolidation of the visual and the aural.

Yet the effort to consolidate implies a consolidator, the narrator we can sense in the liberality of her lexical markers. For a current beams through this passage, streaks through its multitude of definite articles and its trio of protatic figurations. We can sight it in the twelve-fold "the" affixed to "tree," "random breeze," "birds," "dragon-fly," "far hum," "river," "reeds," "glass," "cattle," "bucket," "house," and "tap." Tacked to its definite article, each substantive publishes the pinpointing of a genus "fixed" by its cataloguer who—seized—seems to grasp each for the first time with the concentrated intensification such ample employment of "the" commands. The nouns themselves manifest the ponderousness of being loaded with a charge which the narrator's protases model, each "as if" conceiving "the birds" engorged with air and "sound," "the bucket" brimful, so that when "the tap" drips into voice, it is as though the current charging these nouns rayed out in a kind of speech. At once half-veiled and present in her locutions, Woolf's narrator may come to us steeped in what she sees; nevertheless, by virtue of the past tense that frames her words, of the having-been incumbent on writing—since the person of the writer will always lie elsewhere—she remains "outside" what she says. She may provoke our understanding that the predicative cannot exist without the mediation of a speaker who, in turn, is alloyed with the words eligible for her use: even so, she opposes authoritative seizure. And this opposition augments the weight of what she says, for "saying" is all we have of her.

If the narrator's act of "saying," distended, furnishes us with the integrity of the book we read, and if, like Woolf herself, the narrator escapes a terminal residence in the thing she fashions, the impossibility of confinement works in both directions. The book will not be owned or claimed by author, narrator, or by the individual reader, but will "share in" each, as each will "share in" it. The concept of an integrity divisible into parts, of parts reflecting a whole, carries us to Woolf's 1931 avowal—to Ethel Smyth—that "all writing is nothing but putting words on the backs of rhythm" (*Letters 4*, 303). Materialized by its figure, rhythm shows us a body of reticulated spines skinned over with words and represents Woolf contemplating the profusion in the "one." We can hear her contemplation when she writes to John Lehmann, just before the novel's appearance, that in *The Waves* "there should be many characters" and "only one," together with "an infinity, a background behind" (*Letters 4*, 381). Reverberating Plato as his Socrates contends, in the *Philebus*, that "the universal body has a soul" whose "causation" inspirits and "coordinates" that body's "considerable indeterminacy" and "sufficient limit" (30a-c), Woolf indicates the mutuality native to the infinite and the terminable. Indeed, we note her thinking of a largeness apportioned in the small, divided into the small, without rift, so that while whole gives birth to part, genus to species, class to member, the "one" admits of no schism from the other. *The Waves* may forward death as a constituent of life; its architecture may quiver under the prick of loss, yet it does not crumble. Such is rhythm's wardship.

We seem, under the tutelage of the "book," of rhythm, to be dealing with essences invulnerable to the "sufficient limit" of generated things, to the entropy which companions them. Thus, given their tutelary functions, "book" and rhythm appear to parallel the Platonic diction of *paradeigma*, of *eidos*, which, in the *Republic* for instance, shepherds us to the purlieus of patterned forms which particular objects both exemplify and fall short of (472c, 402c). But Woolf supplements Plato's conception when she avers that the "book" of "literature" *wants*: capable of desiring "change and relief," the "book" behaves like a created thing, simultaneously beyond and within the world of appetite in which all generation is infixed. This infixing of one entity in its customary opposite escorts us back to the sixth AB sections of *The Waves*, to how their materials betray a sort of quaking in response to Percival's death. Yet—so Louis tells us at dinner before Percival sojourns to "'India'" (135)—"'death is woven in with the violets'" (141), a weaving prophesied by the novel's initial AB pairing when, in childhood, Neville hears of "'the dead man'" in "'the gutter'" and finds the "'apple-tree leaves . . . fixed in the sky,'" the tree "'implacable'" because its very sap "'is woven in with'" a designing filament "'which we cannot pass,'" cannot propitiate (24–25). But we can hail, can hark, to that interweaving, according to what we make of it.

And so it is that Woolf and her narrator offer us the prolepsis of the fifth A section in which the sun flares on "sand," "desert," on "the southern village" (148) which anticipates Rhoda's "'climb'" up "'this Spanish hill'"(205); so it is that the fifth B material, announcing the loss of Percival, compresses its voices to those of Neville, Bernard, Rhoda, while its sixth incarnation gives us those of Louis, Susan, Jinny, and Neville. If "'all deaths are one death,'" as Louis informs us, many-backed rhythm, even under the brunt of depletion, can yet impart to what we read the yield of a shift in tempo (170). Indeed, though "'India lies outside'"

(135), by his irrevocable passage there Percival reveals to Rhoda, to us, the bounty within the ruin, the "'gift'" of seeing "'the thing'" (163). For, in a concert hall, Rhoda listens to "'players'" beginning to bow the sonic "'square'" of a string quartet (163). The "'players'" "'take the square and place it upon the oblong'" formed by the audience in such a way that "'very little is left outside,'" in such a way that "'players'" and score, music and listener, are interlined in a knot whose nucleus nevertheless preserves the fact of an "'outside'" outrunning what we say or sing of it (163). I want to "place" Woolf's procedures here relative to what Derek Attridge mandates in *Peculiar Language* (1988) in regard to Joyce: "language that is recognizably deviant, lexically, syntactically, or stylistically, does not simply register a degree of distance from a norm for artistic effect but raises questions about the stability of any possible norm" (184). Yet the power of our imaginative productions (among which we must count the normative)—what Rhoda terms the "'house which contains us all'" (205)—remains their variability, their friability, their failure, even as we gaze at them, to sum us up.

Once we reach the ninth and final B segment, however, the very magnification of its rhythm urges us to ask—how might the struggle to "'sum up,'" despite its requisite failure, be said to serve us (238)? For we must always escape our summations, given that we cannot inhabit the verbal "house" they strain to erect around us: even the dying Percival eludes the book whose linguistic condensations authorize our deducing that he was there. Thus, faced only with the deposit of Bernard's voice, with his syllabic surge over the totality of the closing B section, we encounter a prolonged tempo shift which at once beats out the priority of presence and acknowledges "'the illusion'" that "'something adheres'" to lift up over the verity of loss (238). But such lifting up requires an addressee, necessitates the "'you'" who sits "'at a table opposite'" Bernard (238). Unaffiliated with a proper name, both singular and plural, "'you'" comprehends the triumvirate of interlocutor, transcribing narrator, and reader. Hence, we implicate ourselves in the communicative toil of "'story,'" of the "'design'" traced in it (239), which can gesture towards "'what we cannot account for'" (243), the "'deep below'" the "'precision'" of what we say (255):

> 'I begin now to forget; I begin to doubt the fixity of tables, the reality of here and now, to tap my knuckles smartly upon the edges of apparently solid objects and say, 'Are you hard?' I have seen so many different things, have made so many different sentences. I have lost in the process of eating and drinking and rubbing my eyes along surfaces that thin, hard shell which cases the soul, which, in youth, shuts one in—hence the fierceness, and the tap, tap, tap of the remorseless beaks of the young. And now I ask, 'Who am I?' I have been talking of Bernard, Neville, Jinny, Susan, Rhoda, and Louis. Am I all of them? Am I one and distinct? I do not know. We sat here together. But now Percival is dead; Rhoda is dead; we are divided; we are not here. Yet I cannot find any obstacle separating us. There is no division between me and them. As I talked I felt, 'I am you.' This difference we make so much of, this identity we so feverishly cherish, was overcome. Yes, ever since Mrs. Constable lifted her sponge and pouring warm water over me covered me with flesh I have been sensitive, percipient. Here on my brow is the blow I got when Percival fell. Here on the nape of my neck is the kiss Jinny gave Louis. My eyes fill with Susan's tears. I see far away, quivering like a gold thread, the pillar Rhoda saw, and feel the rush of the wind of her flight when she leapt.' (288–289)

Bernard admonishes us to see the interlineations of loss and gain, how the scrape of "'hard shell'" against outside "'surfaces'" ejects us from the nomenclature of antithesis and friction, from the echolalia of "'I, I, I'" which insists on the gulf between one thing and another (296). But now "'objects'" only seem, their "'fixity'" as apparent as the "I" who questions it, both released from the naming-system which rigidifies all it invokes, delivered to the permeability of seeming as though in a kind of birth. Nevertheless, it is a language intent on stabilizing the summoned which grants Bernard—and, by extension, his listeners—the gain of formulating his interrogative stance, so that the linguistic registry which "'shuts'" us "'in'" can, if reconceived, let us out. Yet this birth, this egress, is preceded by another, by "'Mrs. Constable'" raising the baptismal "'sponge'" whose immersing stream initiates Bernard into the world of responsive flesh. Arrowed with "'sensation,'" that flesh becomes a "'new body'" (239) enlisted in the domain of "'separate bodies'" (241). A "'sediment'" forms; "'I'" forms (253), only to be enrolled in the normative "'convenience'" of a "'military progress'" (255) in which "'Tuesday follows Monday'" (257), in which "'we marry'" and "'domesticate,'" in which words collect in "'phrases'" whose conventions "'compel us to walk in step'" and echo those who antedate us (259). But we are shown another sort of gathering-in here beyond that of the "'consecutive,'" the "'orderly'" (251). Baptized, Bernard secures admission to a body imprinted with "'sensation'" other than its own—the "'blow'" of Percival's descent; the "'kiss'" connecting Jinny and Louis; the suffusion of "'Susan's tears'"; Rhoda's vision while she "'leapt'" into the outside which embraced her when she fell. Such imprinting may render the body more than itself, may turn narrated "'symmetry to nonsense'" and so describe the benevolence of gain (243), but how can we speak of a death that exceeds the little "'syllable'" of its name (295)?

For "grief" arises from the communion of the twinned "'blow,'" "'kiss,'" "'tears,'" and "'pillar,'" when those we love, for example, tangled in the plexus of dying, return to the exterior through which we move and which we attempt to proportion to what we say of it (264). Yet "'grief'" awards us "'a kind of transparency,'" the benefaction of "'things seen through'" so that "'things'" and seer seem to glean an "'immunity'" from "'division'" (264). Even so, the "'canopy of civilization'" recurs (296); "'immunity'" does "'not last'"; we forget our dead when we "'remember inevitably what had been said'" of them "'by others'" (264–265). Thus, our dead become "'symbolical,'" sapped-over with "'this lily-sweet glue'" which culminates in a conventional wreath of imported "'phrases'" (265). But at this point we must pause, haul our eyes from the page, and wait on what that page tells us.

Bernard's struggle, our struggle, the struggle of Antigone before her immurement, of Beethoven while he revivifies the modal world in a present which forgets it, is "'not to let the lilies grow,'" to resist the ignominy of a double burial in which we "'cover'" over our dead with the conventions which purport to organize our experience of them (265). Like Bernard, we may identify death as "'the enemy'" against whom we "'fling'" ourselves, though that battle we can only lose (297). As Woolf forecasts in *Three Guineas*, however, our potential achievement lies in remembering that "by our thoughts and actions" we can "change" the "figure" we make of the dead, rouse their memory up out of the gradual heave of neglect. And, when "'the dead leap out on us at street corners, or in dreams,'" our watchfulness fails to let them rest; indeed, that watchfulness honors the attention we owe to them, told by how our language use acknowledges the weight that words may be said to carry and to redistribute (274). If—from the vantage point of the ground we share, readers of and actors in a "magnetic" world—we stand on our dead, if our dead stand on us, the load of reciprocity cannot be shirked. Such is the burden, such is the gift, of mutual guardianship.

3.

Imaging Figures

Chaque jour j'attache moins de prix à l'intelligence. Chaque jour je me rends mieux compte que ce n'est qu'en dehors d'elle que l'écrivain peut ressaisir quelque chose de nos impressions passéees, c'est-à-dire atteindre quelque chose de lui-même et la seule matiére de l'art. Ce que l'intelligence nous rend sous le nom du passé n'est pas lui. En réalité, comme il arrive pur les âmes de tréspassés dans certaines légends populaires, chaque heure de notre vie, aussitôt morte, s'incarne et se cache en quelque objet matériel. Elle y reste captive, à jamais captive, à moins que nous ne rencontrions l'objet. A travers lui nous la reconaissons, nous l'appelons, et elle est délivrée. L'objet où elle se cache—ou la sensation, puisque tout objet par rapport à nous est sensation—, nous pouvons très bien ne le recontrer jamais. Et c'est ainsi qu'il y a des heures de notre vie qui ne ressusciteront jamais. C'est que cet objet est si petit, si perdu dans le monde, il y a si peu de chances pour qu'il se trouve sur notre chemin.

[Each day I attach less value to the intellect. Each day I realize more clearly that only away from it can the writer repossess something of our past impressions, that is attain to something of himself and to the one subject matter of art. What the intellect gives us back under the name of the past is not it. In reality, as happens with the souls of the departed in certain popular legends, each hour of our lives, as soon as it is dead, embodies and conceals itself in some material object. It remains captive there, forever captive, unless we meet with that object. Through the object we recognize it, we summon it, and it is released. The object in which it conceals itself—or the sensation, since every object relative to ourselves is a sensation—we may very well never

> meet with. And so it is that there are some hours of our lives that will never be resurrected. For the object is so small, so lost in the world, there are so few chances of it crossing our path.]
>
> —Marcel Proust: "Projets de Préface"
> *Contre Sainte-Beuve*, 211. (1908–1909)

Echoing Conrad's Preface to *The Nigger of the 'Narcissus'* (1897), Woolf argues in "Walter Sickert" (1934) that "the novelist after all wants to make us see," yet the operations incumbent on the act of seeing—the need to stimulate "the eye of the mind and of the body"—necessitate that we should linger "on the verge" (241), on the threshold of envisioning the "silent land" which "lies before us," for it is a sharer in the eyeshot of our view (242). Given that we come "within sight of it many times," this "land," this muteness brimming with words we cannot comprehend, spurs us to "feel something" that has "nothing to do with the story" we will ourselves to tell of the world we know (242). Indeed, Proust and Woolf instruct us that telling the "story" involves relating what cannot be told of the "land" whose silence baffles mere recounting. Though they organize their instructions differently, both offer us a means of conceptualizing objects—while Proust refers to those agglutinations of time and matter such as stones, their scale dwarfed by the ground which always recedes from them, Woolf points to the paintings or novels issuing from the marriage of mind, eye, hand—and both begin with a sense of numinous things. Even so, the numina at once concealed in and actuating the life of things remain vulnerable to how we may misprize them. We may fail to find them on our way, fail to render ourselves a Proustian tuning fork for the vibrations with which things inspirit us when struck by mutual recognition, or we may equate Woolfian paintings and novels with the "impediments" of their representations (236). As a "zone of silence" lies "in the middle of every art," as "artists themselves live in it" (236), art, maker, and the things whose tactility he figures participate in the "other world" of which each "is mysteriously a part" (237), so that to identify the object with the "facts" of its narration (236) is to lose sight of "meaning" which "cannot be expressed in words" (243), to replace the "something" larger than the "story" with the simply sayable. Thus, to make—and, by extension, to regard the having-been-made—entails our engagement with "something" finally beyond ourselves. And the finality of that "beyond" brings us face-to-face with power.

Nevertheless, in terms of Proust's directive, power signifies a problem by virtue of how its application realizes a manner of considering objects unendingly exposed to our exploitation. The Proust of *Contre Sainte-Beuve* may abdicate the mind's capacity for intellection, yet to abdicate here is merely to readjust the office of intellect itself: if the "eye" of the "body," raised over that of the mind, must gather up, pick out, read, cognize the objects galvanizing it, the noetic "eye" details the harvest of its apprehensions in words identical with the sensations they typify. Hence, we orbit within a ring of equivalences; since, through the vehicle of sensation, the bodily "eye" becomes interchangeable with the things on which it grazes, it at once nets and eliminates the integrity of its very objects. And such an undertaking requires that we ask: What notion of congress does Proust describe? How might it articulate a double loss? Given that our lost time nests in the materiality of things—as though each moment were ceaselessly hungry for incarnation—and that, in regard to those who live by means of it, time's successive character can only depend on privation, Proust visualizes an alliance between the container and the contained, the latter in thrall to the object of its internment. Moreover, thralldom registers a compromise between the perpetual absence accompanying moment-to-moment succession and the imperative to resist oblivion, even though such resistance secures time's bondage to its deliverer. But how should we see the deliverer itself, the stone, the tree-branch, the leaf strewn across the ground at our feet?

The merit of the thing itself rests in what it imprisons, Proust implies, and solely in reference to its detainee can we begin to consider the virtues of its physicality. Any attempt to contemplate the thing divided from its captive deems the path on which we walk the dominion of the diminished, as—so slight, so susceptible to breaking—the thing must be unworthy of recognition or of the recovery Proust esteems. Thus, the object is made to tolerate a multiple divestiture. Divested of its solidity when our eyes penetrate its surface in order to regain the internee for which we yearn; divested of its value when, pages later, Proust pictures time in the accoutrements of personhood, its arms outstretched in a plea for resurrection, reverberating Aeneas, his underworld descent, and the divine progress which the *Aeneid*, Book VI proclaims through a dead father's reawakened voice—the object remains on the path below us, stripped, naked, victimized by concepts to which it had no choice but to surrender. For we—and my "we" includes Proust together with his readers, since both conceive of the world, its constituents, and their relations—are the cardinal summoners of the contained, of the imprisoned which we free by the detection of our gaze, by the incantation of a word, as though gaze or word could return us to ourselves through the rising up of the not-yet-lost. Rejecting Woolf's "zone of silence," Proust and his eidolopoeia image the phantom forms within things and the speech attributed to them, casting the world in the shape of a columbarium in which each object is an urn for the restless, apportioned dead. But, in "'Robinson Crusoe,'" (*The Second Common Reader*, 1932), Woolf gives us something to position against this impoverished summoning: a "large earthenware pot" (45). We should heed her.

We can linger with Woolf by marking the "reality, fact, substance" of the "pot" itself, how, like all things "staring us full in the face," it "thwarts us and flouts us," so that our expectations of it and the world in which it participates are "rudely contradicted" (45). Indeed, contradiction signals our drawing close to the gift of proximity: however Defoe, as Woolf declares, keeps "consistently to his own sense of perspective" (45), that "perspective" is proportional to the "plain earthenware pot" standing "in the foreground" whose "solidity and earthiness" discharge the effulgence by which author and reader see (48). Hence, Woolf proposes that we fathom the thing before us—and the range around it—through the thwarting and flouting of our desire, whether desire goads us to render the thing an apparatus for recuperating time's continuous debit or impedes our vision of the object which declines to duplicate our self-regard. To edge near, to contact the heat of things (the luster of stone, tree-branch, leaf, or "earthenware pot") is to grant them their difference from us and from our method for apprehending them, as to proceed otherwise is to eliminate things and world, if both suggest a domain beyond the shaping load of our will. Woolf allows us to infer that the thing closely seen jolts us, just as her introduction of the unembellished "pot" jolts us, because to be schooled in the art of looking is to acknowledge the jar, the nudge that posited difference permits us to experience. She extends to us not an exercise in indirection, but a launch into necessary revelation: unlike the Proustian schema, with its vocabulary of forfeiture and restitution, its decree that the thing should be made a surrogate of the self buckling under the onus of time, Woolf intimates that we must deliver ourselves to the task of looking at things as though they were distinct from our mode of comprehending them, that by means of distinction-making we may come under the umbrella of their light.

Real, factual, substantive, the "earthenware pot" instances the patronage of things and is luminiferous, seeing that Defoe, Woolf, and we ourselves can generate a "perspective" by dint of it. Notwithstanding such benefaction, we need at once to remember

Wittgenstein's claim, in the *Tractatus* (1921), that "the world is everything that is the case" (1) and Paul Engelmann's safeguarding inference from it: as "an image of a fact," a "proposition" may delineate "an element of the world," though if "true propositions form a picture of the world, they can say nothing about their own relation to the world, by virtue of which they are its picture" (101–102). For, if objects are the lights we see by, if we achieve "perspective" through our propinquity to those lights, the world will nevertheless escape our descriptions of it. That is the world's distinction—to repulse the comprehensive "picture." Yet while each person remains a "common seer," as Woolf avows in *Roger Fry* (1940), each must revere the thing whose illumination traces a "mind mark" in the tissue of his irradiated organ and balk at substituting the traced for the tracer, the picture for the pictured, the descriptor for the described (105, 85). And we should know what we mean by the activity of sight.

If Woolf adverts to the reciprocal stewardship of persons and things, adumbrating how the one can only be the custodian of the other, what manner of seeing structures the import of custodial care? We are meant, I think, to interpret care not in the penitentiary sense, not as though the two categories were locked in a mutual keeping founded on the compulsion to comply with, to assent to, the imposition of being kept; rather, Woolf asks us to intuit that we glean "perspective" by admitting entities other than ourselves, that to look encompasses something in addition to the looker, that by augmentation we enlarge the probe of our view whose components must guard over, watch over, wait on each other in order for the viewable to endure. By implication, Woolf counsels us to suppose that "seer" and seen dovetail in a corresponding gaze, though the semantics of the grammar accessible to us conventionally forbids us the opportunity of saying that the things we observe look back and meet the decisive flare of our attention. But in their postulating a multiple ministry of the ocular—the twinned glance, concentrated, poised—Woolf and the Conrad with whom she resonates in "Walter Sickert" exhort us not to confuse the means of seeing with an end. For Conrad's Preface adjures us to concede that the "power of the written word" can make us "hear," "feel," and, "before all," it can make us "*see*" (52); thus, through the concussion of the "eye of the mind and of the body," under the impulse of, in the presence of, vision, all our senses are loomed together. If—to rearrange the figure—"fiction" transmits the "appeal of one temperament" to "all other temperaments," the drive to address "must" be "conveyed" through the envoy of the "senses," since the network of the sensory cables our connection (51).

Yet to what end? As "art" may "be defined" as the "single-minded attempt to render the highest kind of justice to the visible universe, by bringing to light the truth, manifold and one, underlying its every aspect," both maker and the made commit themselves to the service of a "universe" of forces absolute to the extent that no "temperament" can command the jurisdiction to loosen, check, or subdue its sway (49). Nevertheless, the "universe" of the human "binds" the "dead to the living," the "living to the unborn" (50), so that the notion of the "visible" incorporates the unseen, the intimations of "the other world" (237) which Woolf reads in Sickert's paintings and which, semaphored by "line and colour," contribute to the somatic world afforded us by the exertions of our eyes (242). While Conrad and Woolf accord us a way of thinking about contiguity and distance, never effacing the utility of our struggle to distinguish them, Proust maintains that the provinces of "art" and selfhood are identical, that both function to reassemble a "seer" who cannot accept the authority of time which will always refuse the right to such convocation. Under the impress of the appetite for assembly, there are no others here—no stone, leaf, branch, or "pot." Each must replicate the self which, conflating the means of sight and its desired end, discovers itself in what it is not, however confined, however avid for liberation. But the things themselves cannot look back, obliterated by a pair of eyes refusing them the rectitude of a devoted watch.

Consolidating means and ends, insisting that the perceptual act must be amalgamated with a reconstitution of the self beyond the mathematics of duration, the voice with which Proust presents us describes the imaginative transference which power exacts when its business is to commandeer, to dispossess. When that voice—under the auspices of the answered gaze—mimes the vigor of an intensity always unconditioned by what we ask of it, the art of making arrogates to itself the very time whose vitality it disallows. Indeed, to disallow the unstoppable is to mask a longing for its prerogatives, for the potency to stay the self's dissolution; so that, converted into a sort of plenum, the self evacuates the fact of anything outside it. Yet evacuation consequently empties the appetitive arena in which we replenish the pool of our energies—and, without access to the radius outside us, we starve ourselves of the food we need. Hence, Proustian selfhood represents power as satiety, a surfeit voiding the ability to nurture its own continuance, unless it should embark on a self-devouring which would occasion the decline whose mournfulness, whose powerlessness, it so strained to circumvent. In "Sympathy" (1919), however, Woolf evokes another way in which the limited can "picture" a near-junction with the illimitable:

> But how death has changed everything!—as, in an eclipse of the sun, the colours go out, and the trees look thin as paper and livid while the shadow passes. The chill little breeze is perceptible and the roar of traffic sounds across a gulf. Then, a moment later, distances are bridged, sounds merged; and as I look the trees though still pale, become sentinel and guardian; the sky arranges its tender background; and all remote as if exalted to the summit

> of a mountain in the dawn. Death has done it; death lies behind leaves and houses and the smoke wavering up, composing them into something still in its tranquility before it has taken on any of the disguises of life. So, from an express train, I have looked upon hills and fields and seen the man with the scythe look up from the hedge as we pass, and lovers lying in the long grass stare at me without disguise as I stared at them without disguise. Some burden has fallen; some impediment has been removed. Freely in this fine air my friends pass dark across the horizon, all of them desiring goodness only, tenderly putting me by, and stepping off the rim of the world into the ship which waits to take them into storm or serenity. My eyes cannot follow. (109–110)

We can earn a "perspective" from Woolf's story by orienting ourselves towards the kindred pathos to which its title conducts us, towards the "withness" of companioned feeling which attempts to enunciate the energy animating the inexpressible and which the above passage depicts as an analogue of the observable. We can note the beneficence of analogy at work in the unidentified first-person voice as it refrains from the collapse ushered in by equivalence—for, struggling to remark "how death has changed everything," it introduces the likeness couched in "as," in "so," and demonstrates that encountering what cannot quite be seen or said promotes likening the unknowable to the known, even while the former bolts from similitude due to the failure which the effort to liken presumes. I say "presumes" because the endeavor to assert resemblance, when it does not conceal a ravening hunger for making the (almost) seen identical with the viewer's experience of it, for an entwining in which one element vanishes in another, counters the human wish that parallelism should be synonymous with equality. And the erasure summoned by identity is precisely all that Woolf's modeling subverts; indeed, her speaker's miscarriage with regard to striving to "follow" what will not be followed re-conceives what success might look like.

Informed by the newspaper of Humphrey Hammond's death (the man who seemed always to mean "something that he could not say"), the voice we read calls on the "fancy" to build up the "moment in other people's lives that one always leaves out," the "moment from which all we know them by proceeds" (108). Thus, our speaker—whose namelessness drafts a simulacrum of personhood—guesses at "the meaning" of the "outward sign" of Hammond's widow, the Celia for whom "emptiness" has "its ghost" both sensate and incapable of decipherment (108). A type of the indecipherable, death may lie "behind" things and function as a "composing," dispensing, distributive order, but Woolf's project in "Sympathy" presages the declaration of Simone Weil when she ruminates on the *Pater Noster* in *Attente de Dieu* (1942): "il faut seulement changer la direction du regard" (167). For Woolf advises us that this is what success looks like—to look, only to look again.

Safeguarding, reciprocal stewardship, custodianship, the necessity of revelation: my terms betoken risk, its correlative devotion—seeing that staving off a needless ruin warrants the magnetism of our concern—and point to the voltage which fires them, which we know merely by reference to its effects, suggesting that to deny the diction of jeopardy, to rescind the devotedness which defends what we can and cannot see from oblivion is to vacate both of their contents. To look again, always again, thus assumes our capacity for comprehending how we have looked at all, as to alter the direction in which we look supposes the potential multiplicity of our vantage points. And the thing which merits our notice, the Celia who "wears the white veil still," the Humphrey Hammond supine on a bed when "one bee" hums "through the room and out again," the stone sitting in our way, shares with us in being a receptor for geomagnetic and superlunary voltages recognizable solely by means of what follows from their burgeoning charge (111). So that to repudiate the fact of the thing is to revoke the electrical enkindling whose origins our eyes cannot give us, to proceed as though the seen were not supported by the invisible. Such support calls to us throughout Woolf's story when death merges "sounds," bridges "distances," fuses "boundaries" (110), strips life of its intimacy with semblance, with simulacra, with seeming, and confers on our speaker the certainty of a coupled "stare." For Woolf's speaker is "ours" because our predicaments are isomorphic: newspapers lie or we misread them; analogies founder; the things we "fancy" we see "deceive" us (111). Yet deception enforces our reassessing "stare," since Humphrey Hammond lives and Celia is no widow, but mourns the "father-in-law" whose name resounds in that of her husband (111). Hence, we and Woolf's narrating "I" must revisit the act of looking in order to right the ruin we have made and which it is the toil of "Sympathy" to picture for us.

Much of the above may appear contradictory, given my contention that Woolf's unnamed narrator quests for a likeness antithetical to identity whose attainment the story itself withholds. But withholding, when wakened to, revivifies our chronicler's appetite for allying readerly practice with the text that elicits it. My use of a phrase associated with conjunction assumes that to partner, to marry, to combine, stipulates two parties together with the gap between them, as it is by reason of the interstitial that we enact the enterprises of longing and by means of it that we rouse up our ability to construe desire's dictates. Nevertheless, our hazard mimics that of the Woolfian reporter who conjures it: with ease, with the familiarity posited by ease, we can choose to contract the distance between the desire to identify and to verge-on, since the reporter's images themselves, in their prodigality, seem to quicken an equality between two differential desires, to maintain that the seen cannot conflict with the "how" of seeing. Yet these difficulties—and the recalcitrance in which they result—will not be tranquilized by our wish to silence or to still them. Indeed, the failure to image what exceeds visualization attests to the story's probity and to that of the voice that surrenders it to us, however unwittingly. For we commit ourselves to error when we absorb the world in the pictures we make of it. As Weil tutors us while she meditates on the *Pater Noster*, "nous sommes désir"—we may be made of desire, hewn by its shaping impulses, but the rigor of our watching-post obliges us to interrogate the manner of our desiring (168).

Even as the work of "Sympathy" visualizes collapse, the caving-in intrinsic to misapprehension, it acknowledges a charge that survives the disintegration of its image. If Celia persists, unwidowed, if Humphrey Hammond rejects the final bed our speaker bestows upon him, both remain laden, imbued with the fervency of an electric thrum unenclosed by the tale that donates its simulation to us and from which, in the sphere beyond Woolf's story, writer and reader emanate. But, because to simulate is not to embody, the prime utility of misconstruction here is that it compels our ability to distinguish the one from the other. The narrative's failure in embodying Celia, Hammond, in bequeathing to us an administrative surge without reference to its counterfeit thus frees each of the perceptual loop that strains to circumscribe it, a freedom extended to narrator and reader as they undertake to reappoint the interval between the facility for vision and the story that merits their envisioning. Yet, like persons and the energies invigorating them, such liberty will always tremble just outside our aptitude for grasping it: it is not ours; we cannot own it. We can elect, however, to be modified by its inspiriting sway. And even though, as Weil protests, "le milieu qu'on organize n'est pas l'univers"—even though the circle we organize is not and will never be identical with the universe—encircling vouchsafes that something is there to be surrounded, encompassed, that the hoop may be retraced, differently tied, and that the things within it are sufficiently fervid to require restraint (126). Nevertheless, for Proust the things themselves remain subdued by what they encircle, owned, used by the vanished time within them, just as the latter can only be repossessed (fugitively, evanescently) by a mind outspreading the catalepsy of its own image on what it sees. Indeed, the objects of this picture appear already dead under the importunity of the yearning to regain all that its "seer" could never annex. But if, with Weil, we want to declare that "le regard est ce qui sauve" (147), that it is "le désir qui sauve," we must identify the labor in looking, we must know what we are saving, and how desire becomes the agent of our delivery (150).

For solely by such work will our form-making, our image-making, serve us. My statement postulates that our pictures portend a route to future action, that they chart the hypothesis of an achieved exertion, hence rendering the future and the past correlative and attesting—in their visuality—to a kinship with the world that compasses them. But Proust's imaging power documents the ache for a prelapsarian terrain that we, in our unending lateness, penetrate by virtue of a divinatory seeing in contradistinction to Weil's counsel: "nous ne pouvons pas faire meme un pas vers le ciel" (149). If we cannot take a single step towards heaven, towards the sky that will abidingly surpass us, if "la direction verticale nous est interdite," we must share in the ache and correct its picture, recognize the vertical avenue of our pining yet honor our interdiction from fusing with what we cannot lay claim to (149). Indeed, to mime the unifying force of a realm before the Fall, to ape the coalition anterior to our descent into time, is to aspire to supplant it—to establish the self as the irrigator of all phenomena. That which opposes the summational image, however, will not be exchanged for its representations; a tropism may ease us in the direction of exchange, but "toutes les sources de puissance" lie "hors de ce monde," outside this world which, nevertheless, is saturated with signs of power sources we cannot track (109). Thus, we need at once to concede our tropism and to reorient its turning in order to announce "le oui nuptial," the nuptial yes that Weil and Woolf conjure for us (95). We need to pledge ourselves to conceptualizing the act of picturing in another way.

As a means of clarifying the tasks inherent in such a promise, I ruminate on desire, on power, on the thinking recumbent in them, and on their visual representations that so often structure the ways in which we project ourselves into the continuous space we denominate as world. Doing so, I posit the reciprocity of mind and body, the complementary character of mental actions and the physical behaviors incited by them. If, with Woolf—in "Memories of a Working Women's Guild" (1930)—I want to say that "after all, the imagination is largely the child of the flesh" (233), I should apprehend that when I think, my body thinks with me, that what I picture to myself is coincident with the corporeality I consign myself to knowing. Hence, how we conceptualize, how we grow round with thought and with thought's behavioral coordinates, all superintend our negotiation of the world whose spatial continuity our pensive "flesh" can never conclusively encompass. If these statements are true, if with Weil we appoint imagination "la source des actions" (109), then to retrain our capacity for imagination would be to re-envisage what it means to act. But, since desire undergirds imaginative operations, enkindles the "flesh" in which they occur, vitalizes the gaze we pitch at the object of our yearning, we ought to examine what desire appears to dictate to us. Precisely to the extent that we can do this may we claim our embarkation on the toil of a revised looking. Yet, because of desire's appetitive, alimentary properties, because of its hankering for the ingestion of its object, we behave as though to absorb were necessarily not to think. In consequence, the thing for which we crave, intagliated with a beauty our longing exerts itself to reach, vanishes from sight once we swallow it. The finality we imitate here, however, indicates an energy whose reapplication would ensue if we were to re-educate our manner of directing it.

Our treatment of beauty can commend us to such an undertaking, if, like Weil, we regard "la beauté" as "la seule finalité" here below: we are drawn towards it "sans savoir quoi lui demander," replacing our facility for interrogation with what we do to the thing which offers us "sa propre existence" (124). Indeed, "la grande douleur de la vie humaine" is that looking and eating "soient deux opérations différentes," so that perhaps vice, depravity, and crime, "dans leur essence," manifest our straining to eat beauty—to eat what we should only "regarder" (124). Eve, as Weil suggests, may have caused humanity to be lost by eating the fruit, though "l'attitude inverse," looking at the fruit "sans le manger," should be what is required to save it (124). Rather than hungering for a Proustian repossession of the lost, we must acquiesce in asking what we intend to point to by the terminological network of desire, power, the cognitive actions in which both originate, and by the objects outside any network. We must distance ourselves, in so far as we can, from our entanglement in how we see in order to attain to the personhood indispensable for ample vision. Thus, to save our personhood is to dispossess ourselves of what we thought we knew of it. And aiming our desire—our re-schooled longing—at dispossession, we liberate objects and world from our engorgement.

Such liberation results from the "no" implicit in "le oui nuptial," the "no" which shuns the compulsion of our "fancy" to enchain its referents to the pictures we fabricate of them. Repealing enchainment, we prepare ourselves for committal to a "yes" which establishes a rift, of whatever size, between our desires and their satisfaction—between the mental, verbal, pictorial images forged by our cupidity and the target of unceasing space for which those images will always be inadequate substitutes.

But inadequacy of fit, of accordance, both demonstrates a breach and rescues the world from the imperative that it should correspond to what we demand of it, so that our sense of inadequacy reveals a gulf in which the world may be said to happen and readies us for what Weil terms "la destruction" of the selves we thought we were (108). In denying ourselves, in challenging what those selves manufacture, we become capable of founding "un autre" by means of "une affirmation créatice": "on se donne en rançon pour l'autre"; we empty ourselves in an effort to redeem the "otherhood" accessible to us and whose magnitude our eyes uncover, when rightly used (108). Yet this right-use involves our unchaining what we designate as power and desire from the teleological thinking to which we affix them. If my love of power amounts to a desire to institute "un ordre" among the people and things around me, my predilection for order springs from what I particularize by the name of beauty (126). Nevertheless, my unsatisfied appetite, the mandate that the ring of my hunger must go on increasing, heralds my need for contact with "la beauté universelle" which, on the strength of its dimensional scale, eludes the snare of my encircling (126). Because our manner of disposing such hoped for order is unequal to the world, it can only hide it; and, for us, the propriety of the world's concealment consists in its rallying our skill at untying desire from both dilation and fulfillment. So loosed from the cordon we have made, we face the very attention, "animée de désir," we never thought we stood in need of (151).

This integration of desire and attention returns me to Engelmann's proposal that our images "can say nothing about their own relation to the world, by virtue of which they are its picture." For, when dispossessed of an acquisitive selfhood, when emptied of the desire that recognizes itself by what it eats, we are free to attend to the world's disengagement from equivalence to our pictures of it. Yet the difference between world and picture does not demolish relation but provokes our assembling it, if by "relation" we signify something other than identity's noose. Thus broken, thus voided of concepts we could never use under the name of legitimacy, we look out—at the shock produced by a new breed of image. And Woolf reminds us how to condition the venture of our looking.

Before probing at more length the ways in which Woolf prepares us for reviewing the individual and what he sees, I want to acknowledge the criteria that determine the utility of self-emptying, of self-dislodgement, since for Weil and Woolf those criteria seem so distinguishable. Both consider desires which must be thwarted, flouted, reoriented in the face of things, whether Eve's fruit or the "large earthenware pot" whose clay, under the work of human hands, evolves into another kind of fruit and so signals the materiality of generative things. Both connect desires, the conceptual activities fuelled by them, and the imaging capacities we train on the "solidity" of the world; both suggest that we see, we look, we behave owing to the charges inherent in this connective network, out of which we fashion essays, stories, novels, and paintings that tell of that conduction—each a goad to potential readerly behaviors as each originates in the world wide enough to include it. And both disdain, implicitly, Proust's eidolopoeia which, by its picturing will, wishes to return the always-vanished to a self already dead because of the circular character of its thinking, because circularity here supposes that the world will adhere to the circumference of its injunction. Yet, for Weil and Woolf, the primacy of any image—verbal, pictorial, sonic, all bent upon by mind—is its failing to wind itself round the world of things, so that we judge an image worthy by virtue of its incapacity for, its rejection of, total comprehensiveness. Indeed, such incapacity renders Engelmann's "relation" an avowal of the not-to-be-captured: the educative image turns me towards what it cannot wholly show, towards the incalculable on the other side of it, hence conducing to my awareness of the "other world" whose capaciousness embraces even its failed representations.

But the ends of conduction, for Weil, for Woolf, appear distinct. If we must refrain from positioning ourselves "au centre de l'espace," which Weil holds in her "Cahiers d'Amérique" (1942), published as *La Connaissance surnaturelle,* our forbearance reprehends a perspective that seems to install us there, at the hub of the real (29). Yet the very "condition de la perception," the very requisite for seeing "le réel," extorts from us our emplacement at the heart of it (29). So that to surmount "la perspective" is to recognize no center in the world, only outside "du monde," in order—through love of God—that we should renounce the illusory power he has left to us of saying "Je suis" (31). Any picture that fosters such renunciation merits the labors of our gaze and angles us towards what will not be framed by it.

I think, in regard to Weil's "justice surnaturelle" and to the God who is its origin, of James Hillman's exploration of the mythic in *A Terrible Love of War* (2004), seeing that myth shepherds in the lexicon of the unfathomable which organizes Weil's experience of theodicy (31). Hillman envisions "myths" as the "norms of the unreasonable" whose "effect" plunges us into feeling that there is "no way out," if "out" describes a terrain beyond their purview (9). Before our lack of egress, before the "necessity" which overhangs us, we must take a "leap of imagination" into "myth" (9), into the "meaning without explanation" (11) on which, for example, Bernard and his author predicate the "'methodical absorption'" so fundamental to the images in *The Waves* (157). For, though Woolf does not syllable Weil's God, she nevertheless advances characters who address "'what is abstract'" at the "'end of the avenue, in the sky'" (154), who struggle to "'find something unvisual beneath'" the "'solidity'" they see—an effort as "unreasonable," as beyond reason, as Weil's argued for perspectival shift (156). Thus, like the Bernard who walks through the National Gallery "'picking up fragments'" while he craves for wholes, like Defoe as he presents us with a "pot" whose "reality" is attributable to the background which must outreach it, we stand steeped in a world braced by the "'unvisual,'" beyond sounding (157). Even so, our paintings (our images) intimate what they cannot measure if their makers and viewers abide in "'the perpetual solicitation of the eye,'" "'methodical'" when it adds "'stroke to stroke,'" look to look, outside the incantation of a mere "I am" (157). Both Weil and Woolf would claim that, so abiding, we edge near to the justice of which we are capable.

I am reminded of one of Cézanne's still lifes, say his *Pommes* of 1878–1882—which John Maynard Keynes bought "on his own behalf" after purchasing, for the National Gallery, nineteen works from the Degas collection auctioned in Paris in March 1918—and whose disembarkation tale Quentin Bell reports in "A Cézanne in the Hedge" (1992, 138). On the evening of 28 March, "deposited" on the "walk up to Charleston" (138), Keynes stood the Cézanne in a "hedge surmounting" a "deep ditch" (136), where it remained, due to an abundance of "luggage" which Keynes could not "manage," outside the home of Woolf's sister, Vanessa Bell, until Duncan Grant and David Garnett "rescued" it after dinner (138). We can now find it on loan to the Fitzwilliam Museum, Cambridge. There, we discover what Woolf terms, in her 1918 *Diary*, "the 6 apples in the Cézanne picture" whose coloration ripens "redder" and "rounder" and "greener" under the duration of our looking (140, 141). Because the picture asks that I hang on its clustered luminosity, I delay addressing Woolf's troubled numeration; moreover, I will later elaborate how Woolf amends the defect of her numeracy by delivering to us, thirteen years on, in *The Waves*, six individuals circling round a Percival whose presence they and we can palpate, yet whose voice is denied us, just as we are refused the identity of the novel's narrator but for the typographical indices that she was there—since, like Percival, her quotation marks redouble a superaddition to the visuality that cannot quite be accounted for, even as the book represents it, this inability on our part to explain, to reckon, to reason out with sufficient exhaustiveness. Though the Cézanne yields seven, not six, apples, with Woolf we inquire: "what can" such "apples *not* be?" (140). For the world—of which apples here are figurative shards—will not be exhausted or drained away by the precept that it should defer to our explanations of it.

Alongside Woolf, we can begin to "wonder" whether the roundness (140), the rubicundity of these fruits (scrabbled with green) is meant to reference Atalanta's mythic course to a marriage she imagined avoidable, to memorialize and multiply the beauty, then plumply golden, she could not withstand plucking from the ground; or whether Cézanne's apples, in their curvaceous plenty, can be seen as descriptors of the amatory exertions incumbent on our desire to realize what personhood prescribes for us, the admittance—as Weil formulates it in her *Cahiers* (1933)—that to labor is to feel with our whole selves the existence of the world, that to love is to feel with our whole selves "l'existence d'un autre" (18). If we see the painting subject to the radiance of this latter vision, its apples become visual synonyms both for the persons realized through their adherence to the twofold covenant of laboring and loving and for the bounty that adherence produces. For its maker's apples visualize much more than an intensified "We are," given that, unlike Eve in the garden ensnared in the circuit of her ecstasy, we cannot choose to eat them: they endure the strain of our eyes. And it is the conception of "ecstasy" that takes us to Woolf's "A Sketch of the Past" (1939–1940) in her *Moments of Being*, because the pedagogy of the shock which attends it coaches us for what it is to look and for who may be said to do the looking (65).

My scrutiny starts with an examination of Woolf's title, the limen through which we enter the "little platform of present time" that slides "over the depths of the past" (85, 98). Already, however, we light upon a temporal "platform"—undulant, liquefied—as difficult to divine as the "invisible presences" whose "depths" uphold it (80). Indeed, to sketch the "impression," the pressing in, the bearing down, of such upholding is to understand its recorder (the "person to whom things happened") as the deputy of "any human being" who endeavors to study, from the guardhouse of the moment, a past that diverges from and sustains his look-out (65). Thus, I see Woolf's textual industry as representative of her readers' dilemma, to the extent that those readers militate against failing to allow for the toilsomeness of gazing back at what seems so gone from them. For, as I concentrate on all that Woolf's title connotes, the sketch—in its preliminariness, in its accepting the irresolvable through never being finished—qualifies the past as it images a depth, an entirety, it cannot compute. In this sense, Woolf re-describes Engelmann's "relation" to mean the angle at which we picture a totality beyond our power to measure within the boundaries of any frame, implying that our vigilance lies in accounting for the space that angularity posits. Hence, any picture angles us towards what it cannot enclose and is, by definition, fragmentary, a definition that it is our human business to recollect. But what of the person engaged in recollection? How can we characterize her?

I commence by adjoining two ideas—the idea of the expanse posited by the angular and that of the being put beyond, pushed outside, the precincts of the sensory which "ecstasy" appears to impose upon us, so that under the force of ecstatic experience we are as though withdrawn to the breadth we could never decisively represent. Nevertheless, Woolf sketches both the extrasensory—the being ousted from the sphere of the senses—and the memory that musters its refluent "impression" (65), the "firstness" of her mother sitting "in a train" while it speeds on to Cornwall, of lying "on her lap" and therefore seeing the "flowers she was wearing very close" (64), though this "firstness" is challenged by the following:

> If life has a base that it stands upon, if it is a bowl that one fills and fills—then my bowl without a doubt stands upon this memory. It is of lying half asleep, half awake, in bed in the nursery in St. Ives. It is of hearing the waves breaking, one, two, one, two, and sending a splash of water over the beach; and then breaking, one, two, one, two, behind a yellow blind. It is of hearing the blind draw its little acorn across the floor as the wind blew the blind out. It is of lying and hearing this splash and seeing this light, and feeling, it is almost impossible that I should be here; of feeling the purest ecstasy I can conceive. (64–65)

Given the bifurcated nature of "the first memory," forked by "red and purple flowers" on the "black ground" of her "mother's dress" and by the metaphoric enterprise of the above passage, Woolf exhibits that to "begin" by visualizing the inaugural image is to spawn a plurality of images (64), that there will always be more than one picture assignable to our own beginnings, that incipience occurs within a continuity, inside an "immense . . . force of life" from which each thinking body emerges and into which each is born (79). Thus, inauguration means our envelopment in a continuousness inescapably antecedent to us, to which our "relation" must be prepositional, intransitive, indirect; thus, the pictures through which we describe our experience are always at an angle to what they could never orbit round. For Engelmann, because he equalizes "picture," "relation," and "world," the impossibility of the orbital image can only be understood as a failure to which we should capitulate. But, for Woolf, capitulation to the "impossible" may be cast in different terms, regardless of those terms' nearness to contradiction.

I say "contradiction" since, if we consider the "ecstasy" which Woolf impresses upon us, we confront opposing systems of discourse and of the self that resorts to them. Indeed, Woolf's recourse to depicting "ecstasy"—the delight that heaves us away from the body, though the latter springboards us into exaltation—propels its account to the "verge" of the ineffable. To heed the words shut in the mouth of the past, to regain the experiential images described by those words, to lever up the body: Woolf devotes herself to an eidolopoeia which, while it cranes towards the inexpressible, must be grasped in accordance with some communicable foundation. If the past is never silent, if it murmurs in the ears of the present, that past, with respect to its listener's notational exertions, assents to communication and its exigencies. Taking such a past, however, as one name for what outdoes exhaustive description, we find how the supra-discursive reaches a settlement with what it is possible for us to say, how to render that settlement (that speaking picture) with patience and distinction is to motion towards its very impossibility. And, in this manner, Woolf's use of the conditional guides us in our reading. For, when turning to the logic of if/then, she hypothesizes all that follows from it. She administers, within the category of metaphor, the metonymic transfer of "life" to "base" and "bowl," as though tendering an understructure clarified in a limpid light the trough both additively filled and disposed to further transmittal. But here pattern performs the work of light: it beams at the sequence that ramifies from a framework beneath which it cannot probe. That incapability of probing reflects the character of the target missed, the aim evaded—and rebounds on the writer whose sentences traverse a vigor they cannot "explain" (72).

Such is the seemliness of Woolf's "if" as it measures out a sentential series, each prefaced with an "it is" that conveys the memorial weight carried by the whole. The benefit of "lying" between sleep and wakefulness, between inside and out, becomes the recognition that their abutment is porous, there in the room where the sea breaches walls while it breaks on sand. Through the conditionality that orders her descriptions, the self seems "one" and "two," an antiphon to the liquid rhythm "behind" and before the "yellow blind," since "lying," "hearing," and "seeing" broadcast an accord as "impossible" as the "I" who apportions and is pervaded by it. "Ecstasy" thus designates a pervasion in which the senses are seized, only to be escaped from. We can avow that seizing; to retail our escape is to hazard the threshold of what, with Woolf, we can "conceive" but not altogether say.

Yet Woolf's "next memory" broaches another sort of seizure (66):

> It still makes me feel warm; as if everything were ripe; humming; sunny; smelling so many smells at once; and all making a whole that even now makes me stop—as I stopped then going down to the beach; I stopped at the top to look down at the gardens. They were sunk beneath the road. The apples were on a level with one's head. The gardens gave off a murmur of bees; the apples were red and gold; there were also pink flowers; and grey and silver leaves. The buzz, the croon, the smell, all seemed to press voluptuously against some membrane; not to burst it; but to hum round one such a complete rapture of pleasure that I stopped, smelt; looked. But again I cannot describe that rapture. It was rapture rather than ecstasy. (66)

If the Latinity underpinning "rapture" levels our attention at a stoppage triggered by an onrush of the sensory, this passage exhibits the self's transfixion before a "whole" that voids motility as a proof of its duress. The young girl of "August 1890" and her author are transported to a "stop," a halt, a desisting from withdrawal whose effects may be listed by reference to how they strum on human skin, ear, nose, and eye, though a total articulation of their phenomenal and emotive cause will elude any catalogue (67). For the perceptible superabounds with an ebullience comparable to that of its receptor, as the latter is both suspended in her venous skin and lexically diversified. And superabundance warrants a "stop" put to the progress of our reading, signals the question—what is this selfhood that boils over, that redoubles its representations? Combined, the two passages forward our harking to the primacy of a sumptuous awareness, as if the hospitable "bowl" of the body were a satellite dish, a basin for the reception of impulses actuated by a "life" that stood always outside transmissive instrumentality. The first passage positions its "I" in the vicinity of the "impossible"; the second couples determinate personhood with a "one" generalized because of its global individuality and abstract because the "hum" of "pleasure" that spirals "round" it draws a course which words "cannot" dispatch. But the "one" who deploys them can, by their use, discriminate "rapture" from "ecstasy," differentiate between the being riveted to sensation and boosted beyond the body's ambit—and such activities, correlative due to their dispensing "one," are encrypted in the semicolon usage so prevailing in the second excerpt. As semicolons punctuate a series of verbal materials whose members require internal commas; as they station, within the flexure of the sentence, independent clauses not linked by coordinating conjunctions—they arbitrate between organ and body, distribute part to "whole," and spring back on their distributor. Intermediate between the mind's moving forward and the attainment of an idea's full "stop," they also notate the intake of air essential to the long exhalation of a sentence and, with regard to clauses, witness correspondences they do not elucidate. As such, they make a gift to us of the elucidating act.

Leashing together all these significations, we find how the passage mounts variants of them on the page: sentences one, four, and five recruit the semicolon to demarcate successive elements, both phrasal and participial, devised to qualify what it is to "feel" when seized by the current of the observed; hence, their combined constituents should aid us in ascertaining the properties of the pronoun—or, in the case of sentence four, those of the scene—they modify. Yet combination posits a "whole" which mathematics will not award us. Indeed, Woolf's unconventional semicolon employment, her string of participles and incomplete clauses, tells us that here we meet with the myopia of an eye fixed on the part. And, since the linguistic indicators of personhood, sometimes discrete, sometimes multiplying discreteness, parallel the treatment of the seen—the ways in which its concatenated units "stop" on the page before the "whole" they surmise, its pieces sieved by the senses of touch, sound, sight—we are countenanced in taking the categories of person and environment as counterparts of wholes, abstract in so far as both seem deducted from and summaries of ever more voluminous entireties. Thinking later of her father, Woolf will commend to us the dual abstraction I am propounding: she culls "from a whole single qualities" which form "part of that whole," the "whole" being "different from the qualities" of which it is "made" (110). If any depiction ratifies its referents, however notionally, infelicitously, Woolf's culling obliges us to tarry in our study of abstraction and its purposes. I thus rephrase my earlier questions: who are these persons insusceptible to the arithmetic of their "qualities"?

Prior to making a rejoinder to my query and discussing what Woolf dubs the "ancestral" (68), those "exceptional moments" magnified by the "sledge-hammer" thumping of their "blow[s]," I enlarge upon the commonplace wisdom which construes the abstract in antithesis to the real and which utilizes opposition as a taxonomic principle (72). My taxonomies at once allude to the substantives they invoke and to our propensity for depicting them—to the enigmatic "conception" laboriously limned, to the thing behind or ahead of us in the space whose scale cedes us the benediction of movement (73). But if to think the concept is to commit it to becoming an apprehensible thing; if to think the object is to seal it in thought, in thought's classifying concerns, the antagonism so habitually stressed appears predisposed to dissolution. We are parties to this undoing because of the certainty that concepts are not things, though we beget the latter by means of them, that our creations overtake their makers when, disregarding the process of their begetting, we re-conceptualize them as adherents of the ground, as heirs of a nature authenticated by a radiance which will not be "stopped." Such rethinking can, of course, function inversely: we may confound the organic object with the "conception" by whose agency we order it, so that—suborned by the play of a "force" which oppugns our possession and by which we are quickened—object and "force" are remade as simply ours. Regarding these fabulations and their consequences in the veridical world, Woolf's approach to the "picture" will assist us in adjudicating the concord or the dissonance between abstraction and what we girdle round with the term "reality"(66, 137)—and in realizing how adjudication submits to "paint" (66).

"If" she "were a painter," Woolf would stain her "first impressions in pale yellow, silver, and green," their federation seeping "blind," "sea," and "passion flowers" on canvas (66). She "should make a picture that was globular" in its semi-transparency; "should make a picture of curved petals" and "shells," of "things that were semi-transparent"; she "should make curved shapes, showing the light through, but not giving a clear outline" (66). And "everything would be large and dim": "what was seen would at the same time be heard; sounds would come through this petal or leaf—sounds indistinguishable from sights" (66). Woolf brakes the fluency of her image-making when she remarks, farther on, that "picture" is "not the right word" for what flows from it: the ocular and the auditory, "so much mixed" (67), counsel us that we follow a synaesthetic "whole" which the conditional brush could not impart to us and which a conjurer of words "cannot describe" in the present indicative accessible to her (66). Though "what makes all images too static" is their being steeped in the fixity of their surfaces (79), their misapprehending what we "cannot analyse" slants us in the direction of the "indescribable" (111, 79), so that the abstract and the real—the palpability of "paint," of canvas, of words on the page—seem inclined to run "together" (123). I listen to the anaphoric pulse of Woolf's "first impressions," to the way in which repetitive insistence marks what it cannot enumerate, the "many other than human forces" endlessly "at work on us" (133). I think of Iris Murdoch, who testifies, in "Art Is the Imitation of Nature," that "abstract paintings," their objects "dissolving into something else," are not mere "idle daubs or scrawls, forms wandering round at random in spaces": they tilt towards "light," "colour," "space," their makers residing "not in a state of total freedom" but "relating" themselves "to something else," to the "world where we normally take colours to be parts of objects" (*Existentialists and Mystics*, 256–257). Yet what can be said of personhood as it dissolves into that "something else"?

Up to this point, we have sifted through the incarnations of images from which time has been absented, the "movement and change" attributable to "one of the invisible presences" which tug us "this way and that" and which "position" us, preserve us in a meshwork of dynamics greater than—in the case of time—our globe's axial revolutions round a burning orb (80). Hence, whether by the lip of a figurative "bowl" or by membranous tissue, the Woolfian self envisaged here conceives a twofold curb, that of a "life" measured by the "container" of its vessel and of an outside that cannot quite get in without exposure to the subjection of measurement (67). But the limitation inherent in these pictures answers to their virtue and to their poverty: human lives overleap and are overleapt by their representations, the self is not all, and I am sent back to the "no way out" which Hillman associates with myth, even as "A Sketch of the Past" institutes a different set of images for what it might mean to brave the butt intrinsic to a phrase so removed from a "state of total freedom." The intervals in the "nursery," in the "garden" among the "hum of bees," may induce astonishment at the self's "impossibility," at a feeling inimical to narration in the explanatory sense (70); such intervals may look to a "meaning without explanation," initiate discernment of the "unreasonable," though—under the throng of the psyche's "mind mark"—their pertinence to the idea of others and to a life "lived in common" remains uncertain (83). Nevertheless, the imagistic collection subsequent to them convokes the intractable, nearly "unveiled," "intensified" (93) by the "sudden shocks" (72) at all that Woolf and those who read her cannot "pass" or "escape," and illustrates that the impassable constitutes much of what we live "in common" (71). Abstract because of our difficulty in grasping it, the impassable is thus akin to "reality," just as Woolf's predicaments typify our own.

Indeed, suicide, a sometime impotence inside the shadow of a lunging fist, and sexual molestation should not be unknown to us; as human possibilities, they are at least parts of the imaginable world. Whether as probability or as fact, they wrest from us our admission of what will brook no denial and are "ancestral" since, together, they comprise a portion of our inheritance with respect to how our species moulds time, shapes time, crafts time as though its periodic pattern were "stuff"—and merely ours. Seen in this last light, each of the above actions becomes a vestige of the mythic, given that each is instigated by the dominion of a human hand replicating, in diminished form, the "unreasonable" there seems "no way out" of. But, picturing these actions, Woolf wants us to reexamine our need to extrapolate from the particular to the generalized, to assess the ways in which extrapolation impugns our putative individuality. Thanks to the calculus essential to extrapolation, to how mind speeds along thought and its embranchments, Woolf fuses the "suicide" of "Mr Valpy," a Cornwall neighbor, with the "apple tree" whose "grey-green" bark swells at once with maturation and resultant decay, networking man and "tree" due to their filiation from a common "force" (71). She recalls "fighting" with her brother "on the lawn": while observing the impulse to "hurt another person" in a "trance" of apperception, the girl she was expanded into a "person" who revoked the principle that punch should retort upon punch, even as her fallen fist "let" her brother "beat her" (71). Yet if velocity of mind projects a thought forward, it can also move by retrogression, figuring an occurrence against the backdrop of its origins. For what shadows the aforementioned events, what precedes them, reveals a retrograde line of reasoning and remonstrates that our singularity is a lie.

"There," on the "slab outside the dining room door," Woolf's half-brother begins to "explore" her "body" (69). He digs down "under" the "clothes" into "certain parts" which "must not be touched"; the sense that "it is wrong to allow" them to be fingered "must be instinctive," inborn, of an agedness greater than the duration discoverable in the girl "stiffened" on a "slab" (69). But if instinct, in its priority, "proves that Virginia Stephen was not born on the 25th of January 1882," such a confederacy of the instinctual "proves" that her readers join her in being "born many thousands of years ago," that we "had from the very first to encounter instincts already acquired by thousands of ancestresses in the past," that the self is backlit by its antecedents (69). I am an otherness amid what I think I know, a plurality which predates myself, and everything I seem to have is not mine, but theirs. All this the "shock" of the outside coming in makes "real" for me—and for the "us" I am (71, 72).

Or so Woolf would have us think.

And yet to read with sufficient fullness the moments over which we have hovered, to detect how they are "connected," we must reassemble them (71). Reassembly centralizes our attention on parts tending towards a "whole" which undoes their mere totaling up; it also underscores our participation in what envisioning means, since we will have remade the "scale," the "scaffolding," by which any human life is upheld, even if it must be more, that life, than the metaphors appendant to it (72, 73). Our metaphoric profusions, the ways in which we transfer the attributes of one thing to another along a line of likeness, of kinship, nevertheless affect the comportment of our thought together with that of the behaviors conjugated by it—and all dispense the vision that we undertake "in common." Adapting Hardy's *Moments of Vision, and Miscellaneous Verses* (1917), Woolf neither replaces "vision" with "being" nor conflates the two terms: in its collective significations, "vision" signposts "moments of being" and the "shock" which heralds their advent (73). To undergo exhumation, to succumb to our unearthing from a tumulus of inattention, to accept that the pictures of our succumbing will always be unfinished—these verb phrases meet in the momentary "being" of sudden sight. But the far-sightedness open to us must be prepared for, equipped with our cognizance of an apprehending eye, mind, and the "shock" which actuates both. However brief the "blow[s]" that enkindle me into "being," I can remember them; out of their sequencing, I initiate a thinking through the irradiation of their images. Doing so, I rally what it was—and will be—to have been.

For, with Woolf, we can recognize: I irrupt into an outside always incomplete with respect to me. When my sense-faculties encroach on completeness, on within and without consummated, divisionless under the rush of feeling, my body foils its anticipated union: the unfeasibility of my being "here" reinstates an "I" inevitably unyoked from a "whole" it cannot recover. Enraptured, that "I" may be unable to relate the thoroughness of its arrest, yet it can educate itself in the slow "stop" over the details of the visible and learn not to covet their capture. Thus far, "shock" names a psyche bruised by where it cannot go, what it cannot do; such negations nevertheless instruct me that to think calls for things exterior to the thinker, forerun my collisions with an outside whose "horror" it is possible for me to meet (71). The interiority of mind required for that meeting shows me what thinking can effect: ascertaining the "suicide" of a "Mr Valpy," of someone else seen by though unknown to me, I struggle my way into watching the moment before declination, speculate on thoughts amassed in a succeeding fall—the world contains nothing but my despair of it, or anything except my skills in abiding an extent wide enough for a mind that imprints itself on, that excises itself from, a span I do not know how to match. Such speculations, notwithstanding their accuracy or imprecision, demonstrate the imperious belief that loss must be repaired by the spotting of its ocular equivalent; as if human minds were slung together, the one compensating for what the other could not persevere in, I revive, remake the lost in the kin I propose for him, an aging "tree," a fallen branch, any object fashioned and subverted by time whose progressive infringement on things is all I grasp of it.

A probable definition of "horror" here, out of so many, is that the lost is not mine; a thing among things, he declines the restoration I ordain for him and the pronouns by which I submit that he was there. In that lies his gift to me, as both he and the world are unequal to my need that they should be requisitioned. But there are other forms of restitution, of revision, and these can be tested under the searchlight of "reason" (72). Furthermore, "reason['s]" practice of parsing out—of resolving—an ensemble into its constituent elements through engrossed cogitation inserts an indefinite hiatus in the midst of action, signalizes the trial of a new "shock"; so that, if the outside will come in by means of a penetrative fiat, I at once suffer that piercing and behold it from a prepositional standpoint, from a mental distance, in order to "explain it" (72). Of course, to "explain" my penetration is to recast those actions within my reach, as well as that "I" fledged by the mindful interim between itself and the inescapability of its penetrator. There is a yielding which consorts with rejection: when my brother or any other figure hurls himself at me as though to enforce the nuptials of one punch and another, I can—as my fist unclenches, descends to the ground—disdain that enforcement and reclaim the capability of failing to be requisitioned, an aptitude I retain while the pumping volley does not "stop," since (for my antagonist) I am solely a shred of matter under the gravity of his will. And if the "instinctive" can be contemplated, its liaison with what uplifts it allows for a reasoning out, a winnowing out, a "revelation of some order" beneath its drift (72). Hence, even when overmastered, I can think in concert with all that the body appears to tell me.

Yet, in regard to syntax, to its customary organization in the air or on the page, "mind," "body," "I," and "me" are discriminative terms moored to articles fixed by their severance from one another, whereas my overmastering rejoins the once separable and furthers thought under the aspect of what it is to act. Despoiled of interiority by a subject whose prodding maintains that inside will replicate out if both are converted into a redundancy of flesh, a void of stuff raided from diverse positions by what must go on looming over it, I am, for my violator, the evacuation he assigns to me. But even under his fingers—those of my half-brother, of his behavioral counterpart—I am not the lacuna he makes of me nor identical with my despoliation. For the incantation of my "resenting, disliking it" befogs my capacity for lighting on "the word for so dumb and mixed a feeling" which, because of its dumbness, of its hybridized properties, appears so large, so monumental, that its anteriority subvenes in this very moment when I sit propped on a "slab" (69). I intuit myself, by means of a depredator's hands, of the instincts they smart in me, as a meditative body that retrogresses from effect to cause: since the former outbalances its patent instigation, effect and cause seem preponderated over by prehistories I cannot know, he cannot know, though one description of duty may be our recognizing how the prehistorical neighbors on us, renders us more populous than two individuals latched to a singular event. We can each temper "feeling" with the cognitive distance fundamental to reasoned, reflective thought; and such a feat will carry us, if we let it, to the intuition of origins whose remoteness seems to belie the lone particularities we understood we were. Yet, lowering my eyes, I see a man who pinpoints his concentration on plundering an integrity already vaporized before he touches it. While his hands—inspectorial, motivated by a hunger more unsparing than its name—dig under my clothes, while a finger starts the slow push in, he perceives neither the psychic footage between himself and his exertions nor what could otherwise have been done with it, how, under the gravitation of desire, he need not have become equivalent to that desire's object. Thus, going in, he finds nothing but himself, a thing mechanized by an autocracy he failed to contemplate and to be responsible for.

The "shock" of his entry nevertheless goads me to retrace those other "shocks" startling "being" into play: I have lain in a fetal bed between house and sea, among the intercommunion of sound and sight; have stood in a "gummy" film before a world I did not know how to reach; stirred at the "horror" of a death I could not change; rejected a fist pounding out its disregard for that rejection; and, penetrated, I have sat suffused with instincts not simply mine (66). "Being," however, appears unthinkable without the backdrop of having-been; tracking the "instinctive" and its derivations back through distinguishable time-scales, through variable circumstances, social conditions, I discern countless pairs of bodies compassed by repetitive despoilments. Each pair generalizes impulses animating the assault precedent to it; each re-enacts a primordial moment almost remembered. Going further in my descent, I come to how we begin inside a coherence which each birth dismembers, so that to be born is to look in both directions, behind and ahead of the single parturition detached from a "whole" all the while in contact with it. If this "intuition" is true (72), it "proves" that though we repeat "ancestral" behaviors, we are individuated according to the degree and manner in which we honor, recollect, the cohesion which backs us and from which we originate; that deliberative thought trained on the instinctual is a form of action; that "one's life is not confined" to the "body," to "what one says and does"; that we live "all the time in relation to certain background rods or conceptions"; "that there is a pattern hid behind the cotton wool," underlying what we may neglect to see (73). Hence, how we meditate on "relation" will determine the personhood within our imaginable reach.

Such ideas bring Woolf and her readers to what she "might call a philosophy" (72):

> at any rate it is a constant idea of mine; that behind the cotton wool is hidden a pattern; that we—I mean all human beings—are connected with this; that the whole world is a work of art; that we are parts of the work of art. *Hamlet* or a Beethoven quartet is the truth about this vast mass that we call the world. But there is no Shakespeare, there is no Beethoven; certainly and emphatically there is no God; we are the words; we are the music; we are the thing itself. And I see this when I have a shock. (72)

I want to slacken the pace of the "we" so noteworthy in the above passage as well as to suggest that the thinking "behind" Woolf's pronoun has an "ancestral" history, that the "truth" she cites counts the multiform among its possibilities. If "moments of non-being" outnumber those which countercheck them, "shock['s]" foremost strength belongs to how it heaves us into consciousness out of the fuzz of our own stolidity, out of the "nondescript cotton wool" in which each of us is "embedded" (70). Ejected from—ousted from—the humus of our indifference, we wake to an influx into "being" whose plenitude may be thought out while experienced, remembered after its copiousness appears to dwindle once we revert to the recumbency inherent in our natal soil. Since plenty, recalled, accommodates analysis and what can be born by virtue of it, the spell of "being," however abridged, expands when memory's composing powers remake it, refashion it, set it free in the "work" which materializes our ripeness for fecundation. Thus, the importunity of "being" is generative if we prolong its experience in the mind. But, with her emphasis on the "work of art," does Woolf simply aestheticize its potential maker, notwithstanding the latter's corporate features?

It seems to me that Woolf saves herself from this indictment because of the "horror" she rates deserving of the lengthened concentration expended on it, a "horror" whose liberality—its abundant fact which will not be wished away—mentors her acquaintanceship with how many of our human actualities, of which suicide, the clash "on the lawn," and molestation suffice as models, are structured by us, made by us, hence accessories to those who propagate them. And, giving us "the other face in the glass," Woolf does not retreat from implicating herself in that "horror" (69). Though it may appear, whether "dream" or authentic event, that the "incident of the looking-glass" imitates Jacques Lacan's insights concerning the specular image in his *Les Complexes familiaux dans la formation de l'individu* (1938), Woolf neither idealizes nor squares herself with the projection shuddering "in the glass" (69). Such disavowals measure out a prime lesson: severing itself from the "background" and moving as though "alive," the thing enciphered in the mirror, the "animal" domiciled in the mirror, prefigures Simone de Beauvoir's conceptualizing, in *Le deuxième sexe* (1949), the socially calibrated alterity of the female body and exhibits that any human corpus, like "la beauté universelle" propounded by Weil, must be other than our expectations regarding it (69). I do not dismiss the "relation" of sex to those expectations; I take Woolf's difficulties as paradigmatic of all our own, given that she repudiates glossing the relational as parity by another name, that the patterned subsists on the ground of what fringes it, that mirrored animality mimes in degraded form the otherness of our provenance, that Woolf's "we" expounds our membership in the word. But, if we are "something else," "something" other than our wellhead, the tract stretched between "we" and its source can be expressed reciprocally: our inception must differ from the "human beings" effectuated by it. On account of the prominence granted here to distinction, is it the case that Woolf exalts either of her divisions to a transcendent order? To respond to that question, to illuminate Woolf's use of the first person plural, I spring back on Hillman and his engagement with the mythic.

Hillman disambiguates the mythical and the ways in which that sector pertains to what it is not. When an impasse coerces us into the conviction of there being "no way out," our catapulting "leap of imagination" may aid us in seeing the certitude of deadlock with eyes revitalized by myth's "meaning without explanation," since that phrase solicits our attending to a "meaning" beyond "explanation," greater than the intelligibility which sense-making stipulates. As "norms of the unreasonable," however, myths must be in contraposition to the reasonable, to terrestrial "reason" and its performances, the one high above the other by virtue of its altitude; thus, the two fields remain in isolation, except for the human "imagination['s]" supplicating "leap." While he blocks out our vault into myth, Hillman implies the unidirectional quality of movement itself: that which excels us, ensphered by its own elevation, abstains from descending to the districts below it—the transcendent will not come down. Yet, if transcendence qualifies all that we entitle by myth, Woolf, Weil, and Murdoch pose how the real and what climbs above it, what lifts above it with respect to eminent rank, join in interplay, in mutual intervention; with them, I advocate that such reciprocity, regardless of its demonstrable truth-value, benefits those who observe it. And, unlike Hillman, all three authors speculate on the equivocal nature of the relationship between the mythic and the verifiably tactile. The two will be difficult to scissor up, so interwoven; one advantage of equivocalness rests on its asking those who admit it that they should risk the snags fundamental to reading an ambiguity deserving of decipherment by more than a single light. Risking readers, in acceptance of that ardency, may envisage "relation" as something other than simple opposition or identity, terms that nullify the very concept they purport to define. But Hillman's bounding "leap," sprung into distance, pits myth against its contrary, ensures their antipathy, and forsakes the means by which "imagination" bears on embodied minds in action.

"La source des actions," the "child of the flesh," our imaginative faculty emerges from what Weil, in her "Cahiers d'Amérique," diagnoses as "la souffrance" which inspires "horreur," "le malheur" which we endure against our will, seek to escape, beg to be spared; nevertheless, our attention to it teaches us that to sustain "un choc," this individualized "shock," is to induce an "imagination" disposed to recognize how the asymmetry between the transcendent and the real—which Weil and Woolf do not deny—need not render their interconnectivity impossible (26). Indeed, we participate in that intercommunication, with or without reference to the "shock" acknowledging it and, in company with the things around us, do so according to a "common" rhythm. The raying out of the sun stores itself in the tree, as Weil reminds us, wood being a "conserver de la lumière," a reservoir of light (210). We may unite with her in longing for the chlorophyll through which we might feed on luminosity, "comme les arbres," though our suspension in desire ought to trigger the remembrance that each green leaf, each fruit within the circles of our mouths, enacts our capacity for eating the transmuted light by which we remain alive (245).

Much would follow from these observations, if we were to keep to them. We would support the claim that diffuse "forces" enwreathe, saturate the human subject and the thing inert on the path before her, both maintained by intensities beyond all evidence of their sustaining powers. Like Murdoch when she writes of Platonic discourse in "The Fire and the Sun," we would hold high "our ability to use visual structures to understand non-visual structures," an "ability" central to "explanation in any field" (445), seeing that the "original role" of Plato's Ideas "was not to lead us to some attenuated elsewhere but to show us the real world," the "work" of being here (*Existentialists and Mystics*, 427). As a thing, Woolf's "we" is "connected with" that "work" through the mutuality she upturns over the hierarchy implicit in transcendence. For, together, the "visual" and the supra-visual extrude the "world."

In regard to that extrusion, a great deal will revolve around how we think out the principle of "connected[ness]" so preponderant in "A Sketch of the Past." To determine that we live "all the time in relation" to constitutional "rods," "conceptions," to "a pattern" lurking "behind the cotton wool" of the given is not to decide that the substratum triumphs over what stands upon it; encoding the former and the latter in visual vocabulary, Woolf allows for our inference that perhaps both emerge from interdependent derivations. But, when she asserts that "one" is "not confined to one's body," to "what one says and does," Woolf fails to produce the consequence that the individual's approach to that which fortifies the visible may be described as straightforward, effortless, tranquil. Since "shock" beckons the seeing of "connected[ness]," to "see" well is to abide by the pricking pain that enhances what the eye can take. To register that twinge, that enhancement, necessitates a "body" whose commitment to unstinting vision will affect its conduct inside the "cotton wool" bequeathed to it from birth and within the "pattern . . . behind" that bequest, a correlation accentuated by how Woolf's representative language pleaches together the two nominal phrases as visualizing systems. With linguistic precision, Woolf settles that, for all of us, a wakened access to any spatiality is never direct, never unmitigated, never of limitless duration; and her prepositions throughout the last excerpt, in concert with the nouns they govern, with the verbs whose "relation[al]" qualities they nuance, steer us towards the variety of connection she judges to be at once meritorious and real. For, whether or not we struggle to perceive with adequate limpidity, so much intervenes between ourselves and the nucleus of our attention: the past as it bridges the present; how we orient ourselves in the direction of the moment; the personhoods evolved across both time-divisions—these collect in interposition while we entrust ourselves to the perceptual act. If a "pattern" conceals itself "behind" the "cotton wool" of daily "non-being," to arrive at one, we must pass through the other, and we will carry with us the content of that passing as we embark on our journey, though to stay in the state of arrival demands a brunt of time to which our attentive skills can only be unequal (70). Yet in what ways does Woolf's vaunted "we" express the "connected[ness]" she surrenders to us?

Out of laboring to modify an abounding first person plural, Woolf applies divided significations to the verb "to be" whose foremost, shaded sense—predicative, hinged on the prepositional phrase—she preserves until her penultimate clausal chain, when manifesting a condition metamorphoses into "being," into the fullness of coinciding-in-identity-with. After fixing on our angularity, "connected with," "parts of," something more extensive than ourselves, we thus achieve agreement with the implemental character which defines us. But, because we begin in indirection, at a tangent to an entity more voluminous than ourselves, our names will not unfold us: there can be "no Shakespeare," "no Beethoven," "no God," "no" crowning maker, since the "whole world" overshadows the conceit of discreteness summoned by a lexical fiction to which the thing so named cannot quite conform. Our coincidence must be with the mission of "the words," of "the music," "the thing itself" being an instrumentality developed at divergent speeds through numberless millennia, a linchpin by whose service the wheel of the "world" goes on spinning. Of the "thing[s]" Woolf gives us here, one is beyond reference to its use—the "whole" of "a work of art" in absolute congruence with itself. Yet the vision of such congruence, issuing from "shock['s]" concentrated "force," will, by definition, fade. Its perceiver returns to the "cotton" blur, invoked by a name, unsure of her utility in a "world" she cannot see, its curves revolving with and without her, all composing the background into which sudden sightedness breaks. However dim or broken, remembered "shock" nicks hollows in the uniformity of that blur, revives the experience of a "whole" superinduced by the near-artisanal tools that we are.

But what drives the telling of "the truth about this vast mass that we call the world"? How can we identify the teller? Once detailing the "intuition" of her "philosophy," Woolf herself alleges how "it is so instinctive that it seems given" to her, "not made" by her, and we can mine the Platonic dialogue for a paradigm of such "given[ness]" (72). As early as the *Ion*, for example, Plato supplies us with a Socrates who quarries from his interlocutor whether the "art of poetry" (532c), the "art" of making, is rightfully a "skill" or the motion of "a divine power" (532d, 533d). Like all "rhapsodes" (530b), like all Homerian declaimers, Ion may be grouped with the "interpreters of interpreters" (535a), yet in what does poetic and declamatory "expertise" consist (531a)? If we intend to say, along with Plato's Socrates, that "a poet . . . cannot compose before he gets inspiration and loses control of his senses," so that "his reason has deserted him" (534b); that "it is the god himself who speaks," addressing us "through" the mediate category of poets (534d), themselves "nothing but the gods' interpreters, each possessed by his own possessing god" (534e), the skein of our logic will depend on our understanding of what interpretation imposes upon its practitioners, among whom Ion must be counted as he listens to the exigencies in Homer's words while declaiming them.

In a note to his translation (1987), Trevor John Saunders aids us in considering the reeling incumbent on the divine "mouthpiece": "only in Plato is the poet as passive" as such a representation avows; "on the ordinary Greek view," neither "the god" nor the poet is a "ventriloquist"—the former "consigns" his "message" or "information" to the poet "for casting" by him "into words, rhythms" (56). Regardless of how the poet achieves that "casting," regardless of his "knowing or being able to describe how" he does it, "it is he himself who is the composer of his poetry, not the god" (56). I want to twist all this together with the tonnage in Woolf's employment of "given," since the latter and what is done with it, made out of it, need not be accounted exclusionary acts. While "possessed by" the "god," by the "whole" of the Woolfian "world," the "possessed" and her possessor stand yoked to each other by the explaining, "in common," which interpretation enjoins on them. And, minding the "given" "message," Woolf must dower it with the form through which the communicated becomes the communicable, an undertaking not unsuited to "reason." But in what ways might our conception of knowledge contribute to that dowering?

In the *Meno*, as he attempts to ascertain if "virtue" is "something that can be taught" (70), Socrates argues that he cannot "know a property of something" when he does not "even know what" that something "is" (71b). Thus, the difficulty of knowledge inaugurates the dialogue's toils: "how on earth" are we "going to set up something" we do not know "as the object" of our "search?" (80d). Plato's actors and their readers seem enclosed in a question whose globularity disowns any conceptual action outside it; and, precisely due to that imprisonment, Socrates deems the question's undeclared "argument" a poor one (81). Explaining "how it fails," he moves to an outside epitomized by "the truths of religion" (81) of which many "divinely inspired" poets speak (81b). Those "truths" begin by presuming that the human "soul" is "immortal," locked in a cyclical pattern of apparent terminations and begettings, coming "to an end" merely to be "born again," without "extermination" (81b). "Born many times," never ending, "the soul" has "seen all things both here and in the other world, has learned everything that is" (81c); hence, "when a man" recalls "a single piece of knowledge"—or when he learns it, bemused by how "ordinary language" mistakes recollection for learning—"there is no reason why he should not" discover "all the rest, if he keeps a stout heart and does not grow weary of the search," for "seeking and learning are in fact nothing but recollection" (81d). Yet, since religiosity postulates a "whole" in which each "part" inheres out of reverent obligation, must we find that the Platonic Socrates has substituted one circularity for another (79c)?

I include Woolf within the umbra cast by this question, as she and Plato appear to describe replacements at once familial and relentless: that of knowledge with "recollection," of experience with encountering "instincts already acquired by" repetitive "ancestresses" doomed to imparting identical lessons. We will be empowered to espy repetition in both cases only if we expunge all notion of the procedural necessary to "recollection" and to wrestling with the always "instinctive." For surely these actions, being actions, occur in time and under conditions that diverge from their sequentially foregoing and primordial origins; surely, we, Woolf, and Plato resemble the "boy" (82b) "seeking" geometrical "truths" "in company with" this particular Socrates whom he cannot have known before the moment of interrogative "teaching" (84d). How we bring ourselves to that time, to those conditions, to that "company," shapes what we make of recollected knowledge and articulates our experiential liberty, an instance of which is "A Sketch of the Past" itself, written on the cusp of world battle, among patterned "shocks" which Plato assists us in thinking out.

So far, the Platonic precedents for Woolf's "philosophy" advise us that poet and potential knower proceed in conjunction with a "power," with a "soul," consecrated to disabusing us of the myth that any self writes, knows, or stands marooned in isolation. To appeal to "virtue," to stand upright in its provident goodness, is thus to dedicate ourselves to remembering the associates among whom we live, presences which religious "truths" and Woolf's populous "we" both presuppose, even when we cannot verify their palpability. But, in the *Philebus*, we learn that "virtue" begins as a problem, apart from its receptivity to being "taught." Plato's Protarchus, "poised to take over" a "thesis" from "Philebus" that "the good is enjoyment, pleasure, delight and whatever is compatible with them" (11-b), must contend with a Socrates who challenges that these "are not the good, but that reason, intellect, memory—not to mention their cognates, correct belief and true calculation—are far better than pleasure for all creatures capable of attaining them" (11b-c). The character of the highest excellence, unsettled at the dialogue's inception, is rendered more indeterminate by "the diversity within" the "good[s]" that wrangle for right definition (14b), by the wobble between "unity and plurality" in "every single utterance" which "speech" appears to steady when it "identifies" the two "in the process" of our treating with words (15d). It may be a part of Plato's project to show us how his foremost player disturbs the equipoise of Protarchus and his readers by divulging the "feature of human speech" which equates an identity-constructing "is" with the predication coincident with "far better than" (15d); it may be that our stir towards the locality of "the good," whatever its determination, entangles us in the condensed difficulty which poise demands of those who profess to demonstrate its achievement. Yet, if qualities enlist their qualifiers, it is in the discussion of the "nature of memory," of "physical feeling" (33c-d), that we find Woolf's prototype for the "shock" which heralds any accession to "being" (33d).

And that discussion, as in the *Meno*, fails to question the existence of the "soul" already hypothecated—pledged to, adopted as self-evident—before the interplay by which dialectic is defined (34a). But the dereliction of inquiry here belongs to how Plato's interlocutors foresee the body itself: if "the life of pleasure . . . is the good, it must lack nothing at all" (20e), so that if we "had pleasure," we would "have all" we "needed," a totality nevertheless obstructing our admission to the "reason, intellect, memory" without which we could not "recognize" our "feeling" of possessing the unimpeachable (21b), an "all" condemning us "not" to "the life of a human being, but of a jellyfish or some sea creature," merely "a body endowed with life, a companion of oysters" shut up in a commotion of the sensorial, pseudonymous because barred from the cognition that harbingers what "soul" dispenses to its enfleshed instantiation (21c-d). These ideas mean that a body is falsely named when seen denuded of the psyche whose radiation authorizes its alliance with the "human." So bared, the body can never be enough; it becomes a "lack," a negation, incapable of judging the "management" of the "life" ceded to it (64b). Yet, if Socratic teaching shows Protarchus the possibility of distinguishing equivalence and predication, discloses that "two terms" anticipate "two things . . . not one," that "the good is not the same as the pleasant," this teaching must also combat the "human" desire to confound them (60b).

Against confounding, the Platonic Socrates assembles "an immaterial system for the management of animate matter" since, with "soul" as the arbiter of body, the latter's conduct can be assessed, retrained by the adjudicator of incarnate comportment (64b), a re-education revealing the plasticity of Murdoch's formulation concerning "visual" and "non-visual" relations because its reversal establishes that the unseen both motorizes the body's visibility and administers its gestural repertory. Such "two-ness" confers on Protarchus, on his readers, a vocabulary for critiquing the specious sorcery of "human" pining—the enchantment that the world must requite us with what we ask of it, the two nouns, self and world, forever in antiphony—and leads to a "shock" intimate with the "nature of sensation," together with what can be realized from it (33c).

Hypothesizing "about any physical feeling," speculating that "some are extinguished in the body before they penetrate to the soul," while "others penetrate both and create a sort of shock . . . peculiar to each part" yet "common to both," Socrates extends his bifurcating vision (33d): "body" differs from "soul" as the perturbation of one must deviate from that of the other, the "soul['s]" altitude over "body" in terms of value preparing the differential nature of the "shock" which psyche and soma "share," traceable to the selfsame source (34a). We may "call" this being "moved together," this "single experience" which pierces doubly, "sensation," with "memory" the name for its "preservation" (34a), but the concept of rank returns when Plato gives us a Socrates who considers "recollection" as "what the soul does internally, without the body, when it resuscitates, as thoroughly as possible, the experiences it once shared with the body," which drops away, already vaporous, always lost, under the principle that it should be animated by an energy other than itself (34b). To lose the body is to empty the corporeal of all desire, to deny "that desire is physical" (35c). Though the aptitude for "memory" depends on the simultaneous piercing of skin and "soul," provides "the impulse" towards "objects of desire," the "argument" here "is declaring that all drive, desire," and "authority, in every living creature, belong to the soul"—a proprietary license whose totalizing vigor ought to be matched by our avidity for disputing it (35d).

Understood as "lack" (35b), "desire" is founded on the longing for "replenishment" which only the faculty of "memory" can "comprehend" (35c). But if "every living creature" strives "for the opposite to his present state"; if a "tendency towards the opposite . . . demonstrates that there is memory of the various opposites" to "various current states," jogs the "recollection" of an internal "soul," such internality is conditioned by the severance of outside from in, of flesh from psyche, and should cue our wonder at its nullifying industry (35c). So negated with respect to praise, to any possible commendation, the "body" must be dangerous, its "management" a hazard. Before the spectre of that danger, uncoupled from the concept of worth due to the "soul['s]" radiating nimbus, all bodies become penurious things, strangely akin to those chunks of matter, inanimate, dead to valuation, which cannot contest an "authority" disposed by necessity to manipulate them. Yet this abounding penury needs to be read in more than one way; we must look at whom the "denial" of desiring corporeality seeks to aim (35c).

When Protarchus and Philebus declare that "pleasure" is equal to "the good," they attribute "goodness" to all "pleasures," classifying "pleasure" as the "most similar thing of all to pleasure, as being itself in relation to itself" (12e). Assimilating "relation" to identity, plurality to oneness, they reveal the "body" as a magnified "thing," an "itself," an organ for the reception of "pleasures" pleonastic because one can always be substituted for any other. The "thesis" of equivalence, since it entails the interchangeability of all desires conducing to "the good," thus holds to a disinterest in, an incapacity for, judgement, discrimination, complexity, terms which pinpoint that one idea cannot be made to fit the world. Such are the characters of his colleagues that Socrates must dissolve the thickening redundancies they keep to, such the exertions that Plato tests our capability of seeing. Even so, if we assent to Wittgenstein's disclosure, in *The Blue Book* (1933–

1934), that "philosophy, as we use the word, is a fight against the fascination which forms of expression exert upon us," we should hesitate in order to ask: has Socrates subdued one "fascination" by deputizing another in its place; does his maker propose that we concur with this supplanting of the "body" by what the "body" is not (27)?

But to answer the second question in the affirmative is to believe that the maker must be the compeer of what he makes, to barter one name for another, a belief which nearly every Platonic dialogue controverts. Its method of argumentation neither apodeictic nor self-explanatory, the dialogue—because it seldom shows us outright the intent goading on its progress—incites in readers the very inferentiality by which it has come to be there, on the page. And, since it represents the conditions from which the groundwork of any human conversation can be derived, that page originates from a hand whose activities must be accounted for, not from the *ex nihilo* subsequent to the conflation of "two things" into "one." Hence, obliged to inspect those conditions, to bring them in under the circumspection of our eyes, we may begin to approach their founder, though his creations impart to us that he is elsewhere.

We venture to see in the depth afforded by the twofold distances between eye and page, between eye and the designer of that page, a Socrates who diminishes the density of the "body" so as to carry his colleagues to the "threshold" of "the good" from which they can survey "desire," once blind because it could have no truck with analysis, misconstruing satiety as the sole criterion of evaluation (64c). Facing his associates' closed-circuit of "body," "desire," "good," Socrates must admit that circuit as his conversational starting-place and undo it, if he is to advocate for an outside in which this wiring-together submits to critical estimation. He disperses the heft of the "body," fictionalizing it, etherealizing it, neutralizing its efficacy, the strain to dematerialize the "body" decreeing the devastations waiting to be wrought by those who, imagining "the good" as "the most perfect thing of all," might "track it down and aim for it, with no concern for anything" not "ultimately accompanied by goodness" (20d). So thinned of purport, the "body" is stripped of its capacity to engender the inventory of actions by which it would consume the world, dissolving "goodness" in "itself."

Of course, such dispersal saves both that world's constituents and our Socratic comrades, their apparent weightlessness readying them "to love the truth and to go to any lengths for its sake" (58d). Unmade with respect to what they thought they knew, they find all the substantiality of the "body"—the "belief" in its power to grasp, to control, to guide (38e)—transferred to the "soul," which "resembles a book"; since, "when memory coincides with perception," psychic "faculties" seem "to write words ... in the soul," their "truth" resulting from that coincidence (38e-39a). Yet when "memory" and "perception," no longer coinciding, are "mistaken in their object" (37e), "an artist" in "the soul's work-force" forms "internal images" of a concordance whose falseness can be settled by the "soul['s]" facility for adjudication (39b). "True" or "false" in its "contact" with the world (39a-b), the "soul" becomes a "picture" of the following paradox (40a): an immateriality capable of "making ... correct assessment" (41d) according to "law and order" always administered by a "truth" (26b), by a "cause," completely "different" from what depends on it "for generation" (27a). Such diction describes a rightness forever beyond what we proclaim of it, its religiosity a universalizing force distinguishing between "itself" and the inclination of all bodies regarding it, concepts which Protarchus and Philebus could not have reached, had they tarried at believing in the unthinking "body."

But I remember, in the *Parmenides*, for instance, that Plato gives us a Socrates who cannot remove himself from the quandary intrinsic to "abstract ideas" and "the things which partake of them"

(130b). Questioned "if there is an idea" of "hair, mud, dirt"—or "anything else particularly vile and worthless"—distinct "from the things with which we have to do, or not," (130c-d), Socrates can only intone a "no"; they "are such as they appear to us," for "it would be quite absurd to believe that there is an idea of them; and yet I am sometimes disturbed by the thought that perhaps what is true of one thing is true of all" (130d). Even for the Socrates who teaches others that entities differ from the "forms of expression" we level at them, the problem, the intervallic space, stretched between "desire" and its "object" remains. And that remaining parades how the problem is ours. We are born to it, inheritors of the distances in which all things coexist and whose extent, despite our being "disturbed" by it, promises our propensity to think, to see, to move. They become, those disturbances, the distance we live by.

Before enlarging on how Woolf adapts the antecedent of Plato's "shock," I persist in searching for what these textual forerunners bequeathed to the woman who read them, for what they remit to those who follow her. With reference to Plato's Socrates and his transcendent noun phrase, whether in the *Philebus* or the *Republic*, where "justice" shadows forth "the good," such coming forth shows Socrates asserting, for his interlocutors, that the latter unceasingly embraces the former (331c, 505a): all we may be said to have here below are reflections of "the good," refractions of its breadth and depth, yet that statement must be qualified by Plato's Socratic visions regarding our flawed humanity, from which Socrates himself cannot be excepted. If we attend to that qualification, we come to how inductive processes concerning the concept of "the good" occur always "in relation to" those towards whom such processes are steered, so that we never achieve a philosophic discourse outside the grounding of an audience and its frailties, its conditions, never gain the footing by which we could hope to scan a hoard of precepts underiveable, unadulterated, absolute. If this is true, we populate an aporia which nevertheless may be useful for us, its readers—because we cannot know, finally, what the Platonic Socrates thinks concerning "the good," for that thinking, as evidenced by the page, stands always "in relation" with other speakers; "the good," notwithstanding its admissible status as myth, narrative, image, or truth, escapes its incarnations. And there will be, everlastingly, a beyond to the circumstances in which we feel ourselves engrossed, even if we cannot stop there, embosomed in its clasp.

Furthermore, the Socrates which Plato ventilates for us respects how the transcendent concept as such must be elsewhere, irrecusably outside our pronouncements on the subject of it, remote from the mastership of human appetites, regardless of its being myth or narrative or undertaken to accommodate to what a specific audience can just tolerate hearing—or of its potential truth-value. But, while we never inhabit "the good" itself in Platonic thinking, we can sample proximity to its avatars—among which we should tally "correct assessment"—though that proximal "relation" will be onerous enough for us to heed, considering our "desire" to think equationally by means of operations which tussle for a simplistic comprehension of unity. Here, I look back to the *Parmenides*, for if "it would be . . . absurd" to think that the things we fail to devote ourselves to participate in notions of value, the absurdity is solely ours: we will have raised so high, under the seeming guidance of Plato's characters, "abstract ideas" assorting their terrestrial "images"; we will have submerged "hair, mud, dirt" in the element appropriate to them, in the ground that must be "dirt" and that prevails merely to suffer our sovereignty over it. Thus, conceptual union and its absence are our bestowments. They repeat us.

Yet, even according to the texts' apparent terms, we cannot say with certainty that Plato's Socrates occupies or is habituated to "the good," as that abstract noun continues comprehensively beyond the claiming of any selfhood. Indeed, that is its virtue and ours. Since we are unable to usurp it, to subjugate it, "the good" can only be inhospitable to those human activities which scheme to eat their "object." In consequence, our Platonic materials advise us to reflect on, to think critically about, our desires, to position ourselves at a tangent to what they command of us, so that we might touch but not intersect with them. We need both to experience and to analyze our desiring in order to salvage ourselves from engulfment and to preserve the world from the annihilation that our hunger's appeasement would produce. For, being "in relation to" them, that hunger is not the world or "the good."

The incessant freedom from arrest, whether or not we are intended to assent to "the good" as myth, accommodation, or verity, divulges the vigilant sophistication of Plato as a writing-mind and that mind's quadruple covenant with its readers. Calling forth the prudent alertness essential to our study of a wisdom unrevealed by the surfaces of the said; coaxing our awareness that interpretive acts never take place in transparency; refocusing the lights by which we read, so that the "how" of comprehension can be neither ready-made nor unconditioned; fashioning form and content as reciprocal envoys—Plato, uncaptured, unimprisoned, unrepresented by the verbal shapes he gives us, cautions against our bewitchment by, our "fascination" with, messages foretokening our partnership in their reception and transference, since those messages will not decipher themselves. To entreat our participation in composing the contours of any message is to brake the latter's implementation in the world, to portion out a lull soliciting our responsibility in the "fight" not to beguile others with an "expression" by which no person should be arrested. And, if Plato himself can bolt from the texts he circulates among us, that expertise in breaking free from detention calls on us to answer it, to remember that we must bridle up at seeing any text as a stopgap for charged contemplation or as a stopover in which, idling, we might doze.

Their forger's refusal to be confined, rejoined by our dexterity in remarking how faraway he is from us, motions towards our discovery that Platonic texts develop from—and prompt our acceptance of—those remotenesses, those gulfs, those intervals, through which we perceive the perceptible and are perceived ourselves. Rather than condemning them to mutual banishment, the standing apart of writer and reader permits their connection, so long as we acknowledge distances as the means by which we commit our eyes to sight. The range of their intermediary spaces may fluctuate: our first three texts mime, by way of supposed direction and in dialogic form, speeches whose fictiveness lies in their being authorless, while our final two—recounting in the present a past whose totality will not be resuscitated—present us with speakers interposed between ourselves and the urgencies they set about reviving. Nevertheless, even in fluctuation, distanced sight endures, a lens for the recognition that inclining-near is not a "given," but a movement, earned.

This movement implied by any resistance to detainment, to imprisonment, appeals to our readerly imperative: for example, we must spurn equating ourselves as readers outside the *Republic* with the many-partnered Socrates inside it. Though we resemble that preeminent voice and its fellows to the extent that our desiring transactions, by necessity, outreach our needs and their "object," "mistaken" for a terminal satisfaction somehow never to be forfeited, once we become their equivalents, we extinguish the text, along with our aptitude for interpreting it. Yet we can countervail such imposture by creating, by clearing, by opening up, a critical discontinuity between ourselves and what we read in order to decide how, as Socrates and his comrades watch a *polis* "coming into existence" in speech (369a), the one noble lie, the "magnificent myth that would . . . carry conviction" to the city

(414c), is a residuum of conceptualizing activities closely aligned with the hazards basic to unconscious metaphoric usage. I mean: if it is the commerce of metaphors to over-naturalize their own behaviors, to betray equivalence as already accomplished, rather than as our manufacture, such commerce serves the human need to aver the wholeness of the world—without recognizing that proposed wholeness may demonstrate the fiat of our "desire" for it, which, in the doing, erases how (so often) we proceed uncritically before integrities which we ourselves fashion.

The nobility here, the magnificence, evolves from the power of the "myth" to honor the mortal fragilities it speaks to, so that our examination of the mythic—our regarding the circumstances that give birth to it, together with how its claim to "increase . . . loyalty" incites consent (415d)—makes it conceivable for those of us outside the text to see the integral as a speculation masking itself as fact, a camouflaging we might guard against if we were to reflect on our own need to confuse a making-method with the world. That world, or another noun in its place, capable of transcending the figurations we sling at it, remains richly other than what we do within its precincts: it will not be, in any final sense, confounded. "Amorous," erotic, we may construe ourselves as the kin of Glaucon (474d); in our eroticism, inflamed, we may "love" the "part" to the "exclusion of" the "whole," as though "love" were a fire whose burning "object" could only be itself, intensified (474c). Whether or not we distinguish between ourselves and his Socratic audience, the inventor of the *Republic* reminds us, by his very absence, that we do not live bound inside the pages of a book, that not living there permits us to "picture," to visualize, to entertain, the "story" both spun on and fixed to the fibers of the page (415a). Not living there fosters our awareness that the *eros* piloting our fictions, our telling of tales, cannot be the ground—but is made from our comportment "in relation to" it.

Preserving these distinctions, we find that the "story" fails due to the instabilities of its narration. Such instabilities, because his characters seem unable to identify them, are among Plato's gifts to us: loitering over them, naming them, we accept their fathering in another place and confess our obligation to judge the worthiness of our own paternity. And what does Socrates, the maker of "stories," contrive in the presence of a Glaucon whose amorousness longs to light upon itself in the things it loves (377b)? He images a creation-"myth" which naturalizes "loyalty" to the dialogic city even as its manner of recounting dishonors the interdictions at play in the "upbringing and education," expounded earlier, of those "Rulers and Soldiers" bred to administer governance (414d). Yet their schooling, the Socratic "myth" insists, "happened to them only in a dream" (414d): accordingly, if "we begin by telling children stories" because childhood "is the time when they are easily moulded," when "any impression we choose to make leaves a permanent mark"; if we "must start to educate" the psyche "before training the body"(377a–b)—all the strictures of that tutelage subsist in the "relation" of a simile, bending towards the "reality" glinting below (379b). Thus, in order to arrive at foundational turf, the following restrictions, once approved, must be penetrated: that prospective "Guardians," for "fear of catching the infection in real life," must refrain from "acting" a "disgraceful part on the stage" in view of how mimesis, when "prolonged" into adulthood, establishes "habits" which "become second nature"(395c); that, so as to inoculate all against the virus of imitation, "if the poet never concealed his own personality," his "poetic" narrative, "devoid of representation," would liberate any audience from mimetic blight (393c-d); that to misrepresent "the nature of gods and heroes" is to commit "the worst fault possible" (377d-e); because anything "not harmful" cannot "do harm," the "god" really "is good" and "must be so described," regardless of generic concerns (379b). Hence, "without deceit or falsehood in action or word," God "does not change himself, nor deceive others, awake or dreaming, with visions or words or special signs" (382e).

To sum up the aforesaid "dream," soon to be absorbed into the familial essence of citizenship: we begin in plasticity, are perfectly educable and can be perfected spiritually from without, as if bodily behaviors simply reproduced those teachings which the "soul" had suckled from; in contrast to human flux, the "god" must be "good"; he does not lie, does not change, so that divinity, idealized, is in analogy with the Ideas against whose permanence all phenomena occur. Natal oscillations may unite humankind here, though the subsequent "myth" attempts to cancel them out. For, regarded "as brothers," the city's residents are indistinguishable from the "earth" which mothers them (414e).

Or so the Socratic progenitor of "myth" would persuade "our whole community" to "believe" (414c, 415c). Neither poets nor "engaged on writing stories," Plato's characters see themselves as "founders of a state" (378e–379a) whose gradual "word-picture" (472e), however phantasmagoric, might help them to "remember" the necessity of pursuing "justice with wisdom" in an already founded world (621c). As authors of an "ideal" civic structure (472e), they should "know the type of story the poets must produce" and, rejecting "any that do not conform" to that model, "need not write" tales "themselves" (379a). But, fascinated by the gleam of igniting, among its citizens, fealty to "the state and to each other," Socrates cannot quit the seduction of conjuring "stories"—he will not have the impulse to bewitch idealized out of him, even if a prior "education" legislated, in a "dream," that the imitator must be surpassed by his imitations, despite his having guarded against that profligacy (415e).

But we who read him, who keep watch over the invisible hand behind his words, ought to note how the inaugural "myth" is as doused in figuration as the pedagogy which precedes it, observe how both conflate custom and nature, *nomos* and *physis*, in order to divine the stability designed to render them connectible. Though "education" and "myth" seem in opposition, together they struggle to stay human lability by means of ordaining its "representation[s]," the former taking mimetic virulence as an almost organic "given," the latter enrolling a communal brotherhood in which the "god" has "added" metal to the "composition" of every member ("gold" to the "Rulers," "silver" to the "Auxiliaries," "iron and bronze" to the "farmers and other workers"), so that the metallurgical figure will "assign" each his "proper value" in the place "where" he "belongs"—a corporeity prophesying ruin when the "State" has "Guardians" outside the rule of "gold" (415a–c).

Underlying both tales is, of course, the fear of human vulnerability to change and evanescence: I am so easily the victim of my figures, so easily jeopardize the *polis* that professes to order me. While the conflation of *nomos* and *physis* unavoidably domesticates religion, understands religion as subsumed under culture's shadow, if we deem such fabricated perspicuity a regulative fiction, we might vary the "pattern" we make of it, since, like the real "in relation to it," our fiction is never unalloyed, static, final (592b). The failure of any metaphor to stabilize its objects is thus akin to inexhaustibility, a paragon of success due to that failure's steadfastness, advancing what cannot be exhausted as a value in which we inhere—because it supports us.

Everything I have expressed above presumes a distinction between Plato-the-maker and the image of Socrates in our texts. The texts themselves, born of a wakefulness to the fact of human fallibility and desire, stage our appetitive maneuverings as the breeding ground for the metaphors by which we construe what it means to live. Yet, if the customary linguistic deportment of metaphor matches two entities via the figurative "representation" of equivalence, it need not follow that we should discern the figure itself as a mere substitution for what it appears, with such facility, to coagulate. Instead, we can grasp that the figure, when understood analytically by its maker and by those to whom it is addressed, prizes the corporeality which is, above all, its index; moreover, as the figure represents how the twinned materialities of perceiver and perceived adhere to each other, it endures being always double in at least this sense: it describes a making-method in contact with something outside it, and its description carries the weight of that transport. For these reasons, metaphors do not replace the real with a fiction; they attest to the real being there, to the complex nature of the real itself. Regarding possible Socratic "fascination"—all bewitchments are not equal; some allow us to see more rather than less, such as those metaphoric couplings through which we who read Socrates can realize that sightedness is never incontestable, that it must be borne witness to by our deliberations over it.

The attestations I trace out here seem potentially ethical acts to me, a seeing-through our skills at beguilement. And the obligation—incessant, magisterial—for each of us to grant, and to give testimony to, those interdependencies whereby the real is composed directs me to Maurice Merleau-Ponty's ideas in his posthumously published *Le visible et l'invisible* (1964). There, we find illuminated an intercorporeity (185) in which "le petit monde privé" of each thing is "non pas juxtaposé à celui de tous les autres" but surrounded by it, levied off from it, and all together are "un Sentant en général devant un Sensible en général" (187), an intercorporeal being, the surface of a depth, which, "inépuisable," inexhaustible, we can properly term the visible—of which "nous ne sommes pas" the titulars (188). If we cannot lay claim to the titular ownership of this intercorporeality because we belong to it, because we survive and perish by virtue of it, each thing is bound up, opens on, is endlessly interrelated with, other things, so that the world becomes a web of the relational; so that no thing abides in isolation from other things; so that isolation, like unhampered congress, numbers among our fictions, reprehensible, unavailing, if not wakened to.

While systems thinking champions such ideas, as treated by Ludwig von Bertalanffy in *General Systems Theory* (1968), by Bela H. Banathy in *Designing Social Systems in a Changing World* (1991), and in *The Guided Evolution of Society* (2000), and while much of quantum theory reinforces them, I do not ask the sciences to stand surety for the power or for the truth-functions of those ideas. Rather, I propose that, from them, we might envision an ethics of the intercorporeal, which would argue for the virtues in comprehending that we do not stand alone, fall alone, live, die alone: we *are* always with respect to the intertwinements of which phenomena are made. To believe otherwise is to beguile others in a darkness of our own fabrication, in an obscurity without use, to counter that we must by necessity be "mistaken" in our "object[s]," even though they are not ours, since we will have breathed among them.

Having scanned some of Woolf's Platonic ancestry, we are now ready to contemplate how the woman who studied Greek with Dr. George Warr, Clara Pater, and Janet Case—as Hermione Lee reminds us in the biography (1997)—modulates a "shock" whose textual inception seems to underscore the division between "being" and "non-being" (141). I begin my contemplation, however, by approaching the organism which Plato and Woolf regard according to dissimilar assumptions, to variant ends; I start with the body that "walks, eats, sees things, deals with what has to be done," with what cannot be dodged, with the faculty of judgment so significant to "A Sketch of the Past" and, for instance, to the *Philebus* (70). With respect to both minds, telling "the truth about this vast mass that we call the world" implies an account of the soma whose dispositions affect the revolving of that "world." But, below any recital of physicality, underneath our two writers' discrepant viewpoints concerning its valuation, we encounter this: the body and its sensorium *stop*; our experience of the corporeal is limited by its termination, a limiting whose attributes we can neither review nor report on, as the ordeal of that curb undoes us. Even our capability of asserting that "the ordeal undoes us" exemplifies the manner in which our very language supposes that self and body are separable, that the former must survive, or disengage from, the concretion which hauls it along the curvature of the "world," so far as syntactic logic admits the announcement that I will outlast my own undoing. The soma's disgrace thus rests on its being doomed to desert us, speakers who negotiate grammars trumpeting a continuance they cannot, in fact, deliver.

Yet the foundering of such delivery, while it summarizes the body's danger, its exposure to a decline which we may not know how to countenance, abets our endeavors to compensate for it. Perhaps from desertion, from declination, issue those displacements which, in their prevalence, Plato desires we should own to: disbanded from the body, mind, self, and "soul" become synonymous and eternal, their everlastingness a reparation for fleshly defeat. Nevertheless, the eternity promulgated here, once elevated as a measure of excellence, is as though upraised over the things of the "world," over "hair, mud, dirt" and their non-human analogues, all deemed equal to how "they appear to us," to the inertness we read in them—we who are not their kinsmen, according to this stance, and whose concept of perpetuity originates in the need to disconnect from a soma which unendingly decays.

Woolf may inherit these ideas; as one of his many heirs, she may accept that Platonic indirection starts with the accidental from which ascends, over the range of the dialogues, the purposing, the planning, the schematizing, which Socrates and his companions uplift by way of exhibiting how flux can be transformed into the invariant. But the method itself disappoints, uproots, any reader's longing to halt at her "fascination" with the invariable: in view of how the circumstantial initiates the dialogues' sequenced thinking, given a different set of circumstances, another assortment of persons and their inclinations, everything would be otherwise. Hence, though our five Platonic texts appear to affiliate externality with "non-being," to federate the internal, the incorporeal, with a "being" always beyond decrepitude, their structures surrender us to the extrinsic as our foundation and as our founding trouble. Woolf extends that trouble—that ambiguity lengthened between the touched and the touching—to what Merleau-Ponty espouses as "les choses," the things we contact and are contacted by (247). Through such extension, Woolf prepares us for a transcendence that integrates human physicality and the things among which it lives, notwithstanding her claims to the contrary.

When she studies her "habit," at "six or seven," of "looking at" her "face in the glass," reveals that "the looking-glass shame has lasted all" her "life," that its duration uncovers how her "natural love for beauty was checked by some ancestral dread," Woolf concedes that such "shame" did not interfere with her "feeling ecstasies and raptures," provided that both "were disconnected" from her "own body" (67–68). Yet, rather than registering a discrete fact, being "ashamed or afraid of" the body is to despair at learning that the flesh cannot be seen by itself, solitary, anomalous, whole, just as yearning to unhitch our regarding the body from the means by which we scrutinize it, or to sever "feeling" from carnality, is to confirm insufficiency as our heritage (68). Unlike Woolf herself, I fit our "ancestral" lack of insularity to the image she sketches a page later: if she was "looking in the glass one day when something in the background moved," that movement, that aliveness, pertains to spatiality, to bodies, and to the mirror which donates them a piecemeal "representation" (69). Certainly, "the glass" cannot fasten to itself the things hedged in by the rigidity of its frame, for the traffic of the body, of our desiring "beauty," of space, of things themselves, overtops all representational circumscriptions.

I coordinate this legacy of spilling-over with Merleau-Ponty's admission that "on n'est jamais à la chose même": because one is never at the thing itself, the experience of disconnection from the body bespeaks the entitlement of having once been anchored there, insulated from the overspill bequeathed to flesh and to things, though both can neither be perceived nor arrived at as if they were lone, one, entire (245).

Even the mirror thwarts the "myth" of insulation when we move away from it, a thwarting which lies like a ground underneath the Woolfian "ecstasies and raptures" we have examined. Since her narrations of ecstatic and rapturous incidents end with "feeling" how "it is almost impossible" that the self "should be here," with an inability to "describe" being seized by a time and place which drum up a vibrative "hum" along the frets of the senses, Woolf's first person usage airs that any "I" is never at the thing itself, never knows parity with the irresolvable by which selfhood may be characterized or with the certitude of being altogether taken. And what holds true for persons presides, in this instance, over things themselves, as the two divisions inhabit a mutual distancing: "I" am that which encroaches on things, they are those entities that seem to encroach on me, and both warrant the spaces between them to preserve the world they share.

But, while she succeeds to Plato's inaugural "shock," to a causality effacing bodily significance in order to elevate a "soul" fated to judge its relations with "animate matter" beyond the limit of a single life; while Platonic fiction struggles to save the "matter" of the world from the wreckage produced by our indiscriminate coveting, do Woolf's "sudden shocks" ask us to partition off the "real thing" and "appearances," to divide value from the body (72)? The differential immensities of "being" and its apparent opposite need not destine both to compartmentation; rather, their differences secure the possibility of reciprocal encroachment. To express this idea in other terms: when adducing disconnection from the body as the criterion for "ecstasy" and "rapture," Woolf does not foreordain the nugatory status of the flesh; she cites fleshliness as a perplexity worth the neural expense of aspiring to survey it, to "explain it," an aspiration which accepts that neurological enterprises assume the material in which they are enmeshed (72). Though both narratives of the body (as pulled away from itself, as taken by an outside it cannot "describe") suppose a physicality exalted or transfixed, the following assurance predetermines their reception: even as our alignment with the corporal, with "appearances," with a "thing" identifiable as "real," like any acquaintanceship with connectivity, can never be prearranged, the indirectness of our pathways to alliance invokes our aptitude for edging towards its accomplishment, despite the latter's necessary momentariness. For, if we consent to considering, with Merleau-Ponty, that we ought to pass from the thing "comme identité" to the thing "comme différence," as transcendence, as behind, beyond, as always "lointaine" (249), we resemble the things among which we live in compliance with the multi-directionality ascribable to the human, to the inanimate, both sustained by an intermundane space (73), which confers on them a more than uniparous birth. Once acceding to these considerations, we join Woolf in being carnalities inclusive of, but not assimilable to, the properties "of which" we are "made," so that possession by right or by force becomes annulled—forever imperfect, unfinished—due to our prepositional grip on the body that any language allows us to call our own.

Thus, since memory and forgetting are discontinuous with regard to experience, our sense of self-foundership must be remade, reclaimed, as will Woolf's ability to "put the severed parts together" under the briefly unifying "blow" (72). When she wonders, however, if "things we have felt with great intensity have an existence independent of our minds," Woolf imagines that, one day, she "shall fit a plug into the wall" and, listening to "the past," discover "garden" and "nursery" emanating from a current by which "we shall be able to live our lives through from the start," as though to listen were to bypass the flexuosity, the bending-in, central to interpretation (67). Yet this deposit of feeling and prospect shows us how a woman, leaning a present ear in the direction of "garden" and "nursery"—murmurous, distant, strangely close—would heed them not alone through the technology of a mediating "plug" but thanks to contemporary attention tilting towards, bordering on, those sounds lost to a "past" in need of decipherment because it could never simply unravel itself. Such near sight-reading exertions, under the possible future of Woolf's image, signal the "third voice" that we hear again as she speaks "to Leonard," as "Leonard speaks" to her, both sensing a tertiary thing circulating among the said (133). As she sketches this "past" that does not seem to die, as we read her, so much intervenes: "light glows"; an "apple becomes a vivid green"; an "owl" throws its vowels "under" the "window," each not an aid to disconnection but to our remembrance that what appears to come between, the "vessel afloat on sensation," the "plate exposed to invisible rays," a "voice" born of other voices, produces the relations of which "words," "music," and "the thing itself" are made, the latter a "whole" other than, though proposed by, the multiplicity of its parts (133).

Hence, to say that we do not live "confined" to the body, to the part, is to envision a kinship with "scenes" through which "floods" a "reality" beyond and inclusive of evident circumscription, to invite the "shock" whose violence tells us that the body's "sealing matter," by definition, "cracks" open on to other things (142). And, if our Platonic texts emerge from a top-down construction which situates, at its core, the body forever constrained by a "soul" it cannot see, Woolf's "life-writing," her writing-on-behalf-of-life, trains itself on "presences" seen and unseen, their interdependence exceeding the limits of any sketch (80). We can remark, with her, that "I see myself as a fish in a stream; deflected; held in place; but cannot describe the stream," knowing how the Heraclitean simile approaches a fluidity whose dimensions we cannot quite measure, although they grant persons and things a kind of swimming, that the courage in admitting the incapacity to "describe" comprehensively is itself a way to swim (80).

Yet the problem of comprehensiveness need not denude any of us of the ability to examine how we have swum at all. For my part, when I have utilized the first person at moments throughout the preceding pages to demonstrate my inclusion, like that of all potential readers, in the communal character of the "blow" prized by "A Sketch of the Past," that usage stresses an argument I raise now on the support of many foregoing inductions: to augment the purview of the self, to expand the single "I" so that, dilated, it incorporates past and future "ancestresses," is to disown the commonplace that any embodied consciousness can be fastened on as unaccompanied, shut out, debarred from participating in the swarm basic to dilation. It means that the self, seeing the things around it as subdued by the gravity of human will, can only be a falsehood tied to the lie inherent in the almost-discreteness of its name, when seen without reference to those kin behind, before, and on all sides of it. It means that we must "describe" always again, reassess how we engage in the activity of naming, because the thing we call with words will be somehow other than its invocation. It means, as we join with the thronging self, that the leaf, the branch, the stone we often deduct from the concept of value cannot exist in seclusion, that our rich participation in the category of selfhood will affect our behavior with respect to the division of things—indeed, that the very idea of partitioning must be challenged, the boon of such a blur being how the thing regarded may be as multitudinous as the one who commits himself to looking.

At the back of those approaches to looking which I have considered, behind the pictures fabricated by means of them, lie at least two tactilities: the handcrafted art object, the "pot" that preserves and transports, which Defoe depicts, which Woolf so earthily specifies, and the ground on which fall leaves, branches, stones, its pliancy appearing to welcome the metamorphosis effected by that attentive scrutiny of human hands capable of seeing, in dwindled "hair," sopping "mud," arid "dirt," a materiality beyond mere wastage. But, as my enumerating these palpabilities situates them in adjacency, as one concreteness seems to greet the notice of another, such welcoming ought to be reciprocal. And the art object, in company with our resolute heeding of it, can stimulate reciprocity in a world whose members justify a mutual hearkening—if that world is to continue.

I advocate, moreover, that in all our texts the continuation of the earth and the forces interpenetrating it is the nodus appealed to, begged for, pursuits which predetermine actual readers, viewers, listeners standing alongside of the object that springs perceptual experience into play and who trust in—thinkingly, unthinkingly—this ensphered solidity which will go on enduring. The latter's endurance nevertheless hinges on our abstaining from the human tendency to devour the nutriments, the richnesses, the resources that, for many of us, must be as illimitable as the self, its end deferred, ever elsewhere, even when imagined. Yet, since resources bring us back to the phylum of things, how we envisage substances will prepare the trajectory of our behavior towards them. I thus contend that art objects, afforded substantiality through the manner of their fashioning, can reorder how we comport ourselves in a world that is not for us, so long as we read them amply, espousing the strain which extensiveness of vision assumes.

My "for" in the previous sentence suggests that what we indite as "world" cannot be apprehended as stationed in requital of, as the price paid for, our avarice when confronting a global plenitude which could only effloresce, without cessation, the bloom sacrificed to the magnitude of our need for it. Because this avariciousness supposes a transitivity, unfailing, unidirectional, between the self and all it covets, instigated by the former, sustained by the latter, it will not accept that taking a thing directly can redound upon the taker, that unchecked taking will, in some predictable future, desolate both the taker and the taken. To frustrate that desolation, we should enrich our view of things, see reciprocation as the process that perpetuates both persons and things, admit the obliquity of our recourse to any object due to the necessity of our reading it—and acknowledge that the work of art which enlarges our aptitude for construing a mutuality of exchange, as well as the diverse pathways to the things we long to perceive, educates us to alight on the means of retarding a near-universal annihilation. But nihility, retarded, imposes on us a respect for slowness so reproved by the speed with which we award inertia to the object spellbound by our use of it that we appear invited to misidentify ourselves with a rapidity that dominates for the reason that it can. Despite celerity, despite misidentification, the thing and the vitalities upholding it may, spurning the deadness awarded them, recoil upon those who would repulse their being numbered among the class of entities sufficiently generous to allow for the human and the non-human, not in the teeth of their formal differences, but on account of them. To avert nothingness, to prevent recoiling, we will need a sense of relation that cultivates things, since they are our kindred.

With regard to the associatory character of kindredness, I observe that any "I," as the offspring of its parents' charged coming-close, is at once in alliance with and distinct from the two whose engendering frictions rubbed it into life, an affinity liable to discernment on the ground of the spaces between "I" and its forebears. Such spaces do not invalidate kinship; they render its production possible. I recollect Merleau-Ponty, in the *Phénoménologie de la perception* (1945), promising that "c'est dans mon rapport avec des 'choses' que je me connais" (439). Marking this promise that assures me I am accountable for my demeanor concerning things, I recast it in the plural: it is in, through, by the agency of, our relation with things that we know ourselves—and the dispensation of our knowing, spread across all environments available to us, will ripple through what it touches. Abounding prepositions here predict the labors inherent in them, for the prepositional transacts how the relation between two things must be intransitive, indirect, to the extent that what relatedness means is neither self-explanatory nor interpretable according to the speed which the rapacity to equate one thing with another pre-ordains. Merleau-Ponty consequently asks us to recognize that the conceptions, the pictures, the essays, the scientific reasoning through which we describe the known are always on the advent of, tangential to, their referents. The wisdom of that proximate meeting lies in its inciting us to think again, to sit in the toil which critical thought enforces, to concede that our attentions divulge us. Undoubtedly, the "always" that Merleau-Ponty's sentence postulates, but does not say, should give us pause.

On the way to building up a means of fighting for the cultivation of things, rather than for our licence to devastate them, I revert to Woolf's "moments of being" and "non-being." Both rely on the body, that emblem of "appearances" which a hasty reading would permit us to belittle in comparison with "some real thing behind," always "behind" the vegetable repetitiveness of dealing with "what has to be done," which "non-being" appears to exact from the bodily. Yet, for their participant, both proceed in conformity with contrary tempos: the "sledge-hammer blow" discharges "a whole avalanche of meaning," the day's vegetative rhythms return, and the body is the point of their intersection (78). For Woolf herself, a rapid "shock" may be followed by the "desire to explain it," but the languor of "non-being" supplies her with the time to persevere in fitting the divided "parts together" (72). We should emulate Woolf's quest for "wholeness" as well as her capacity for asking, "what is the meaning of 'explained' it?" (72, 81), though our emulation binds us to inquiring how—as concepts—rapidity, slowness, and selfhood relate to one another.

"A Sketch of the Past" charts a partial answer to that inquiry, since we who read it, regardless of profession, once applying our human skill in "putting into words," into any expressive medium, the "revelation" of an "order" from which we have been driven out, scan a "whole" that "non-being" bequeaths to us (72). The latter's dense lag, while it triggers our memorial work, our grasping at the ensemble which that work undertakes to effect, along with our dexterity in debating its accomplishment, thus renders us a threefold bequest, so that the recollection by which we intervolve Woolf's two existential realms may stall a too easy understanding of forward motion. When we intend to move onward, we ought to know what we are moving; on behalf of that knowing, I swivel round to Merleau-Ponty's call concerning the connectors between persons and things.

Before discussing those connectors at length, however, I observe how our texts have begun to speak to one another and what that speaking suggests. As Lee so rightly tells us, "the elusiveness of the self almost becomes" Woolf's "subject" (18), along with her "sexual assault by Gerald Duckworth," a much older half-brother, "in very early childhood," and both are concentrated on highly visualized recollections of the Stephen family's Cornwall summer home (123). But memory's picturing work, intimate with that of the imaginative faculty, "is largely the child of the flesh," so that mind and matter, rather than being antagonists, are co-realities.

The necessity of co-existence sits at the center of *Le visible et l'invisible*, due to Merleau-Ponty adjuring us to admit that the things among which we live, conventionally pictured as "brute," material, unthinking, "offer themselves" solely to "someone who wishes not to have them but to see them, not to hold them as with forceps, or to immobilize them as under the objective of a microscope, but to let them be," to "witness their continued being" by "giving them the hollow, the free space they ask for in return, the resonance they require" (101). Such a person becomes "a question" searching not for "an *answer*" but for "a confirmation" of the "astonishment" at discovering "perception as this interrogative thought which lets the perceived world be rather than posits it" (102), a "thought" that equals "not only philosophy": "it is first the look that questions the things" themselves (103). And, as Hans Jonas advises in *The Phenomenon of Life: Toward a Philosophical Biology* (1966), "since most of what we now know to be inanimate is so intimately intertwined with the dynamics of life that it seems to share in its nature," earth, "wind, and water—begetting, teeming, nurturing, destroying—are anything but models of 'mere matter'" (7). Instead, they are "the basic setting for experience—a horizon of co-reality" whose amplitude will outdistance the pictures we fabricate of it, even while their failures point to what surpasses them (84).

If we discern ourselves, then, by means of our "rapport" with objects, our experience of personhood develops from and is modulated by how we answer to the precondition that we must carry, conduct, convey those things which, in their precedence, in their being forever in advance of us, dispose our identities and their significations. This thinking prescribes that a world untenanted by things would also be emptied of persons, their cognition determined by intercourse with what they are not. Our attitude towards transporting objects, towards the ways in which they seem to gratify our solicitations should, in consequence, champion a mutual abiding. But, because knowledge, relationally gained, takes time, the swiftness of our desires may exhort us to sacralize a self that gets rather than carries, that owns rather than shares in. Such speed, however, when multiplied by all who are electrified by it, quashes the very getting it sought for—once the supply of what can be got begins to narrow.

For these reasons, I submit the necessity of our desanctifying a selfhood misapprehended as the raging voracities of a maw, as an acquisitiveness that, far from being hallowed, chews into fragments a whole it had no interest in divining. And I judge that our obligation to renounce the sacral character of our liberty-to-obtain, to derange the belief that we are what we appropriate, will uplift our consciousness of "this vast mass that we call the world" that our texts so diversely counsel us to recognize and to sustain. Since we tend to preserve what we rate essential, since how we enter into value-thinking shows up in our evaluative actions, to re-envision the self is to interrupt maintaining an entity ranked over those things designed, presumably, to satisfy it, to allow that the grader forsakes the graded when assessing skills, when the wish to be always elevated, risk the sustenation of a "world" throughout which human lives and things are distributed, a coequality any evaluator ought to plan for.

Woolf furthers this interruption-of-maintenance, this review of a self misaligning valuation and undisputed ascendancy, so long as we commend ourselves to her qualifying how "it is almost impossible" that her self, that any self, "should be here." On the border of impossibility, intermitted between "here" and not-"here," we cannot by right procure the experience of a presence unmodified, coincident with a wholeness which must be "lointaine," farther away than our calculations respecting it, whether or not we pinpoint that distance as a dream or as a certainty belabored because we suspect its enduring attainment. If we never arrive at the thing itself, at the thing segmented off, broken off, alone, we have neither our selves nor things, on the condition that having hails undisrupted possession as its target. Instead, according to the "rapport" through which both are constituted, our persons and things jointly intervene in, break into, intrude on, one another, the "world" fortified rather than endangered by the "mass" of their enmeshments, by what Merleau-Ponty, in *Le visible et l'invisible*, salutes as the "co-fonctionnement" of human life and all that seems so other than it (268). We ought to exhibit that co-functioning in how we value; the fact of it should destabilize our demoting what appears below us due to a supremacy which, like our indissolubility, like our "almost impossible" wholeness, is always—can only be—interrupted. The something more implied here, the devotional connectivity worth our commitment to it, takes me to what I regard as Woolf's spatial religiosity.

Though she focuses "that great Cathedral space" on the purlieu of her Cornwall "childhood" (81), Woolf permits us to broaden, to globalize its bounds and temporal span on account of how her thinking phrase discovers that to speak of one dimension is to distend towards another, the two extents of space and time interfused in a mutual occasioning, so that it would be toilful to enclose their outlying limits, if we were to try. The "great Cathedral space which was childhood" thus roofs over the many other time-scales that proceed from infancy. Yet, so generalized in import, Woolf's figure turns us to considering all the spaces we sit in while our lives lengthen along the surfaces of the earth which, always moving, revolves those tracts open to the possibility of our knowing them. I emphasize, as does Woolf's diction, the reverence we owe to spaces, to the earth that displays their repertory; I stress the religious thought incumbent on, ceded to, "Cathedral," even as I have not forgotten that, for Woolf, "there is no God."

But non-belief in the godly and our choosing to sanction hallowedness need not be adversarial postures: over many millennia, our kind has exercised its aptitude for making more than one sort of vow at the service of divinities as multiform as the covenants with which we have honored them. Despite their multitude, our divine compacts profess the bond between human life and that which will not sponsor the need that it should become intelligible, measurable through our grasping it, which transcends our acquisitive maneuverings and assures us that the latter cannot be pronounced the chief criterion of value, especially if we depute their success or lack thereof to the supernal which, from such a prospect, is our substitute. These concordances across time periods show our faculty for devoting ourselves, however troublesomely, to conceiving the more than human, to a sanctity seen to last—as must the sky or the "space" in which materialities, co-existing, co-evolve.

To be deficient in the sanctifying impulse, in the propulsion to hallow what we can neither penetrate nor gauge with thorough accuracy, would seem thus to incur the deficit of failing to imagine the co-existences whose co-evolutions populate the world, this imaginative smallness preparing those beggared by it for envisaging the human and the non-human as equal to the liabilities by which both may be commandeered. I set Woolf's "Cathedral space" against our species's predilection for jumbling together tenancy, ownership, usurpation, because that spatiality betters any title-deed due to each of us being born inside its expanse; because, if we cannot desist from entertaining possession as a concept, so multiplex, continuous, "space" could be said to hold us; because our deference answers for its longevity and, contracting our managerial care, is religious—nothwithstanding the particular "God" we venerate or disallow. The pertinence of these deliberations to Woolf herself lies in the "battle" pounding at "its crisis," with every "night the Germans" flying "over England" (100), "space" becoming a "broken surface," pitted by the bombs we have invented for its ravaging (98). And what can be ravaged is, of course, susceptible to vanishing.

We will find textual examples of that near-vanishing if we search behind and just ahead of us. Behind us, we hear Socrates recommending to the discussants of the *Republic*, themselves potential leaders in a future which their conversation rehearses, the "magnificent myth" whose persuasive weight rests on illustrating that "space," though stretching beyond the body, is domiciled within us, that we are its residences, hence necessitating the isomorphism between inside and out which the city, dialogically constructed, extrudes, its order uncountered by chaos, so that Plato fits his readers—contemporary, distant—for responding to these successive presumptions: Socrates died as an opponent of the state; dying, he judged the city which executed him; reconceiving order devolves to being our task, regardless of how its enactment disrupts those structures which are, indeed, our progeny. Just ahead of us in terms of urgencies regarding "space" and a religiosity of attitude that might defend its continuance, we can look to Tim Flannery who, in *The Weather Makers* (2005), asks us to connect our behavioral covetousness with proliferating "greenhouse gases, global warming, and climate change" (19).

Flannery starts by retracing the depths in that phrase invented by Alfred Russel Wallace as a description of our atmosphere—"the Great Aerial Ocean" whose swell joins "everything with everything else," thus performing "many services that we take for granted" (12). Since "our lungs" heave with the "Earth's great aerial bloodstream" in an uptake that "inspires us from our first breath to our last," we may, over-habituated to the regularity of breathing, neglect the stipulation that coursing air maintains all we undergo, including our own forgetfulness (12). We may overlook the ways in which, "indivisible and omnipresent," this "bloodstream" has "so regulated our planet's temperature that for nearly 4 billion years Earth has remained the sole known cradle of life amid an infinity of dead gases, rock, and dust"; although such "a feat is as improbable as the development of life itself," we must remember that "the two cannot be separated, for the great aerial ocean is the cumulative effusion of everything that has ever breathed, grown, and decayed" (13). Wondering, "perhaps" that "cumulative effusion" is "the means by which life perpetuates the conditions necessary for its existence," Flannery directs two interrelated questions to his readers: "how can the individual components that constitute life coordinate their efforts; and (more immediately relevant to ourselves) what can be said of species that threaten that equilibrium?" (13). Before replying to these queries, however, Flannery adverts to James Lovelock's *Gaia* (1979), which plunges so thoroughly into them. Because our conceptions of "space" affect our inhabitancy of it, we need to follow him.

Lovelock "argued that Earth was a single, planet-sized organism, which he named Gaia after an ancient Greek earth goddess" (13), her body encompassing all terrestrial phenomena whose vastness rendered her a multiple creature, built up by the inter-working of organisms she succored and subsisted on. The "atmosphere" may be Gaia's prime "organ of interconnection and temperature regulation," yet Flannery cites Lovelock's attempt to particularize what he means by "organ": it is "not merely a biological product, but more probably a biological construction"—"not living, but like a cat's fur, a bird's feathers, or the paper nest of a wasp, an extension of a living system designed to maintain a chosen environment" (13). If "anyone who has lived close to nature will recognize the thing" which Lovelock describes, "his arguments" nevertheless "discomfited many scientists," due to their seeming "mystical"; even so, "scientists" themselves must be members of the "living system" into which their births initiate them and which scientific zeal ought to probe, discomfiture proving, I think, the merits of that inquiry (13). Flannery details "the evidence in favor of Lovelock" produced "since 1979" (14), though—in spite of "the growing sophistication" with regard to "our understanding of how life works to affect Earth's temperature and chemistry"—much "debate" remains "about Lovelock's Gaia hypothesis" (17). Going on to ponder the ways in which mythological hypothesizing might benefit our idea of "space," Flannery specifies our wardenship of it:

> Does it really matter whether Gaia exists or not? I think it does, for it influences the very way we see our place in nature. Someone who believes in Gaia sees everything on Earth as being intimately connected to everything else, just as are organs in a body. In such a system, pollutants cannot be simply shunted out of sight and forgotten, and every extinction is seen as an act of self-mutilation. As a result, a Gaian worldview predisposes its adherents to sustainable ways of living. In our modern world, however, the reductionist worldview is in the ascendant, and its adherents often see human actions in isolation. It is a reductionist worldview that has brought the present state of climate change upon us. (17)

But none of the above is a guarantor that "Gaian philosophy inevitably makes for good environmental practice" (17). When, Flannery reports, he "frequently" hears "people say that all will be okay with climate change because 'Gaia will sort it out,'" he epitomizes to what extent those benighted by, fascinated with, a form of "expression" will abbreviate the very "philosophy" that cannot "sort" anything "out" by itself, the human element's subtraction from it dooming "Gaian" thought to the "isolation" it countermands (17). And, even if "Gaia" does "manage to rid herself of us, we would take so many other species with us that the repair job to Earth's biodiversity would take tens of millions of years" (17–18): "so," Flannery urges, "let's use the term *Gaia* as shorthand for the complex system that makes life possible, while recognizing" that the living outgrowths behind the mythical figure "may result from chance," not from the teleology that submits humankind as its apex, its proof, which much Darwinian thinking, with its insistence on generative variations, entreats us to reassess (18). Indeed, once characterizing life's "development" as "improbable," as issuing from "chance," we begin to tolerate the saving of it, redeeming that potential destruction which *The Weather Makers* prognosticates at such length. Since fortuity honors the multidirectional, we may "chance" upon the powers to abridge imperiling all the "organs" of the "body" from which human conduct cannot be excepted—"Gaia" as a concept subserving both that abridgement and the opportunity to prohibit sentencing ourselves to being the "species" that threatened a planetary "equilibrium" whose care, whose exactions, it could not see meeting. Yet, if "it is almost impossible" that we "should be here," our "almost"-absence counts as an equal possibility.

Below, I enlarge on the argument I have been puzzling out because that enlargement enforces a rethinking of relation, an expanding rather than reducing, an interlinking rather than isolating, and gives us the concepts by which we might "coordinate" our "efforts" at the behest of an "equilibrium" so exposed to our disregard of it. To feud with indifference is to contend for the fostering of things, to grant that, while objects and persons do not form two embattled tribes but an intercommunity, their wreckage would be our own final censure. I assume the "rapport" between our abilities to conceive and to act; I assert our capacity to choose a conceiving which, instead of numbing its participants, wakes them. In order to prompt that wakefulness, I suggest we now combine the ideas of Merleau-Ponty, of Woolf, of Flannery's adherence to "Gaia," over which we have long loitered. Doing so, we come to this: the "great Cathedral space which was childhood" stretches throughout all earthly spaces, ranges over the childhoods formed by experience of them, over lives developing by virtue of such experience, and in that "space" there are no individuals—excised, in "isolation," unrelated—but "living system[s]," each accessible to being seen singly, each affected by forces, by conditions, by things other than itself and affecting these in turn, so that all are co-founded.

To see any person as severed from that interplay is thus to mutilate a self of one's own foundation, while to welcome him "comme différence" means that he is a proceeding, a process which abuts on and overlaps with others, undetachable even in "extinction," never by themselves entire, their coordinations setting up the domain of human flesh. Yet the "Cathedral space" inclusive of that domain holds more than flesh: it superintends the emergence of what our ordinary language invokes as things, the trees, stones, sticks among which we move, together with those objects we model from their instrumentality, the members of both categories alike in being deemed inanimate, devoid of breath, though all are maintained by the "bloodstream" which infuses us with animation.

What can be said of human life, according to the ideas we are combining, must, however, befit its contrary, owing to a "rapport" whose dual orientation directs the classes of person and thing towards each other. So directed, both classes intercorrelate, in consequence of which the dynamism we attribute to the human ought to simmer in the thing, which can only be more expansive, more intricate, than our little name for it. Consistent with this intercommunicating vision, there are no things here, ossified, crystallized out into shapes whose permanence lies in their disambiguation, if that noun describes, for instance, "mud," "dirt," fallen "hair," exiled from interdependency on account of the yearning to see each as graspable—and an "it." But the one who exiles, the immobilizer, is himself immobilized, an "it" clutching at another of his own contrivance, both "vile and worthless" inasmuch as their penury could have been otherwise. I appreciate that our combinative idea-building doubts the utility of what Woolf represents as "the daily world" (139), as the "sway of a society . . . too old for us" (147), occupied with "making an end where there is no such thing" (135). I appreciate, too, that our social occupations, inciting us to aspire after obtainment, are, because of their very seniority, ripe for the remaking.

Yet the "sway" that we have once made can be the helpmate of conversion, if, temporizing our eagerness for seizure, for being seized, we postpone recognizing that "sway" as an "it" invulnerable to debate, there, inexorably, in all its age-old concretions. Our idea-work leads us to affirm that, instead of what we call by custom a thing, an "it," we should see: multitudes of overlappings, abutments, conjoinings, imbrications, their key aspect not a unit-like "it" which perceptual experience yields to us with alacrity, not a form separable because always inactive, but a structuring process, a going forth of weight upon weight, multiplied across "space," throughout duration, an overbrimming which, as it coordinates the non-human and the human, is coordinated by a "world" that goes on gyrating. That "world," that earth, ought to partake of the co-functioning we elaborate here, so that, rather than an agglomeration of rotating matter, the "world" must be a sequence of numberless, englobed relations. This observation extols connectivity over severance; this observation reminds those of us who keep to it that our kind cannot lay claim to the relational as a thing, cannot subject it to our own convenience. And, when I say we are responsible for the manner of our participation in it, I acknowledge that the vocabulary available to me makes it difficult not to discuss a process as though it were another wad of quiescent matter, despite its never staying still.

The dominant problem, relevant to persons and to non-persons, to all phenomena, remains the ease with which we seem so free to weigh the discriminative over the procedural, to reduce the dynamic to what can be uncoupled from it, hence making the latter, that corporeal island we will have meted out, identical with our desire for it. Though I assert that to revere interconnectivity means we cannot relegate networking operations to our own convenience, I know how much of human history narrates such relegation, as well as its costs for those adjudged to be inconvenient, know our bias towards confusing power with proprietorship, towards seeing the inexpedient as the merely inappreciable. I admit also that "the daily world" underwrites the management of our desires. But, "comme différence," the thing perceived as cut off from relation must be contrary to our employment of it, an inexpedience promoting our self-examination; seeming freedoms look in a multiplicity of directions; we should challenge a "daily world" which disposes us to believe that aching has an "end," particularly when that disposition routes us to the world's "extinction," a course rendered appreciable because the earth, relative to the "shunted out of sight," recalls in its perturbations all that we have "forgotten." So long as "daily"-ness is fictive to the extent that we have spun its story, and stories can be told again, narrated differently, any bias, since it suggests at least a twofold looking, asks for reassessment.

I argue for exercises in attention—and present "Gaia" as one of its images. There are, of course, many other illustrations of a materiality energized rather than inert. I think of Patricia S. Churchland's "Feeling Reasons," from *On the Contrary* (1998), a collection written with her husband, Paul M. Churchland, which fights for our comprehending that the "brain is a complex dynamical system" (245), its "cortical network" intrinsic to how each child, together with the person he becomes, "must learn about the physical world by interacting with it and bearing the consequences of his actions, or watching others engage the world, or hearing about others engage the world" (251). If Churchland indicates the reciprocity among "network," person, and "world," she cues our memory of the ways in which "the great and lasting stories" aid us in transacting reciprocation, as they "provide a basic core of scenarios" through which we "imagine and feel, if only vicariously, the results of various choices, such as failing to prepare for future hard times" (250). While I cheer on the ethical pressure of a "dynamical system" capable of connective expansion, we need another sort of picturing story, one which does not scruple to take the human as its paragon, one whose amplitude, interlaced with the human, exceeds it. For, prodded by a "reductionist worldview" pandering to our own advantage, we have compressed the distance between "future hard times" and the present, lugged that "future" so close that we face an intimacy for which we are inadequately prepared. A diversity of processes, a multiformity of them, can only foil our fervor for mutating process into thing, can only disappoint our isolating vision, as to intervene in one is to alter all, in however graduated a fashion, and this is the story that "Gaia" requires we should remember. As Flannery describes it, "Gaia" differs from the divinity upheld by the *Republic*, its remoteness from us, its being out of time, validating the standard of its "sway." Yet, because "Gaia" images, with regard to human life, a devotion both constructive of future developments and conservative in the sense of staving off ruination, Flannery shows us a religious concept in time, always modulating, our fellowship with it already prepared for. And that brings us to considering the relations between the divine and fiction.

We have met prior intimations of the ways in which these terms might be seen to appertain to each other. Plato gives us, in the instance of the *Republic*, a godliness whose insusceptibility to change corroborates the stabilizing efforts of the "myth" which Socrates concocts, a conceptual enjambment resulting in the following formulation: changelessness, a characteristic of the divine, can be figured by a "story" according to the dictates of socialized human orders—and behold, the "myth" becomes true. For the players inside the text, for readers outside it, this formula may be opportunistic due to its applying absolute invariance to our native unrest, as though the verity of the former expunged from us those fluctuations by which we are constituted and which, in view of the stability enjoining our veneration, must be lies. But that opportunism, all the trouble taken over it, features both the truthfulness of our variability and that we can imagine finding no use for it. Like Woolf, like Flannery, we succeed to conjuring the divine, the veracious, the fictive as concepts in action, and our conjurations ought to be flexible enough so as to issue in another variety of pattern.

Once we entertain even loosely a belief in "Gaia['s]" systemic vision, we estimate that the "whole" inheres in, abides by virtue of, the "difference" among its "qualities," its parts; that the entirety here, while departing from the personalized "God" in whom Woolf cannot trust, nevertheless participates in the sacred because its adaptations, adjustments, diversifying, are prolonged by the fidelity we offer to a wholeness which will always answer it. Such notions of inherence, exemplifying that the divine need not be equivalent to the absolute, that holiness is conceivable in interlocking modifications, movements, exchanges, belie the received wisdom that power is our possession or that we preempt what we "engage." A "complex dynamical system," the brain, in concert with any "network," does not own; it connects, collaborates with. As conscious bodies affected by and affecting the "world," we can, however fleetingly, abstract ourselves from, draw away from, the manners of our connection in order to judge their efficacy. So doing, we will avoid the lot of Plato's city and of his Socrates: co-founders of a "Gaia" more valuable than our ability to threaten it, accepting the obligation to submit our human structures to readjustment, we will live within an intercorporeality that was never ours to demolish.

In making my declaration—or, from a skeptical point of view, in dreaming it—I propose "Gaia" in concord with Flannery's emphasis on belief. That concordance recommends to us the practice of realizing truth not as a fact proved by its aloofness from the fictive, not as a certainty authenticated by virtue of its dormancy, its stagnancy, but as a perceptual exercise in proximity to the fictional, to the "almost impossible," as in consort with movement as the entities whose existence truth as a concept means to certify and to arbitrate. I am implying that "someone who believes" in "Gaia['s]" cooperative intimacies will, allowing for the protean, envisage sanctity, truth, and fiction in agreement with a fluidity which does not eliminate their boundaries, though it cautions that "someone" while he deliberates over the problem of determining them. I am positing that, cautioned, warned not to mistake rigidity for right ascertainment, "someone who believes in Gaia" will recollect the ways in which a great deal of our history covers conceptual inelasticities inciting behaviors which extirpated more than they preserved. And, if we commit ourselves to becoming Flannery's collective "someone," we will promise that the criterion of an actual and notional fluidity must be that, by means of merging under it, we will repair rather than go on wounding, save rather than destroy.

Woolf herself supplies us with a prototype of the pliancy I argue for concerning the terms we choose to esteem and why we should appraise their relations as problematical. Near the beginning of *A Room of One's Own* (1929), deciding that "the true nature of woman and the true nature of fiction" will "remain," for her, "unsolved problems," Woolf recognizes that she will "never be able to fulfil" the "first duty of a lecturer": to deliver to her listeners "after an hour's discourse a nugget of pure truth to wrap up between the pages" of their "notebooks and keep on the mantel-piece for ever" (4.) Moreover, "when a subject is highly controversial—and any question about sex is that—" if "one cannot hope to tell the truth," unconditional, unqualified, cloistered from modification because of its purity, "fiction here is likely to contain more truth than fact" (4). Woolf suggests, already, that so long as we look for "truth" to be lifted up out of the muck of "daily life," we look in a place of our own invention, which, by necessity, can spew forth neither the hoard we require nor function as the principle on the strength of which "daily life" should be judged, given its seclusion from it (4). What follows from this lack of antithesis between veridical "fact" and "fiction"—Woolf's "making use of all the liberties and licences of a novelist" to tell the "story" of how she developed her "train of thought" (4); her muddling the perspicuity of any "I" when she exhorts her listening readers, parenthetically, to "call" her "Mary Beton, Mary Seton, Mary Carmichael or by any name you please," since "it is not a matter of any importance" (5); under the exigency of that "call," her inquiring "whether there are two sexes in the mind corresponding to the two sexes in the body," whether "they also require to be united" in order to gain "complete satisfaction and happiness" (98); her assertion regarding the fatality of being "a man or woman pure and simple; one must be woman-manly or man-womanly," and "fatal is no figure of speech": "for anything written with that conscious bias" must be "doomed to death" (104)—is Woolf's revelation to us, as "Mary Beton ceases to speak," that "in a question" unavoidably "controversial" because of the depths beneath it, "truth is only to be had by laying together many varieties of error" (105).

Such "laying together" necessitates interpretive labors, presents "truth" not as a terminus, reached, not as a furlough inviting our disembarkation, but as a process akin to that "collaboration" which "has to take place in the mind between the woman and the man before the act of creation can be accomplished" (104). Once "consummated," once "fertilized," the veracious becomes a way, a passage, a transit, which ought to "grow in the minds of others" (104), so that "it explodes and gives birth to all kinds of other ideas" as though enacting "the secret of perpetual life" (101). If Woolf characterizes "truth" without defining it, predicates "truth" while refusing to identify its equivalent, we should sojourn in the ethics she sketches for us: though it may be "had" in the sense of our drawing near to the possibility of experiencing it, "truth" can be neither an "end" nor a "nugget" nor "pure"—nor, regardless of my preceding diction, an "it," trouble-free. Bewildering our affection for polarities, for their never mingling, the true will forever engender our inconvenience due to the precept that we must participate in a doing, in a going forth, in fertilizations we can never scent the "end" of. The virtue in that problem, so far as we discountenance a bemused yearning for "isolation," is that we can live by means of it, live by means of a "Gaia," which "births" the struggle to "coordinate" our "efforts" on behalf of a "space" not "doomed to death" because we consent to seeing its variability, its proceedings, as sanctifiable.

All this returns me to where we started from, to Woolf intuiting the "silent land" which Sickert's paintings seem to open out, to what the wish "to make us see" might mean to a "species" in need of as much depth-charged seeing as it can bear to give to a world whose saving will depend on it, depend on its capacity for exploding poorly critiqued desires and the behaviors initiated by them. Throughout, we have looked at the act of sight as a breed of divination, as a conjecturing that ought to challenge the too readily unquestioned in order to dynamite our derelictions, our leavings, our failures so often to understand the relational in terms vivifying, noisome, and difficult, these two last, at least, ruffling our own ease. Further, "someone who believes," with Merleau-Ponty, that we are never at the thing itself will speculate that the human, like all materiality, begins from and issues in transcendences, in so far as, since we cannot ever hope to arrive at one sole place, at one lone thing, we are always "on the verge" of being elsewhere, and things join with us in that physical, in that corporeal, ongoingness. I believe such speculations will assist us in schooling our desires and their applications, will promote a "Gaian" thinking that tells us how the earth we stand on is never finished, allowing us to comprehend that the "biological construction[s]" of our texts, of *The Waves* itself, are "extension[s] of a living system," their design maintaining an "environment" quite different from our ideas of it—thus worthy of persistent engagement. And, if we look, our absorption, our engrossment, if mindful, will inform us that the "silent land," this "other world," is *here*.

. . .

Her *Diary* entry for 23 November 1926 permits us to overhear Woolf experiencing the genesis of what will become *The Waves*:

> . . . I am now & then haunted by some semi mystic very profound life of a woman, which shall all be told on one occasion; & time shall be utterly obliterated; future shall somehow blossom out of the past. One incident—say the fall of a flower—might contain it. My theory being that the actual event practically does not exist—nor time either. But I don't want to force this. (*Diary 3*, 118)

Nearly three months later, on 21 February 1927, Woolf begins to see a sequence of contemplative actions governed by the concept of merging:

> Why not invent a new kind of play—as for instance
> Woman thinks: . . .
> He does.
> Organ plays.
> She writes.
> They say:

> She sings:
> Night speaks:
> They miss
>
> I think it must be something in this line—though I cant now see what. Away from facts: free; yet concentrated; prose yet poetry; a novel & a play. (*Diary 3*, 128)

We know from the letters and from the diaries that the novel's working title was *The Moths*, the latter in some way transmogrifying into waves. We also know, as Quentin Bell reveals in his biography of her (1972), that Woolf found herself hypnotized by the account, in a May 1927 letter from Cassis, of "moths flying madly in circles round" the body of her sister and "the lamp," Vanessa Bell ending her tale with the wish that Woolf should "write a book about the maternal instinct" (126). If we add all these materials together, along with her nephew's reflection, in the biography, that Woolf appears to "apprehend processes of thought and feeling as though they were pictorial shapes" (107), we must consider how the picturing activity orders the motion of *The Waves*, what that activity centers on, and who produces the images which make up so much of our reading.

As an image articulated in any medium serves to affirm the discernment which is its origin, to maintain that Woolf distinguishes "thought and feeling" as "pictorial shapes" is to imply that internal "processes," once exteriorized, become tactile, palpable, real, their ability to be handled predisposed to affect those who make contact with them. But how can we meditate on the character of that effect with regard to Woolf's inaugural visions of *The Waves*? We can understand that Woolf organizes, in the first excerpt, two elements which, according to conventional thought, seem contradictory, for "the fall of a flower" exists by virtue of the very "time" whose obliteration Woolf intends to represent. Much will depend, of course, on our comprehension of "time" itself, on our detecting it as the medium by which our losses accumulate, the loss of one hour to another, of one age to another, or—conversely—as that by which we gain what a life can be said to gain, only to undergo a final leaving. Yet these postures set up the temporal in the light of a subtracting-from, a separating away-from, while Woolf rejects, in the two passages above, all notion of an "itself." If to build up an image is to embody a way of seeing, Woolf's capacity for "pictorial" shaping connects "thought," "feeling," "woman," and "flower" in an "incident" focused on the reader who handles it, so that challenging "the actual event" presents the nouns at our disposal as members of ever more capacious wholes or, say, as particles of a fluidity in entrainment. Woolf herself, however, exhibits the difficulty in attempting to raise the connective over the disparate, since a flower's "fall" must consort, in some fashion, with sequence and narration, terms which point to the "time" that "shall be utterly obliterated" by a perspective yearning to associate the traditionally discrete in an ensemble at once "prose," "poetry," "novel," and "play." Perhaps an associative image benefits reading viewers even when it fails, slowly signaling its constituent units; perhaps that failure pictures our enlistment in a world influenced by our perceptions of it, because the need to associate again warns us to disbelieve in the finality of our associations.

I do not reference lightly the militarized denotations inherent in "enlistment"; rather, I postulate that our acceptance of conscription in, of being altogether written on, the world will militate against our defeat of it. To that end, Woolf supports my postulation by offering us an image not cut apart from, not shorn free of, a materiality more extensible than its illustrations: indeed, "woman" and falling "flower" are encompassed by, inducted into, a visual domain capable of intimation according to how our attempts to represent it must remain incomplete. Woolf's imagined "life of a woman" will thus be "semi mystic" because all of us are, in terms of knowledge, partial initiates of a whole we can never fully appreciate. I am indicating that depictions whose relational components must be wrestled with, composed of genres and discursive methods seen routinely in opposition, characterize an attitude to the reality we ought to soldier in, though we cannot perceive it in the round. To strain under Woolf's images is to practice, on another scale, soldiering in the world upon which her approach to the visual dilates, a world figured wrongly as a contest, with human dominance the only victory, a world made of relations neither linear nor transparent. It is possible to respect what we know imperfectly, possible for us to look, hard, at a struggle there may be no end to. And, in her diary, on 30 September 1926, Woolf writes a brief portrait of such struggling: "one sees a fin passing far out" (113).

The Waves permutes this four times, on pages 182, 189, 245, 273, permutations which, like their original, level us at Woolf's incipient sense of what the novel "might contain." A few paragraphs before she draws out that sense find her leaguing together life and its apparent contrary: once visualizing the former "as the river" that "shoots to Niagara," the latter is already there, death "active, positive," a spume of water on water, cascading without conclusion (117). Since Woolf's forecasting of *The Waves* shows the human in relation to the non-human, a woman's "life" somehow contiguous to dying "flower," prophesies their expression in an ebullience of usually separable literary forms, I attach that "fin passing far out" and shooting "river" to the "maternal instinct," which her sister forwards as a potential subject. For we are concerned with a mind that denies excision, regarding what resembles extraction or removal as conditioned by the connectivity that nothing can escape from, that involves one image in a panoply of others, entangling "prose" in "poetry," a "play" in the "novel." The mind that fights for these involutions allows us to intuit the travails which are ours so far as we cannot decamp from them, their quality neither sickly sweet nor noxious, but tough, stubborn, necessary, terms which pressure me to join my sometime military diction to the "instinct" that mothers all by allusion to Woolf's liquid metaphor: we are in the water, not the water itself, and our inability to extricate ourselves from that prepositional stance should foster our reflections on it as well as the faculty by which we determine their rectitude. If, relative to the watery figure, life and death are concordant surges, if the "fin" in the water cannot get out of it, even when dying, mothering in this instance embraces the toil of the continually unfinished, to the extent that fluid phenomena encircle alike the living and the dead, cradling both, without interruption. Hence, to frame human lives as battles bent on the winning is to perpetrate the sort of lie we cannot use, one which takes relation to mean mere despotism and subjugation, the impoverishment which energizes it arising, most probably, from its perpetrators' craving for rupture from the water in which all pieces of matter, regardless of their enrollment in animation, whether living or dead, move.

In view of the thought we are examining, to undulate towards maturity would be to admit that there is a strife which has no recourse to conquest or to defeat; to be cognizant of striving with the processes by which we are mothered; to attend to the "incident," to the falling-in, of our experiencing them, aware that "the actual event" and "time" do "not exist," so long as they propose release from the liquidity that buoys and constrains us. It appears to me that such ideas, were we resolved to listen to them, could only marshal the "coordinate . . . efforts" whereby Flannery advises us constituted life would survive our current threatening of it. As we have come upon those ideas by prising open a number of Woolf's concatenated images, as this enchaining together displays grit—the pluck needful for hurtling without end—at its heart, we deal not with a Woolfian rarefaction of the real, not with a staunching of its rush, however aqueous, but with facing its inescapability. The mind commending that relentlessness counters a "daily world" so often mistaken for the immobile and, asking for our participation in its pictures, appeals to the possibility of our discomfort at their assortment. Yet discomfiture may be one of many signals that we know we are being carried, that we begin to endure the carrying. I think of Bell, in the biography, musing on Woolf's "desire to make literature 'radial' rather than 'linear'" (107): How might that "desire" pertain to persons, to their representations, to the world radiating both?

I understand that my introducing Bell's interest in the "radial" seems to spawn a wobbling of the figures in my preceding paragraph, a waver between irrefutable fluidity and rays, spokes, staffs irradiated from a center, an image which Bell hopes will account for the attitudinal swerves predominant in Woolf's fiction. But, though "the river shoots to Niagara," it does not do so in a line, straight or otherwise; even the "Niagara" of dying becomes another humid heave, unstopped; all fluctuations are not identical for those who experience them, just as their endpoint is a moving curve rather than a fixity. Since both modes of picturing, however, deploy ocular vocabularies aimed at the "'unvisual beneath'" them, at the forces we do not see, for example, which palpitate throughout what we do, I recommend we liquefy Bell's vision of radiality, so that the points of view, the actions, emanating from a human core wobble and bob, as will the self presumed to be their center. Divergences, undulations, together with the variability at their hub, do not drown the corporeal among which we live but witness its complexities, as well as those in the invisible, which underprops the seen. Woolf's imaging that complexity thus fights against the "daily world" which simplifies it and, for viewing readers, may elicit the "desire" to prefer nurturing to endangerment. Yet the inclination to nurture obliges us to acknowledge what we have not seen before.

In what follows, I claim that Woolf, in *The Waves*, will harmonize her notion of the image with Cézanne's representative discipline as exemplified by his *Pommes*; that the latter, founded on a looking at objects from multiple perspectives, models the ways in which the thing divined, in company with its diviner, must be of a multitude proportionate to the viewpoints from which seer and the seen are derivable, their untold number rendering both beyond calculation in that the reckoned will surpass our reckonings, notwithstanding their multitudinousness. I imply, with Cézanne, that person and thing border on each other, that we can learn to see this bordering-on, this being together-with, and that any image which promotes such an education will be as manifold as those who gaze upon it. Moreover, because training ourselves to envision the multiplex occurs in a "society" which tends to equate its members with their putative positions, that training will, while it disfavors rigid positionality, expose how the intricacy of our circumstances can function as the means by which we see them. When I say that by adhering to the difficulties native to the intricate, we do not abandon the world, but commit ourselves to the vigil of being jointed to it, I concede that, for Cézanne, seeing demands such a vigil and that my reading of him conflicts with the Roger Fry of "The Double Nature of Painting" (1933), published in Christopher Reed's *A Roger Fry Reader* (1996).

There, Fry paraphrases the famous analogy from *Ars Poetica*: "*ut pictura poesis erit*—painting must be like poetry, said Horace" (382), only to ruminate over his belief "that there do exist paintings in which the literary element [primarily associative] and the plastic element [architectural, volumetric] enter into a very intimate combination . . . a sort of chemical combination," offering Cézanne as one exemplar of a visuality produced by the jointing together of two artistic procedures (388). I agree with that assertion; I dispute Fry's inference from it. For, discussing *Still Life with a Basket* (1890–1894), observing that "no one . . . would feel like eating his apples," since "they function only as volumes receiving the light in a particular way, becoming the occasion for particular plastic harmonies," Fry extrapolates that "Cézanne removes these objects from our world; they are transposed into a purely spiritual world in which by means of their harmonies and contrasts they achieve a visual symphony endowed with a deep and inexpressible eloquence" (388). But to associate need not be to associate-away-with, to spiritualize matter out of existence. Rather, Cézanne, like the Woolf who contemplates him, shows us that our personhoods ought not to be rooted to a singular looking, that the multiplicities of our standpoints are answered by those at play in any object begot by processes visible and invisible. The multilateral image, a mobile intermixture of eye, object, space, will guide us towards seeing multilaterally, towards rethinking what our actions effect: to do so, that image requires merely our allowance of being guided. These "incident[s]," it appears to me, occur in a world whose sustenance depends on them: to remove them from that world is precisely not to see them.

I turn now to material from Cézanne's letters—five from 1904, the last from 1905—all written to Émile Bernard. Painters and, by extension, those of us who "desire" to testify to the integrity of the visible, should treat "la nature par le cylindre, la sphère, le cône," their ensemble put into perspective so that each side of an object is directed towards a central point; nevertheless, since nature, "pour nous," is more depth than surface, we need to introduce into "nos vibrations de lumière," represented by the reds and yellows, a sufficient sum of blueness "pour faire sentir l'air" (300). For the real and immense study to be undertaken is "la diversité du tableau de la nature" (302), one which records how we see by building up articles of transport, of communication, the cylinder, the sphere, the cone in contact with the ways in which we feel the air our eyes cannot give us, the image aiming at "un enseignement" (302), at the education of painter and viewer, both of whom inhabit a world where seeing ripely, by means of depth, is never automatic. But, in order to progress, the eye "s'éduque à son contact"; it becomes "concentrique," shares a center with what it discovers through the force of looking and working: "dans une orange, une pomme, une boule, une tête," there is a culminating point, and that point is always—despite the tremendous effect of light and shade, of color sensations—the closest to our eye, though the edges of objects flee towards "un centre placé à notre horizon" (304–305). The eye's educative progression thus hangs on our ability to relate the close, crowning points of things with the manner in which their joints seem to depart for a centrality distant from persons and non-persons, the picture a registry of, a carrying of, the tensions between the near and the far away. If, however, "une sensation optique" is produced in our visual organs, which allows us to classify the planes represented by color sensations as light, "la lumière n'existe donc pas pour le peintre"; non-existent as an object, light is the process that grazes over, that pulsates on, what it is not, including our depictions of it (308). And here Cézanne deepens his theme:

> Or, la these à developer est—quel que soit notre temperament ou forme de puissance en présence de la nature—de donner l'image de ce que nous voyons, en oubliant tout ce qui apparut avant nous. Ce qui, je crois, doit permettre à l'artiste de donner toute sa personnalité grande ou petite.
>
> Or, vieux, soixante-dix ans environ, les sensations colorants qui donnent la lumière sont chez moi cause d'abstractions qui ne me permettent pas de couvrir ma toile, ni de poursuivre la délimitation des objets quand les points de contact sont tenus, délicats; d'où il resort que mon image ou tableau est incomplète. (314–315)

That double use of the verb "to permit" chimes with the strenuousness which all six passages articulate, with the effort to forget everything that has appeared before us, to dismiss the sense that our junction with materiality must already be ordained by social standing, by inclination, by familial origins: to disregard these is to set out on seeing, to be permitted to give the personality beneath them to those things which border it. Yet we can overlook only what we have recognized with sufficient clarity, and to give is to remember our obligation to give again. The always unrounded off, the never being finished—by submitting that his perceptions of color, actuated by light, permit him neither to delimit the points at which objects incline towards each other nor to traverse the entirety of his canvas, Cézanne exhibits the ethical choice which underlies this abstracting from the real, this drawing away from delicacies too frangible for the brush, so that the incomplete gestures in the direction of the unrepresented, what will not be pictured implied, but not captured by, its image. If that is a kind of saving, we will find it, too, in the *Pommes*, which Woolf wonders at in her diary, its seven apples seeming to tilt down into the space beyond the frame, each sloping in the vicinity of that central spot shaped by the ways in which seven roundnesses nearly meet at their bottoms, the totality seen from distinguishable angles, the stems truncated, darkened, as though they were a new category of eye. A shadow thickens from middle ground to foreground; bits of canvas, unbrushed, glimmer out an almost-light in contrast with its extension. And patterned strokes, arriving from all directions, fall on curves of fruit, on the surface below them whose end the painting fails to surrender to us, one form of making not eliminating another, spiritualizing another, but contiguous to what continues, unstopped, outside its picture.

By giving us a painting which gesticulates towards its own fabrication, Cézanne directs our understanding that to dedicate ourselves to the manifold picture of nature is to realize all that the long look imparts: how and what we see will always be in friction; altering the angle of our outlook on the thing we hope to discern cannot, while it reformulates that friction, expunge it; though we transpose our exposure to the frictional according to our capacity for gaining more than one perspective on an object, labored sight will remain undone. Thus, because sightedness never operates by fiat, because the fullness of the seen never capitulates to our injunctions concerning it, we should comprehend that, for us, seeing must be mediate; it connects as it intervenes, granted that the human eye attends to the burden of its charge not to usurp, not to dematerialize the nature it undertakes to envision and so to represent. Such incompleteness becomes, Cézanne's brush tells us, the testimony of the look that probes but does not eat, that resists an emplacement at the center of space, as Weil instructs, in order to "maintain" a focal distance worth any maintenance we can vouch for. We will ascertain these possibilities, however, to the extent that we reject collapsing the painted and the painting, the seen and those eye-movements whose concentration conduces to sight. On behalf of the intransitivity I am detailing, as one of its many instances, Woolf—in *The Waves*—contributes this:

> Some petals had fallen in the garden. They lay shell-shaped on the earth. The dead leaf no longer stood upon its edge, but had been blown, now running, now pausing, against some stalk. Through all the flowers the same wave of light passed in a sudden flaunt and flash as if a fin cut the green glass of a lake. Now and again some level and masterly blast blew the multitudinous leaves up and down and then, as the wind flagged, each blade regained its identity. The flowers, burning their discs in the sun, flung aside the sunlight as the wind tossed them, and then some heads too heavy to rise again drooped slightly.
>
> The afternoon sun warmed the fields, poured blue into the shadows and reddened the corn. A deep varnish

> was laid like a lacquer over the fields. A cart, a horse, a flock of rooks—whatever moved in it was rolled in gold. If a cow moved a leg it stirred ripples of red gold, and its horns seemed lined with light. Sprays of flaxen-haired corn lay on the hedges, brushed from the shaggy carts that came up from the meadows short-legged and primeval looking. The round-headed clouds dwindled as they bowled along, but kept every atom of their rotundity. Now, as they passed, they caught a whole village in the fling of their net and, passing, let it fly free again. Far away on the horizon, among the million grains of blue grey dust, burnt one pane, or stood the single line of one steeple or tree.
>
> The red curtains and the white blinds blew in and out, flapping against the edge of the window, and the light which entered by flaps and breadths unequally had in it some brown tinge, and some abandonment as it blew through the blowing curtains in gusts. Here it browned a cabinet, there reddened a chair, here it made the window waver in the side of the green jar.
>
> All for a moment wavered and bent in uncertainty and ambiguity, as if a great moth sailing through the room had shadowed the immense solidity of chairs and tables with floating wings. (182–183)

We have hovered over her diary entries in which Woolf documents the novel's incitement; we have found how that incitement haunts its experiencer in the image of a woman enduring some flower's "fall," endurance and descent in relation as are the woman and the man who, participants in "a new kind of play," may people an amalgamation of genres which admits their listening to the "night" that "speaks," to a speaking other than the utterances we are taught, by habit, to recognize. If images haunt their receivers, if Woolf's reception of them induces her to craft pictures of our earthly home, that home seems haunted by something which defamiliarizes what we thought we knew, its ghostliness leading us to observe again. And we should not be surprised, turning to the novel, that this pairing of the human and the non-human—the extra or the supra-human—means that moths yield to waves, seeing that the latter represent our difference from the origin whose cradling we forgot long ago, due to a remoteness which Woolf renders in the paradox of its being close by us. We should not be surprised to discover that the novel's twofold sequential pattern, repeated in full on nine occasions, comprises seascapes, landscapes which appear to enunciate their compositions for us, coupled with six voices notated by a recorder who remains unknown, as does the Percival around whom those voices revolve, the gift of speech unawarded to, or unwanted by, him. Woolf thus indicates that her picturing activity here centers on the need that we should see the profundity of what we do and do not readily acknowledge, what we omit, what we elide through omitting. Repairing her innumeracy with regard to Cézanne's seven, not six, apples, she shows that to dismiss the indicators of her narrator's moving presence is an analogue of self-forgetting, that we forget ourselves when we too swiftly accept the certainty of our own presences, hence disregarding how we bear on the seen. She shows us the imperative that we should remember.

If I am describing a "radial" envisioning, at its core lies not one thing but multiplicities of viewpoints, the person presumed to see burgeoning, multiplying, amplifying, neither doomed to one perspective nor disconnected from the aged sea and land, their rhythms discerned as a kind of touching-on. In this case, verging-upon entails our acknowledgement of, our responsibility to, that touching. The above passage exhibits, like Cézanne's *Pommes*, the many varieties of the verge: since the painting consists in its maker's eye and body viewing their subjects from multiple angles, it becomes a dialogue between still life and the portrayal of a self capable of moving, a motility Woolf simulates as she gives us a landscape which the narrator's eyes approach myopically, in paragraph one, though the ensuing materials evince a self adept at seeing in a plurality of ways. We follow those eyes as they appear to leap into the sky, to gaze down on corn and lacquered fields, stay with them while they descend, spying "a whole village" in a "net" of clouds. But we ought to pause, as they do, over the "or," which the narrator aims at the "horizon," as though its distances could not be matched; we ought to note the eyes implicated in words retelling how, far away, "a pane" burns "or . . . one steeple or one tree" rises; we ought to remember that words shape and are shaped by those who come to them, that a perspective supposes a seer, however plural, and never—like a god—disembodied. We should attend to those eyes passing through "the window," apprehending the way in which "the light" and air, combined, seem to cause a window's frame to "waver" in the curving "side of the green jar." And we need to register our probable discomfort at these pictures of our own equivocality, of Woolf's crafting skill: discomfort tells us that we waken while regarding them.

Above all, by means of remarking that "great moth" imaged as "sailing through the room" under the logic of "as if," we may remember the "uncertainty" of our presences, along with the gifts which the indeterminate bestows on us, on things, since any "ambiguity" can be reshaped, reproportioned—remade. From the concept of remaking, we might, just possibly, learn the human duty to rescue what "we call the world" from our destruction of it. Should that knowledge materialize through self-interest, I hope only that moths, that waves, that pluralities of things, survive the time needed for us to comply with listening to it, with heeding what Jonas's essay, "Technology and Responsibility: Reflections on the New Tasks of Ethics," announces in 1972 as "the critical vulnerability of nature to man's technological intervention—unsuspected before it began to show itself in damage already done" (9). Yet, so far as our desires presuppose a visuality that must be there, absolutely, a "Gaia" meant for the taking, the necessity of reparation will, for us, never stop:

> This discovery, whose shock led to the concept and nascent science of ecology, alters the very concept of ourselves as a causal agency in the larger scheme of things. It brings to light, through the effects, that the nature of human action has *de facto* changed, and that an object of an entirely new order—no less than the whole biosphere of the planet—has been added to what we must be responsible for because of our power over it. (9)

While the texts we have lingered over may encourage our aptitude for meditating on the human and the non-human, such encouragement occurs by virtue of the "living system" that predicates their interdependence. Our responsibility for the character of how we touch-on, how we verge-on, that interdependence remains a lesson meriting all the dedication we can bear to concentrate on the task of learning it.

Afterword: Rethinking Transcendence

Faire l'inventaire ou la critique de notre civilisation, qu'est-ce
à dire? Chercher à tirer au clair d'une manière precise le piège
qui a fait de l'homme l'esclave de ses propres creations.
[To make an inventory or a critique of our civilization, what
does that mean? It means trying to clarify in a precise manner
the trap that has made man the slave of his own creations.]
—Simone Weil: *Cahiers* (1933–1934), 71.

We can fight with the mind.
—Virginia Woolf:
"Thoughts on Peace in an Air Raid" (1940), 244.

You know, we never talked about responsibility at the
university, not in my time. We never discussed ethics.
We were never taught value-thinking. . . . We were taught
in our closed rooms that we were doing pure science, in
the pursuit of pure truth—the noble pursuit of pure truth.
—Floyd Byars and Fritjof Capra: *Mindwalk* (1990).

What is the true value of knowledge?
That it makes our ignorance more precise.
—Anne Michaels: *Fugitive Pieces* (1996), 210.

The illusion that one has understood the past feeds the
further illusion that one can predict and control the future.
—Daniel Kahneman:
Thinking, Fast and Slow (2011), 204–205.

For some time now, close to the semester's end, I have turned with my students from laboring at the critical analysis of written texts on behalf of crafting exploratory essays to watching Keith Jarrett play movement 2d of his *Tokyo Solo* (2006), filmed live at Metropolitan Festival Hall, in 2002. There is, however, a back story to that turn: during my sixteen years in the New York University essay-driven classroom, I have used varieties of music in terms of genre, instrumentation, and time-period as a means of fostering students' abilities to critique the patterns among which humans and non-humans live. I appreciate, of course, that we belong to a culture generally disinterested in, and disinclined to value, musical education; that, because of this disinterest, we are led to experience music according to whim, frivolous to the extent that personal preferences often remain ignorant of the analytical rigor in the sound they presume to judge, so that sound itself is doomed to an inconsequence ordained, already, by culture's educational vision. And I appreciate that the human and the non-human alike exist on account of patterning acts which order what both categories know as the world.

Sharing my multiple appreciations with students, I advise them that we ought to take music as one instance of the pattern-making whereby we set about the activity of living, adding that what any culture deems unworthy of its schooling-time need not be called simply trivial. Yet my students counter that music is so "abstract" for them that it seems unreal. My reply: though the Latinity of "abstraction" may mean to draw off or away from, these prepositions point to the world of things on whose authority our conceptual acts stimulate our seeming to lift off, away from that world, abstraction and reality thus becoming nouns related not by contradiction—but by their necessary coordination. I understand, nevertheless, that my students' sense of musical unreality has been prepared for by their lack of training; I know that the latter shapes their manners of seeing, hearing, engaging. But we, in or outside the university, are here to enlarge that capacity for engagement.

I offer students musical texts, in the hope of enhanced engagement, beginning with our first day together, selecting pieces ranging from a twelfth-century ode by Hildegard von Bingen, praising Mary as a "door . . . that has been opened," to the incantatory voice of Salif Keita, from Mali; to a section of John Adams's *El Niño* (2000); to "Sun in My Mouth" (2001), by Björk, whose swooping, upturned vocal line never quite summons the finality of cadencing, its female voice in a rhapsody of longing to "leap into the ripe air, alive / with closed eyes." All these texts share and manifest a devotion to the difficult. They teach us that our contact with the troublesome thing arises from exposure to a form capable of affecting us, in company with our behaviors, with the concept that human conduct can be rethought, re-patterned, provided that we linger in the meditation which any irksome text enjoins on its participants, and resist seeing interpretation as being in the business of expunging from our attention those charges fixed to it.

At the service of imagination and what it can produce, I ask students to listen; to watch (if the text's format is audio-visual); to write, simultaneously, in response to the prompts I have outlined for them. I oblige them to describe, in writing, what they hear, see, along with any tensions in the works themselves, any textual elements which appear not to coalesce with their intuition of the wholeness at which each individual piece aims. Such tensions indicate that the text must be different from our expectations regarding it, that the shaped thing is not our duplicate. Unfamiliarity with musical form supports, ironically, the perceiver's (possible) avoidance of confusing what she thinks she knows with the sounds she struggles to draw close to. And this lack of duplication, this making way for the differential, facilitates that mutual speaking by which any dialogue proceeds.

Finally, I request that students qualify the character and performance of the patterned sounds themselves, that they detail how these aural shapes affect them, going on to say that they must identify what specific components of the music impede their qualifications, if that impasse should occur, as the effort to enumerate what obstructs us does not destroy relationship but affirms our re-commitment to its urgencies. When they balk at these multiple promptings, when students express amazement at their difficulties, I recall how they were required to negotiate concurrent phenomena on their way to class, for example, how they undertake—all the time—coincident tasks in their mathematics lectures, most likely without complaint. But the entitlement to complain issues from the appeal to partiality to which music and the other arts have been consigned by culture: it marks their apparent frivolity, even if all arts demand from their partakers the perceptual, cognitive, imaginative skills by which any person continues to survive.

While the complaints diminish after months of such work, the arduousness to which students must entrust themselves does not, though their experience of it improves over time. Yet, nearing the term's end, over-worked, under-slept, students tell me that, at first hearing/watching Jarrett's performance, they see only an old man in oval glasses, hunched over a piano, sometimes almost moaning, his hands passing over the keys in an umbrella of light that makes the auditorium a sort of cave. And they insist: How can that hunching figure teach me anything; what will I gain from listening to him? These are good questions; they require additional context concerning Jarrett and his career; they demand another envisioned listening.

Much of the above suggests, as does Liv Ullmann's character in *Mindwalk*, that students and teacher may find themselves in "closed rooms," but they bring the outside in with them on their clothing, their books, in the air they breathe, the thoughts they resort to when faced with class-materials that disallow ready-made thinking. Because outside and in always intercommunicate, nothing "pure" ever happens here, in the sense of remaining unadulterated, unmixed, the "truth" to which university coursework aspires being at once initiated by, modified in relation to, redirected at, the world on the other side of our classrooms' walls. To proceed ethically, in recognition of such reciprocities, would necessitate our remembrance that what occurs within those walls influences the human management of a world whose physics of friction and balance permits them to go on standing. So, after learning that Jarrett began his career as a pianist at the age of six; that he toured and played with Miles Davis for a number of years; that he never forgot his grounding in classical vocabularies, which extends his ability to silhouette jazz melodies against the harmony that supports them; that his preparations for each solo, improvised concert last a year in which he flexes and nuances the muscular operations of hands, forearms, shoulders, only to "sit at a piano, bring[ing] no material" with him, "clear[ing] his mind completely of musical ideas," as he tells us in the liner notes to his recent release, *Testament* (2009), all the while acknowledging that "utmost chemical importance" of the audience, since the quality of its members' presence can catalyze, "change the potential and shape of the music" more easily "than the difference of pianos or hall sound," when on tour—my students see, now, more than an old man bent over the keys.

They listen to Jarrett building a nine minutes' long near-waltz, the propulsion of its tempo tempered with the ruminative cast of a melody that rises and falls, beginning in the upper voice, moving to middle and lower registers, cradled by the complex harmonies intersecting it. They hear Jarrett start to hum, halfway through, watch him stand close to full height, look at how his right hand, tracing the melody's ascent, leans its index finger hard on a sustained note, bearing down on the key as if fingering a cello string in order to elongate the croon of its vibratory power. They will sense the crux of this auditory-visual moment, and a few will write, following their second experience of it: it seems that Jarrett's moaning hum is two or so bars in advance of his present placement in the music, a future time-scale intervening in the current instant, both modulated by the past, by Jarrett's listening to the sonic form he began assembling there. Those few students who pinpoint this gathering together of what is, according to received wisdom, separate, disjoined, will assist their colleagues in approaching the claim that a mind in concentrated action allows us to intuit that what divides may, from another perspective, connect, that player and the played modify each other, as do instrumentalist and audience, as do the intervals of duration in which each body exists, all interlinked by the air between them.

Such ideas have many antecedents, among the oldest being those pictured for us in Werner Herzog's film, *Cave of Forgotten Dreams* (2010). Dominique Baffier, the curator of Chauvet Cave, is standing alongside the *Panel of the Horses*, whose images—like everything humanly constructed in the cave itself—originated 32,000 years ago. She asks us to observe the animals' procession across the undulating curves of the limestone wall, to grasp how the cow, the bison, two female lions, rhinoceroses, horses, and aurochs progress in a company of movements thirty feet wide, twenty feet high, from right to left, to mark the ways in which each positive, charcoal outline is impressed on, seems to spring up from, the textured vivacity of the stone, so that drawing, for our ancestors, entailed the ability to remark and to heed those animals recumbent in the wall, to listen for them as they vaulted out under the beseeching, human hand. Pointing to the four horses, arrayed in ascending perspective just above two rhinoceroses, who bunt and jolt their horns in patterned play, Baffier urges us to notice the intermeshing of sound and image:

the lips of each horse are parted; each whinnies as the four heads fan out together, up the wall, the whole a polyrhythmic overlay of horse-neigh, horn-jab, and clack. The kinship represented between hearing and seeing, among animals whose assembly is unusual even in art of the Upper Paleolithic period, takes me to Jean Clottes's speculations, in *The Evolution of Rationality* (2006), that

> to venture deep underground into the complete dark in order to make paintings and engravings is an exceptional occurrence in human history. Those actions cannot be ascribed to any recognizable practical necessity. If such a tradition persisted for so long (more than 20,000 years), it must have entailed the powerful constraints of beliefs passed on from one generation to the next. (142)

If, with Clottes, we "consider" the "spirituality" evoked here "as an awakening of a consciousness that goes beyond day-to-day contingencies, beyond 'simple' adaptation to material necessities in order to get food, to reproduce, and to survive"; if we discern that, through this "spirituality," our ancestors "began to question the world around them, and in it they tried to find a reality different from the one perceived by their senses, the one to which—like other animals—they always reacted instinctively" (133), it nevertheless remains the case that the labored care imaged in the cave exhibits how, for the spirit to climb above, to transcend, materiality, it must hearken to and draw upon the vigor in the stone wall that it has gone to such lengths to meet. Transcendence and immanence thus become co-equals with respect to value: to mount high, the enfleshed spirit must go down, into the earth, and these valued co-equalities, of sound/image, spirit/matter, human/animal, should reflect on the selfhoods committed to their visual enactment.

There is a moment in Herzog's film in which Clottes muses on how our painterly forerunners may have understood what we would term the self. Outside, the limestone cliff atop Chauvet Cave high above his head, Clottes theorizes that the pictures in the earth represent their makers' envisioning the "fluidity and permeability" of human selves, seeing that those panels depicting long trains of associated animals, along with the occasional image of a lone bear, an owl, emanate from charcoal-carrying hands palpating stone in order to elicit the life anchored there, the distinctions between maker and made, between one species and another, liquefied by the forces flooding all together. This emphasis on the out-thrust, on what overspreads our now customary boundaries, remains especially pointed in the cave's end-chamber. On a hanging rock perpendicular to the *Lion Panel*, we discover that the single representation of our kind is a hybrid figure, half bison for the upper part, half human for the lower, where two legs are coupled by an inverted, pubic triangle, the vulva well-indicated. Its hybridity appears to say: here, the human is never in isolation; it does not transcend the species among which it lives but shares in, partakes of, their powers. Yet Herzog's postscript to his film shows us, behind where Clottes stands, just twenty miles away, that the managers of a nuclear plant have constructed a habitat for alligators, their albinism caused by the run-off of contaminated waters, which, embanked, have been made their home. The camera's final shot reveals a pair of them, their white, globulous eyes, the pitted opalescence of their skin. Abiding in toxic pools, they swim, isolated, possessed, patterned by our conceptions of them, forced to live precisely where we have put them, in liquid poisoned by an invention of our own devising.

Herzog's parting image ought to school us in the dangers of this shift over millennia, this veering from the liquidity of the self-in-the-cave and its collaborative qualities to our contemporary species (often) recognizing the human according to its capacity for possession, mistaking itself on account of being ceaselessly in the role of a claimant with respect to other entities: if many of our kind operate from the understanding that elements of nature are ours for the having, such thought—however misguided—serves to dictate that we define ourselves on the basis of the power to manipulate what we appear to own. We encounter the peril of that view, for example, in John Searle's discussion of *Self Comes to Mind: Constructing the Conscious Brain* (2011), by Antonio Damasio, in which Searle asserts that "we need to explain how our conscious states are experienced, not just as a sequence of isolated qualitative subjective events, but as 'my experiences'" (52), since "whenever I have a conscious experience I always experience it as *mine*" (50). The force of that possessive pronoun spreads over "experiences" themselves and includes the creatures who perform inside them, meaning that the self equals the compulsion to stake off ownership, to usurp what must be connectible to it, the whole ensemble of concepts transcendent with regard to anything that might impeach its accuracy or rectitude, elevated, eternally, like the soul that many believe outlasts the fragilities of flesh, which fails us—because it dies.

I do not ask for a sentimental return to nesting in the caves of our precursors. I ask that more of us remember the potency of questioning what we have been taught or come to value, recall the verity that no creature is precisely identical with the conceptions professed to order it. Patterns and pattern-makers change, so long as the latter combat becoming the slaves of their own "creations," enslaving others in that unchallenged process.

Any artwork supporting this resistance can be called worthy: it causes us to think again, to reconsider what merits the time necessary for rethinking. And that, our texts counsel us, is a lesson ripe, always, for the relearning.

These ideas won't save the alligators on the other side of Chauvet Cave or repair their debilitation from being forced to swim in pools that we have made their poisoned haven. But our textual thinking may rescue their future species-members from that enslavement, if greater numbers of us keep to the labor of critiquing the conceptual powers whereby we order the world that will never be solely ours. By virtue of our keeping to that requirement, all—human and non-human alike—can only benefit, and that must be a value worth every imaginable discomfiture.

Acknowledgments

Much of this book has appeared, in altered form, in the following journals: *Environmental Philosophy*; *Women and Performance*; the *Journal of Speculative Philosophy*; *State of Nature Magazine*; *Foilsiú: An Interdisciplinary Journal of Irish Studies*; *Fringe Magazine*; *Able Muse: A Review of Poetry, Prose, and Art*, and *Fogged Clarity: An Arts Review*. I thank the editors of these journals, heartily.

I could not have written this book without the support of New York University's Expository Writing Program, where I have taught since 1996 as part of a community of teachers whose thinking-time nourishes everything I do. To the directors of that program, I owe many very real thanks, especially to Darlene Forrest and, above all, to Pat Hoy—the finest teacher and writer I have ever known, one whose mind sings on and off the page.

Among my colleagues in the academy, as well as my friends outside it, I thank: Gabrielle Starr, NYU's College of Arts and Science Dean; Matthew Santirocco; Denis Donoghue, whose prose remains a model of what words can do; John Bavicchi of the Berklee College of Music; at Barnard College, Peter G. Platt; and, during my time at Columbia University, Victoria Silver, who now teaches at UC Irvine; David R. Sherman of Brandeis University; Tom Lecky; and, with joy, Edward Ross.

I dedicate this book to my brother, Michael, who died too young of a rare cancer and who had the stoutest heart I know. He had the gift of making more alive everything and everyone he touched. That aliveness continues in the hearts of his wife, Lorraine , and of his daughters, Julia and Stephanie.

For their boundless support, I thank my father, Stephen, who died in 2003; my mother, Patricia, who continues to honor life at the age of 91; and my sister, Leslie, who taught me all that music can offer to a world very much in need of that offering. And I thank my partner, Neil Merrick, who helps me to remember the wonders of mutual giving and guardianship: his loving presence shimmers behind every word.

Bibliography

Adorno, Theodor W. *Beethoven*. Ed. Rolf Tiedemann. Trans. Edmund Jephcott. Stanford: Stanford UP, 1998.

———. *The Philosophy of Modern Music*. Trans. Anne G. Mitchell and Wesley V. Blomster. NY: Continuum, 1973.

Aristotle. *The Art of Rhetoric*. Trans. Hugh Lawson-Tancred. NY: Penguin, 1991.

Attridge, Derek. *Peculiar Language*. NY: Cornell UP, 1988.

Banathy, Bela H. *Designing Social Systems in a Changing World*. NY: Plenum Press, 1991.

———. *The Guided Evolution of Society*. NY: Plenum Publishers, 2000.

Banfield, Ann. *The Phantom Table*. Cambridge: Cambridge UP, 2000.

Beauvoir, Simone de. *Le deuxième sexe*. 2 vols. Paris: Gallimard, 1949.

Beethoven, Ludwig van. *Late String Quartets and the Grosse Fuge*. NY: Dover, 1998.

———. *The Man and the Artist, As Revealed in His Own Words*. Ed. And Trans. By Henry Edward Krehbiel. NY: Dover, 1964.

———. Symphonies No. 6, 7, and 8. Cond. Karl Böhm. Vienna Phil. Orch. Deutsche Grammophon, 437 928–2, 1993.

Bell, Quentin. "A Cézanne in the Hedge." *A Cézanne in the Hedge and Other Memories of Charleston and Bloomsbury*. Ed. Hugh Lee. Chicago: U. of Chicago P., 1992.

———. *Virginia Woolf*. NY: Harcourt Brace, 1972.

Bertalanffy, Ludwig von. *General Systems Theory*. NY: G. Braziller, 1968.

Bingen, Hildegard von. "*Nunc aperuit nobis.*" *Canticles of Ecstasy*. Performed by Sequentia. Deutsche Harmonia Mundi CD, 05472 773202, 1994.

Björk. "Sun in My Mouth." *Vespertine*. Elektra Entertainment Group CD, 75596 26532, 2001.

Blackmur, R. P. *Language As Gesture*. NY: Harcourt, Brace, and Co., 1952.

Burnyeat, M. F. "Enthymeme: Aristotle on the Rationality of Rhetoric." *Essays on Aristotle's Rhetoric*. Ed. Amelie Rorty. Berkeley: U. of Cal. P., 1996.

Cave of Forgotten Dreams. Dir. by Werner Herzog. Sundance Selects Films, 2010.

Cézanne, Paul. *Correspondance*. Ed. John Rewald. Paris: Bernard Grasset, 1978.

———. *Pommes*. The Provost and Fellows of King's College. The Keynes Coll., Cambridge.

———. *Still Life with Basket of Apples*. The Art Institute of Chicago.

Churchland, Paul M. and Patricia S. *On the Contrary*. Cambridge, MA: MIT P., 1998.

Cicero. *Cicero on Oratory and Orators*. Ed. and Trans. J. S. Watson. Chicago: Southern Illinois UP, 1970.

Clottes, Jean. "Spirituality and Religion in Paleolithic Times." *The Evolution of Rationality*. Ed. F. LeRon Shults. Grand Rapids, Michigan: William B. Eerdmans Pub. Co., 2006.

Conrad, Joseph. *Conrad's Prefaces to His Works*. 1937. Freeport, NY: Books for Libraries P., 1971.

Craig, Edward Gordon. *On the Art of the Theatre*. NY: Theatre Arts Books, 1911.

Dalgarno, Emily. *Virginia Woolf and the Visible World*. Cambridge: Cambridge UP, 2001.

Daly, Ann. *Done into Dance*. Bloomington: Indiana UP, 1995.

Davie, Donald. *Articulate Energy*. London: Routledge, 1955.

Deleuze, Gilles, and Felix Guattari. *A Thousand Plateaus*. London: Athlone P, 1987.

Donoghue, Denis. *Walter Pater*. NY: Knopf, 1995.

———. *Who Says What and the Question of Voice*. Buckinghamshire: Colin Smythe, 1992.

Duncan, Isadora. *Isadora Speaks*. Ed. Franklin Rosemont. SF: City Lights, 1981.

Eliot, T. S. "*Ulysses*, Order, and Myth." *Selected Prose of T. S. Eliot*. Ed. Frank Kermode. NY: Harcourt, Brace, and Co., 1975.

Ellmann, Richard. *Oscar Wilde*. NY: Vintage-Random House, 1988.

Engelmann, Paul. *Letters from Ludwig Wittgenstein, with a Memoir*. Trans. L. Furtmüller. Ed. B. F. Guiness. Oxford: Basil Blackwell, 1967.

Flannery, Tim. *The Weather Makers*. NY: Grove Press, 2005.

Forster, E. M. "The Eternal Moment." *The Collected Tales of E. M. Forster*. NY: Knopf, 1948.

———. "Virginia Woolf." *Two Cheers for Democracy*. NY: Harcourt Brace, 1966.

Fry, Roger. *A Roger Fry Reader*. Ed. Christopher Reed. Chicago: U. of Chicago P, 1996.

———. *The Letters of Roger Fry*. 2 vols. Ed. Denys Sutton. London: Chatto & Windus, 1972.

Garafola, Lynn. *Diaghilev's Ballets Russes*. NY: Oxford UP, 1989.

Gautier, Théophile. Préface. *Mademoiselle de Maupin*. In Gautier. *Oeuvres*. Ed. Paolo Tortonese. Paris: Robert Laffont, 1995.

Genthe, Arnold. *Duncan Portrait*. Museum of the City of New York. Illus. 2–3 in *Done into Dance*. By Ann Daly. Bloomington: Indiana UP, 1995.

Gillespie, Diane F., ed. *The Multiple Muses of Virginia Woolf*. Columbia: U. of Missouri Press, 1993.

Hardy, Thomas. *The Complete Poetical Works of Thomas Hardy*. Ed. Samuel Hynes. NY: Oxford UP, 1982–1985.

Hillman, James. *A Terrible Love of War*. NY: Penguin Press, 2004.

Hyde, H. Montgomery. *The Trials of Oscar Wilde*. NY: Dover, 1962.

Jarrett, Keith. Liner notes. *Radiance*. ECM, 1960/61 B0004314-02, 2005.

———. Liner notes. *Testament*. ECM Records CD, 2130–32, 2009.

Jonas, Hans. *The Phenomenon of Life: Toward a Philosophical Biology*. 1966. Chicago: Northwestern UP, 2001.

———. "Seventeenth Century and After: The Meaning of the Scientific and Technological Revolution." In *Philosophical Essays: From Ancient Creed to Technological Man*. 45–80. Englewood Cliffs, NJ: Prentice-Hall, 1974.

———. "Technology and Responsibility: Reflections on the New Tasks of Ethics." In *Philosophical Essays: From Ancient Creed to Technological Man*. Englewood Cliffs, NJ: Prentice-Hall, 1974.

Joni Mitchell: Woman of Heart and Mind. Dir. Susan Lacy. Eagle Rock DVD, 2003.

Keith Jarrett: Tokyo Solo. Dir. by Kaname Kawachi. ECM DVD, 987 3186, 2006.

Kahneman, Daniel. *Thinking, Fast and Slow*. NY: Farrar, Straus and Giroux, 2011.

Kerferd, G. B. *The Sophistic Movement*. Cambridge: Cambridge UP, 1981.

Kermode, Frank. *Puzzles and Epiphanies*. NY: Chilmark Press, 1962.

———. *Romantic Image*. NY: Chilmark Press, 1957.

Kodicek, Ann, ed. *Diaghilev*. London: Barbican Art Gallery, 1996.

Kolbert, Elizabeth. *Field Notes from a Catastrophe*. NY: Bloomsbury, 2006.

Lacan, Jacques. *Les Complexes familiaux dans la formation de l'individu*. Paris: Navarin, 1984.

Lanham, Richard A. *A Handlist of Rhetorical Terms*. Berkeley: U. of Cal. Press, 1991.

Lee, Hermione. *Virginia Woolf*. NY: Knopf, 1997.

Little, Judy. *The Experimental Self*. Carbondale: S. Illinois Press, 1996.

Lovelock, James. *Gaia*. Oxford: Oxford UP, 1979.

Macdonald, Nesta, ed. *Diaghilev Observed by Critics in England and the United States, 1911–1929*. NY: Dance Horizons, 1975.

McLuhan, Marshall. *The Gutenberg Galaxy*. Toronto: U. of Toronto Press, 1962.

Merleau-Ponty, Maurice. *Phénoménologie de la perception*. Paris: Gallimard, 1945.

———. *Le visible et l'invisible*. Paris: Gallimard, 1964.

———. *The Visible and the Invisible*. Trans. Alphonso Lingis. Chicago: Northwestern University Press, 1968.

Michaels, Anne. *Fugitive Pieces*. NY: Vintage International-Random House, 1998.

Miller, J. Hillis. "Mr. Carmichael and Lily Briscoe: The Rhythm of Creativity in *To the Lighthouse*." *Modernism Reconsidered*. Ed. Robert Kiely. Cambridge, MA: Harvard UP, 1983.

Mindwalk. Dir. by Bernt Amadeus Capra. Written by Floyd Byars and Fritjof Capra. Atlas Films, 1990.

Murdoch, Iris. *Existentialists and Mystics*. Ed. Peter Conradi. NY: Penguin, 1997.

———. *Metaphysics As a Guide to Morals*. NY: Penguin, 1992.

Murphy, James, ed. *A Short History of Writing Instruction*. Davis, CA: Hermagoras Press, 1990.

Nicolson, Marjorie Hope. *The Breaking of the Circle*. Evanston: Northwestern UP, 1960.

Nussbaum, Martha Craven. "Aristotle on Emotions and Rational Persuasion." *Essays on Aristotle's Rhetoric*. Ed. Amelie Rorty. Berkeley: U. of Cal. P, 1996.

Ong, Walter J. *Interfaces of the Word.* Ithaca: Cornell UP, 1977.

———. *Orality and Literacy.* London: Methuen, 1982.

———. *The Presence of the Word.* New Haven: Yale UP, 1967.

Panofsky, Erwin. *Meaning in the Visual Arts.* NY: Doubleday, 1955.

Pärt, Arvo. Jacket notes. *Alina.* ECM 1591, 1999.

Plato. *Cratylus, Parmenides, Greater Hippias, Lesser Hippias.* Loeb Classical Library. Ed. G. P. Goold. Trans. H. N. Fowler. London: Harvard UP, 1977.

———. *Ion. Early Socratic Dialogues.* Trans. Trevor J. Saunders. NY: Penguin, 1987.

———. *Phaedrus and Letters VII and VII.* Trans. Walter Hamilton. NY: Penguin, 1973.

———. *Philebus.* Trans. Robin Waterfield. NY: Penguin, 1982.

———. *Protagoras and Meno.* Trans. W. K. C. Guthrie. NY: Penguin, 1956.

———. *Republic.* Trans. Sir Desmond Lee. NY: Penguin, 1987.

Proust, Marcel. *Contre Sainte-Beuve, précédé de Pastiches et mélanges et suivi de Essais et articles.* Ed. Pierre Clarc avec Yves Sandre. Paris: Bibliothèque de la Pléiade, 1971.

Purcell, Henry. *Dido and Aeneas.* With Lorraine Hunt Lieberson. Cond. Nicholas McGegan. Libretto by Nahum Tate. Philharmonia Baroque Orch. Harmonia Mundi, HMU 907110, 1994.

Sackville-West, Vita and Harold Nicolson. *V & H: Vita and Harold.* Ed. Nigel Nicolson. London: Weidenfeld & Nicolson, 1992.

Searle, John. "The Mystery of Consciousness Continues." *The New York Review of Books.* June 9, 2011. Vol. LVIII, #10.

Sophocles. *Antigone. Sophocles I.* Trans. David Grene. Chicago: U. of Chicago P., 1991.

Stephen, Leslie. *History of English Thought in the Eighteenth Century.* Vol. 1. 3rd Edition. 1902. NY: Peter Smith, 1949.

———. *Hours in a Library*. Vol. 3. NY: G. P. Putnam's Sons, 1904.

Stevens, Wallace. *The Necessary Angel: Collected Poetry and Prose*. Ed. Frank Kermode and Joan Richardson. NY: Library of America, 1997.

Stock, Brian. *The Implications of Literacy*. Princeton: Princeton UP, 1983.

———. *Listening for the Text*. Philidelphia: U. of Penn. Press, 1996.

Stravinsky, Igor. *Les Noces*. Cond. James Wood. New London Chamber Choir. Hyperion, CDA66410, 1990.

———. *Poetics of Music in the Form of Six Lessons*. Trans. Arthur Knodell and Ingolf Dahl. Cambridge, MA: Harvard UP, 1970.

Symons, Arthur. *The Symbolist Movement in Literature*. London: Heinemann, 1899.

Theodora. Dir. Peter Sellars. By G. F. Handel. Glyndebourne Festival Opera. Cond. William Christie. Orch. of the Age of Enlightenment. Kultur DVD, D2099, 1996.

Torgovnick, Marianna. *The Visual Arts, Pictorialism, and the Novel*. Princeton: Princeton UP, 1985.

Twitchell, Beverly H. *Cézanne and Formalism in Bloomsbury*. Ann Arbor: UMI Research Press, 1987.

Weil, Simone. *Attente de Dieu*. Paris: La Colombe, 1957.

———. *Cahiers*. Paris: Plon, 1970.

———. *La connaissance surnaturelle*. Paris: Gallimard, 1950.

Wilde, Oscar. *De Profundis*. *The Complete Works of Oscar Wilde*. NY: Harper & Row, 1989.

———. *Oscar Wilde's Oxford Notebooks*. Ed. Philip E. Smith and Michael S. Helfand. NY: Oxford UP, 1989.

Wittgenstein, Ludwig. *The Blue and Brown Books*. NY: Harper & Row, 1960.

———. *Tractatus Logico-Philosophicus*. Trans. C. K. Ogden. London: Routledge & Kegan Paul, 1988.

Woolf, Leonard. *After the Deluge*. Vol. 1. London: Hogarth Press, 1953.

Woolf, Virginia. *The Common Reader*. NY: Harcourt Brace Jovanovich, 1953.

———. *The Diary of Virginia Woolf*. Vols. 1–3. Ed. Anne Olivier Bell. London: Penguin, 1977.

———. *The Diary of Virginia Woolf*. Vols. 4–5. Ed. Anne Olivier Bell. NY: Harcourt Brace Jovanovich, 1982.

———. *The Essays of Virginia Woolf*. 4 Vols. Ed. Andrew McNeillie. NY: HBJ, 1986 1988.

———. *The Letters of Virginia Woolf*. 6 Vols. Ed. Nigel Nicolson and Joanne Trautmann. NY: HBJ, 1975–1980.

———. "Memories of a Working Women's Guild." *The Captain's Death Bed*. NY: HBJ, 1978.

———. *The Moment and Other Essays*. NY: HBJ, 1948.

———. *Moments of Being*. Ed. Jeanne Schulkind. NY: Harcourt Brace, 1985.

———. *Roger Fry*. NY: HBJ, 1968.

———. *A Room of One's Own*. NY: HBJ, 1981.

———. *The Second Common Reader*. NY: HBJ, 1960.

———. "Sympathy." *The Complete Shorter Fiction of Virginia Woolf*. Ed. Susan Dick. NY: Harcourt Brace, 1989.

———. "Thoughts on Peace in an Air Raid." *The Death of the Moth and Other Essays*. Ed. Leonard Woolf. NY: Harcourt Brace Jovanovich, 1970.

———. *Three Guineas*. NY: HBJ, 1966.

———. *The Voyage Out*. London: Penguin, 1992.

———. "Walter Sickert." *Collected Essays*. Vol. 2. Ed. Leonard Woolf. NY: Harcourt, Brace & World, 1966.

———. *The Waves*. NY: HBJ, 1959.

Yeats, W. B. *The Collected Poems*. NY: Macmillan, 1933.

———. "Hodos Chameliontos." *The Yeats Reader: A Portable Compendium of Poetry, Drama, and Prose*. Ed. Richard

Finneran. NY: Scribner, 1997.
———. *On Baile's Strand. The Yeats Reader*. Ed. Richard Finneran. NY: Scribner, 1997.
———. *Selected Poems and Plays*. Ed. M. L Rosenthal. NY: Scribner, 1996.
Zwerdling, Alex. *Virginia Woolf and the Real World*. Berkeley: U. of Cal. Press, 1986.

Bruce Bromley is senior lecturer in expository writing at New York University, where he won the 2006 Golden Dozen Award for teaching excellence. Bromley earned his BA from Columbia University, and his MA, MPhil, and PhD from New York University. He has performed his music throughout Europe and the US; his essays, fiction, and poetry have appeared in such journals as *Environmental Philosophy* and the *Journal of Speculative Philosophy*, among many others.

SELECTED DALKEY ARCHIVE TITLES

JANICE GALLOWAY, *Foreign Parts.*
The Trick Is to Keep Breathing.
WILLIAM H. GASS, *Cartesian Sonata and Other Novellas.*
Finding a Form.
A Temple of Texts.
The Tunnel.
Willie Masters' Lonesome Wife.
GÉRARD GAVARRY, *Hoppla! 1 2 3.*
ETIENNE GILSON,
The Arts of the Beautiful.
Forms and Substances in the Arts.
C. S. GISCOMBE, *Giscome Road.*
Here.
DOUGLAS GLOVER, *Bad News of the Heart.*
WITOLD GOMBROWICZ,
A Kind of Testament.
PAULO EMÍLIO SALES GOMES, *P's Three Women.*
GEORGI GOSPODINOV, *Natural Novel.*
JUAN GOYTISOLO, *Count Julian.*
Juan the Landless.
Makbara.
Marks of Identity.
HENRY GREEN, *Back.*
Blindness.
Concluding.
Doting.
Nothing.
JACK GREEN, *Fire the Bastards!*
JIŘÍ GRUŠA, *The Questionnaire.*
MELA HARTWIG, *Am I a Redundant Human Being?*
JOHN HAWKES, *The Passion Artist.*
Whistlejacket.
ELIZABETH HEIGHWAY, ED., *Contemporary Georgian Fiction.*
ALEKSANDAR HEMON, ED.,
Best European Fiction.
AIDAN HIGGINS, *Balcony of Europe.*
Blind Man's Bluff
Bornholm Night-Ferry.
Flotsam and Jetsam.
Langrishe, Go Down.
Scenes from a Receding Past.
KEIZO HINO, *Isle of Dreams.*
KAZUSHI HOSAKA, *Plainsong.*
ALDOUS HUXLEY, *Antic Hay.*
Crome Yellow.
Point Counter Point.
Those Barren Leaves.
Time Must Have a Stop.
NAOYUKI II, *The Shadow of a Blue Cat.*
GERT JONKE, *The Distant Sound.*
Geometric Regional Novel.
Homage to Czerny.
The System of Vienna.
JACQUES JOUET, *Mountain R.*
Savage.
Upstaged.
MIEKO KANAI, *The Word Book.*
YORAM KANIUK, *Life on Sandpaper.*
HUGH KENNER, *Flaubert.*
Joyce and Beckett: The Stoic Comedians.
Joyce's Voices.
DANILO KIŠ, *The Attic.*
Garden, Ashes.
The Lute and the Scars
Psalm 44.
A Tomb for Boris Davidovich.
ANITA KONKKA, *A Fool's Paradise.*
GEORGE KONRÁD, *The City Builder.*
TADEUSZ KONWICKI, *A Minor Apocalypse.*
The Polish Complex.
MENIS KOUMANDAREAS, *Koula.*
ELAINE KRAF, *The Princess of 72nd Street.*
JIM KRUSOE, *Iceland.*
AYŞE KULIN, *Farewell: A Mansion in Occupied Istanbul.*
EMILIO LASCANO TEGUI, *On Elegance While Sleeping.*
ERIC LAURRENT, *Do Not Touch.*
VIOLETTE LEDUC, *La Bâtarde.*
EDOUARD LEVÉ, *Autoportrait.*
Suicide.
MARIO LEVI, *Istanbul Was a Fairy Tale.*
DEBORAH LEVY, *Billy and Girl.*
JOSÉ LEZAMA LIMA, *Paradiso.*
ROSA LIKSOM, *Dark Paradise.*
OSMAN LINS, *Avalovara.*
The Queen of the Prisons of Greece.
ALF MAC LOCHLAINN,
The Corpus in the Library.
Out of Focus.
RON LOEWINSOHN, *Magnetic Field(s).*
MINA LOY, *Stories and Essays of Mina Loy.*
D. KEITH MANO, *Take Five.*
MICHELINE AHARONIAN MARCOM,
The Mirror in the Well.
BEN MARCUS,
The Age of Wire and String.
WALLACE MARKFIELD,
Teitlebaum's Window.
To an Early Grave.
DAVID MARKSON, *Reader's Block.*
Wittgenstein's Mistress.
CAROLE MASO, *AVA.*
LADISLAV MATEJKA AND KRYSTYNA POMORSKA, EDS.,
Readings in Russian Poetics: Formalist and Structuralist Views.
HARRY MATHEWS, *Cigarettes.*
The Conversions.
The Human Country: New and Collected Stories.
The Journalist.
My Life in CIA.
Singular Pleasures.
The Sinking of the Odradek Stadium.
Tlooth.

FOR A FULL LIST OF PUBLICATIONS, VISIT:
www.dalkeyarchive.com

SELECTED DALKEY ARCHIVE TITLES

JOSEPH MCELROY,
Night Soul and Other Stories.
ABDELWAHAB MEDDEB, *Talismano.*
GERHARD MEIER, *Isle of the Dead.*
HERMAN MELVILLE, *The Confidence-Man.*
AMANDA MICHALOPOULOU, *I'd Like.*
STEVEN MILLHAUSER, *The Barnum Museum.*
In the Penny Arcade.
RALPH J. MILLS, JR., *Essays on Poetry.*
MOMUS, *The Book of Jokes.*
CHRISTINE MONTALBETTI, *The Origin of Man.*
Western.
OLIVE MOORE, *Spleen.*
NICHOLAS MOSLEY, *Accident.*
Assassins.
Catastrophe Practice.
Experience and Religion.
A Garden of Trees.
Hopeful Monsters.
Imago Bird.
Impossible Object.
Inventing God.
Judith.
Look at the Dark.
Natalie Natalia.
Serpent.
Time at War.
WARREN MOTTE,
Fables of the Novel: French Fiction since 1990.
Fiction Now: The French Novel in the 21st Century.
Oulipo: A Primer of Potential Literature.
GERALD MURNANE, *Barley Patch.*
Inland.
YVES NAVARRE, *Our Share of Time.*
Sweet Tooth.
DOROTHY NELSON, *In Night's City.*
Tar and Feathers.
ESHKOL NEVO, *Homesick.*
WILFRIDO D. NOLLEDO, *But for the Lovers.*
FLANN O'BRIEN, *At Swim-Two-Birds.*
The Best of Myles.
The Dalkey Archive.
The Hard Life.
The Poor Mouth.
The Third Policeman.
CLAUDE OLLIER, *The Mise-en-Scène.*
Wert and the Life Without End.
GIOVANNI ORELLI, *Walaschek's Dream.*
PATRIK OUŘEDNÍK, *Europeana.*
The Opportune Moment, 1855.
BORIS PAHOR, *Necropolis.*
FERNANDO DEL PASO, *News from the Empire.*
Palinuro of Mexico.
ROBERT PINGET, *The Inquisitory.*
Mahu or The Material.
Trio.
MANUEL PUIG, *Betrayed by Rita Hayworth.*
The Buenos Aires Affair.
Heartbreak Tango.
RAYMOND QUENEAU, *The Last Days.*
Odile.
Pierrot Mon Ami.
Saint Glinglin.
ANN QUIN, *Berg.*
Passages.
Three.
Tripticks.
ISHMAEL REED, *The Free-Lance Pallbearers.*
The Last Days of Louisiana Red.
Ishmael Reed: The Plays.
Juice!
Reckless Eyeballing.
The Terrible Threes.
The Terrible Twos.
Yellow Back Radio Broke-Down.
JASIA REICHARDT, *15 Journeys Warsaw to London.*
NOËLLE REVAZ, *With the Animals.*
JOÃO UBALDO RIBEIRO, *House of the Fortunate Buddhas.*
JEAN RICARDOU, *Place Names.*
RAINER MARIA RILKE, *The Notebooks of Malte Laurids Brigge.*
JULIÁN RÍOS, *The House of Ulysses.*
Larva: A Midsummer Night's Babel.
Poundemonium.
Procession of Shadows.
AUGUSTO ROA BASTOS, *I the Supreme.*
DANIËL ROBBERECHTS, *Arriving in Avignon.*
JEAN ROLIN, *The Explosion of the Radiator Hose.*
OLIVIER ROLIN, *Hotel Crystal.*
ALIX CLEO ROUBAUD, *Alix's Journal.*
JACQUES ROUBAUD, *The Form of a City Changes Faster, Alas, Than the Human Heart.*
The Great Fire of London.
Hortense in Exile.
Hortense Is Abducted.
The Loop.
Mathematics:
The Plurality of Worlds of Lewis.
The Princess Hoppy.
Some Thing Black.
RAYMOND ROUSSEL, *Impressions of Africa.*
VEDRANA RUDAN, *Night.*
STIG SÆTERBAKKEN, *Siamese.*
Self Control.
LYDIE SALVAYRE, *The Company of Ghosts.*
The Lecture.
The Power of Flies.
LUIS RAFAEL SÁNCHEZ,
Macho Camacho's Beat.
SEVERO SARDUY, *Cobra & Maitreya.*
NATHALIE SARRAUTE,
Do You Hear Them?
Martereau.
The Planetarium.

SELECTED DALKEY ARCHIVE TITLES

ARNO SCHMIDT, *Collected Novellas.*
Collected Stories.
Nobodaddy's Children.
Two Novels.
ASAF SCHURR, *Motti.*
GAIL SCOTT, *My Paris.*
DAMION SEARLS, *What We Were Doing and Where We Were Going.*
JUNE AKERS SEESE,
Is This What Other Women Feel Too?
What Waiting Really Means.
BERNARD SHARE, *Inish.*
Transit.
VIKTOR SHKLOVSKY, *Bowstring.*
Knight's Move.
A Sentimental Journey: Memoirs 1917–1922.
Energy of Delusion: A Book on Plot.
Literature and Cinematography.
Theory of Prose.
Third Factory.
Zoo, or Letters Not about Love.
PIERRE SINIAC, *The Collaborators.*
KJERSTI A. SKOMSVOLD, *The Faster I Walk, the Smaller I Am.*
JOSEF ŠKVORECKÝ, *The Engineer of Human Souls.*
GILBERT SORRENTINO,
Aberration of Starlight.
Blue Pastoral.
Crystal Vision.
Imaginative Qualities of Actual Things.
Mulligan Stew.
Pack of Lies.
Red the Fiend.
The Sky Changes.
Something Said.
Splendide-Hôtel.
Steelwork.
Under the Shadow.
W. M. SPACKMAN, *The Complete Fiction.*
ANDRZEJ STASIUK, *Dukla.*
Fado.
GERTRUDE STEIN, *The Making of Americans.*
A Novel of Thank You.
LARS SVENDSEN, *A Philosophy of Evil.*
PIOTR SZEWC, *Annihilation.*
GONÇALO M. TAVARES, *Jerusalem.*
Joseph Walser's Machine.
Learning to Pray in the Age of Technique.
LUCIAN DAN TEODOROVICI,
Our Circus Presents . . .
NIKANOR TERATOLOGEN, *Assisted Living.*
STEFAN THEMERSON, *Hobson's Island.*
The Mystery of the Sardine.
Tom Harris.
TAEKO TOMIOKA, *Building Waves.*
JOHN TOOMEY, *Sleepwalker.*
JEAN-PHILIPPE TOUSSAINT, *The Bathroom.*
Camera.
Monsieur.
Reticence.
Running Away.
Self-Portrait Abroad.
Television.
The Truth about Marie.
DUMITRU TSEPENEAG, *Hotel Europa.*
The Necessary Marriage.
Pigeon Post.
Vain Art of the Fugue.
ESTHER TUSQUETS, *Stranded.*
DUBRAVKA UGRESIC, *Lend Me Your Character.*
Thank You for Not Reading.
TOR ULVEN, *Replacement.*
MATI UNT, *Brecht at Night.*
Diary of a Blood Donor.
Things in the Night.
ÁLVARO URIBE AND OLIVIA SEARS, EDS., *Best of Contemporary Mexican Fiction.*
ELOY URROZ, *Friction.*
The Obstacles.
LUISA VALENZUELA, *Dark Desires and the Others.*
He Who Searches.
PAUL VERHAEGHEN, *Omega Minor.*
AGLAJA VETERANYI, *Why the Child Is Cooking in the Polenta.*
BORIS VIAN, *Heartsnatcher.*
LLORENÇ VILLALONGA, *The Dolls' Room.*
TOOMAS VINT, *An Unending Landscape.*
ORNELA VORPSI, *The Country Where No One Ever Dies.*
AUSTRYN WAINHOUSE, *Hedyphagetica.*
CURTIS WHITE, *America's Magic Mountain.*
The Idea of Home.
Memories of My Father Watching TV.
Requiem.
DIANE WILLIAMS, *Excitability: Selected Stories.*
Romancer Erector.
DOUGLAS WOOLF, *Wall to Wall.*
Ya! & John-Juan.
JAY WRIGHT, *Polynomials and Pollen.*
The Presentable Art of Reading Absence.
PHILIP WYLIE, *Generation of Vipers.*
MARGUERITE YOUNG, *Angel in the Forest.*
Miss MacIntosh, My Darling.
REYOUNG, *Unbabbling.*
VLADO ŽABOT, *The Succubus.*
ZORAN ŽIVKOVIĆ, *Hidden Camera.*
LOUIS ZUKOFSKY, *Collected Fiction.*
VITOMIL ZUPAN, *Minuet for Guitar.*
SCOTT ZWIREN, *God Head.*